CAREER EDUCATION:
A Lifelong Process

291 8 9 9

CAREER
EDUCATION:
A *Lifelong Process*

Editors:
Jack W. Fuller &
Terry O. Whealon

Nelson-Hall *nh* Chicago

Library of Congress Cataloging in Publication Data
Main entry under title:

Career education.

Bibliography: p.
Includes index.
1. Career education—United States—Addresses, essays, lectures. I. Fuller, Jack W.
II. Whealon, Terry O.
LC1037.5.C37   370.11′3′0973   78-1994
ISBN 0-88229-200-5

Manufactured in the United States of America
10   9   8   7   6   5   4   3   2   1

Contents

Part 1

Problems and Issues in Career Education

One of the most publicized studies of education in the last decade, *Crisis in the Classroom,*[1] voices a sharp criticism of education in America today through the use of the term "mindlessness." The contention inherent in this term is that we in education fail to ask a fundamental question before we jump on the latest bandwagon. That fundamental question is "Why?" By asking "Why career education?" we delve into the philosophy and rationale behind such a curriculum, and are therefore better able to pursue other questions, such as: "What kind of career education and how much?"

The articles included in this section deal with some basic issues and controversy surrounding career education. In reading these articles, one should discover that career education is a multi-faceted concept that has direct bearing on many areas of learning. The reader is provided a framework with which to build his own philosophy toward the topic.

Are Schools Meeting the Demands of Our Society?

Before one can begin to answer questions about career education, one must first look at society and the role of education in shaping that society. The first two articles in this section give an up-to-date assessment of society at large, the individual worker, and the changing world of work. They have major implications for the development of a philosophy toward career education.

Schools have always been expected to play a major role in shaping society. Many educators, however, believe that too much is expected of schools. The article by Bane and Jencks implies a need for the educational system to redirect its focus if it is to be instrumental in bringing about social reform and equality of economic opportunity.

Is Career Education the Answer?

Sidney P. Marland, Jr., believes that schools can be "agents" of change. Providing all students with an education that enhances their potential for success in a chosen career will bring about societal reform. He explains his position in the article "Career Education: Every Student Headed for a Goal."

Not everyone agrees that career education is the panacea for our social ills. The articles by King and Brownell, Nash and Agne, and Palmer point out some of the pitfalls and dangers of placing too heavy an emphasis on career education without having a firm understanding of the philosophy supporting it.

Career Education: A Multi-Faceted Concept

A well-balanced career education program does not simply provide a person with skills needed to pursue a given career. One must examine his attitudes toward life, people, and himself before he can make an intelligent career decision. The articles by Tuckman and Mitchell illustrate two different concerns related to the affective side of career education.

To use an over-worked phrase, in order for education to be meaningful, it has to relate to the real world. Alvin Toffler, in his most recent book, *The Role of Tomorrow in Education*,[2] states that "by maintaining the false distinction between work and learning, and between school and community, we not only divorce theory from practice and deprive ourselves of enormous energies that might be channeled into socially useful action, we also infantilize the young and rob them of the motivation to learn. Gyspers and Moore, Whealon, and Moyer have suggestions on how education can combine people and their careers into the curriculum of everyday living.

Education for Career Change

It is in error to conceive of career education as a terminal phenomenon. It never has and never will cease to be a perceptual necessity. In fact, latest reports indicate that its continual pursuit will be of paramount importance in the next few decades. A recent release from the U.S. Department of Labor, for example, predicts that a person entering the labor market in the 1970's will probably experience a career change approximately seven times during his working years. That a person be prepared to effectively deal with the dilemma of career change is a cornerstone of career education. The concluding article in this section by James Farmer and Robert Williams offers a guide to making this apparently inevitable transition more palatable.

Notes

1. Charles E. Silberman, *Crisis in the Classroom* (New York: Random House, 1970).

2. Alvin Toffler, *Learning for Tomorrow* (New York: Random House, Vintage Books, 1974), p. 16.

1

The Schools and Equal Opportunity*

*Mary Jo Bane
and Christopher Jencks*

mericans have a recurrent fantasy that schools can solve their
problems. Thus it was perhaps inevitable that, after we redis-
covered poverty and inequality in the early 1960s, we turned
to the schools for solutions. Yet the schools did not provide solutions,
the high hopes of the early-and-middle 1960s faded, and the war on
poverty ended in ignominious surrender to the *status quo*. In part, of
course, this was because the war in Southeast Asia turned out to be incompatible with the war on poverty. In part, however, it was because
we all had rather muddleheaded ideas about the various causes and
cures of poverty and inequality.

Today there are signs that some people are beginning to look for
new solutions to these perennial problems. There is a vast amount of
sociological and economic data that can, we think, help in this effort,
both by explaining the failures of the 1960s and by suggesting more
realistic alternatives. For the past four years we have been working
with these data. Our research has led us to three general conclusions.

First, poverty is a condition of relative rather than absolute deprivation. People feel poor and are poor if they have a lot less money
than their neighbors. This is true regardless of their absolute income.
It follows that we cannot eliminate poverty unless we prevent people

*Reprinted by permission from *Saturday Review*.

from falling too far below the national average. The problem is economic inequality rather than low incomes.

Second, the reforms of the 1960s were misdirected because they focused only on equalizing opportunity to "succeed" (or "fail") rather than on reducing the economic and social distance between those who succeeded and those who failed. The evidence we have reviewed suggests that equalizing opportunity will not do very much to equalize results, and hence it will not do much to reduce poverty.

Third, even if we are interested solely in equalizing opportunities for economic success, making schools more equal will not help very much. Differences between schools have very little effect on what happens to students after they graduate.

The main policy implication of these findings is that although school reform is important for improving the lives of children, schools cannot contribute significantly to adult equality. If we want economic equality in our society, we will have to get it by changing our economic institutions, not by changing the schools.

Poverty and Inequality

The rhetoric of the war on poverty described the persistence of poverty in the midst of affluence as a "paradox," largely attributable to "neglect." Official publications all assumed that poverty was an absolute rather than a relative condition. Having assumed this, they all showed progress toward the elimination of poverty, since fewer and fewer people had incomes below the official "poverty line."

Yet, despite all the official announcements of progress, many Americans still seemed poor, by both their own standards and their neighbors'. The reason was that most Americans define poverty in relative rather than absolute terms. Public-opinion surveys show, for example, that when people are asked how much money an American family needs to "get by," they typically name a figure about half what the average American family actually receives. This has been true for the last three decades, despite the fact that real incomes (incomes adjusted for inflation) have doubled in the interval.

During the Depression the average American family was living on about $30 a week. A third of all families were living on less than half this amount, which made it natural for Franklin Roosevelt to speak of "one-third of a nation" as ill-housed, ill-clothed, and ill-fed. By 1964 mean family income was about $160 a week, and the Gallup poll found that the average American thought a family of four needed at least $80 a week to "get by." Even allowing for inflation, this was twice what people had thought necessary during the Depression. Playing it safe, the Johnson administration defined the poverty line at $60 a week for a family of four, but most people felt this was inadequate. By 1970 inflation had raised mean family income to about $200 a week, and the National Welfare Rights Organization was trying to rally liberal support for a guaranteed income of $100 a week.

These changes in the definition of poverty were not just a matter of "rising expectations" or of people's needing to "keep up with the Joneses." The goods and services that made it possible to live on $15 a week during the Depression were no longer available to a family with the same real income ($40 a week) in 1964. Eating habits had changed, and many cheap foods had disappeared from the stores. Housing arrangements had changed, too. During the Depression many people could not afford indoor plumbing and "got by" with a privy. By the 1960s privies were illegal in most places. Those who still could not afford an indoor toilet ended up in buildings that had broken toilets. For these they paid more than their parents had paid for privies.

Examples of this kind suggest that the "cost of living" is not the cost of buying some fixed set of goods and services. It is the cost of participating in a social system. It therefore depends in large part on how much other people habitually spend to participate in the system. Those who fall far below the norm, whatever it may be, are excluded. Accordingly, raising the incomes of the poor will not eliminate poverty if the cost of participating in "mainstream" American life rises even faster. People with incomes less than half the national average will not be able to afford what "everyone" regards as "necessities." The only way to eliminate poverty is, therefore, to make sure everyone has an income at least half the average.

Arguments of this kind suggest not only that it makes more sense to think of "poverty" as a relative rather than an absolute condition but that eliminating poverty, at least as it is usually defined in America, depends on eliminating, or at least greatly reducing, inequality.

Schooling and Opportunity

Almost none of the reform legislation of the 1960s involved direct efforts to equalize adult status, power, or income. Most Americans accepted the idea that these rewards should go to those who were most competent and diligent. Their objection to America's traditional economic system was not that it produced inequality but that the rules determining who succeeded and who failed were often unfair. The reformers wanted to create a world in which success would no longer be associated with skin color, economic background, or other "irrelevant" factors, but only with actual merit. What they wanted, in short, was what they called "equal opportunity."

Their strategy for achieving equal opportunity placed great emphasis on education. Many people imagined that if schools could equalize people's cognitive skills this would equalize their bargaining power as adults. Presumably, if everyone had equal bargaining power, few people would end up very poor.

The strategy for reducing poverty rested on a series of assumptions that went roughly as follows:

1) Eliminating poverty is largely a matter of helping children born into poverty to rise out of it. Once families escape from poverty, they do not fall back into it. Middle-class children rarely end up poor.

2) The primary reason poor children cannot escape from poverty is that they do not acquire basic cognitive skills. They cannot read, write, calculate, or articulate. Lacking these skills, they cannot get or keep a well-paid job.

3) The best mechanism for breaking this "vicious circle" is educational reform. Since children born into poor homes do not acquire the skills they need from their parents, they must be taught these skills in school. This can be done by making sure that they attend the same schools as middle-class children, by giving them extra compensatory programs in school, by giving their parents a voice in running their schools, or by some combination of all three approaches.

Our research over the last four years suggests that each of these assumptions is erroneous:

1) Poverty is not primarily hereditary. While children born into poverty have a higher than average chance of ending up poor, there is still an enormous amount of economic mobility from one generation to the next. A father whose occupational status is high passes on less than half his advantage to his sons, and a father whose status is low passes along less than half his disadvantage. A family whose income is above the norm has an even harder time passing along its privileges; its sons are typically only about a third as advantaged as the parents. Conversely, a family whose income is below average will typically have sons about a third as disadvantaged as the parents. The effects of parents' status on their daughters' economic positions appear to be even weaker. This means that many "advantaged" parents have some "disadvantaged" children and vice versa.

2) The primary reason some people end up richer than others is not that they have more adequate cognitive skills. While children who read well, get the right answers to arithmetic problems, and articulate their thoughts clearly are somewhat more likely than others to get

ahead, there are many other equally important factors involved. The effects of I.Q. on economic success are about the same as the effects of family background. This means, for example, that if two men's I.Q. scores differ by 17 points—the typical difference between I.Q. scores of individuals chosen at random—their incomes will typically differ by less than $2,000. That amount is not completely trivial, of course. But the income difference between random individuals is three times as large and the difference between the best-paid fifth and the worst-paid fifth of all male workers averages $14,000. There is almost as much economic inequality among those who score high on standardized tests as in the general population.

3) There is no evidence that school reform can substantially reduce the extent of cognitive inequality, as measured by tests of verbal fluency, reading comprehension, or mathematical skill. Eliminating qualitative differences between elementary schools would reduce the range of scores on standardized tests in sixth grade by less than 3 percent. Eliminating qualitative differences between high schools would hardly reduce the range of twelfth-grade scores at all and would reduce by only 1 per cent the disparities in the amount of education people eventually get.

Our best guess, after reviewing all the evidence we could find, is that racial desegregation raises black elementary school students' test scores by a couple of points. But most of the test-score gap between blacks and whites persists, even when they are in the same schools. So also: Tracking has very little effect on test scores. And neither the overall level of resources available to a school nor any specific, easily identifiable school policy has a significant effect on students' cognitive skills or educational attainments. Thus, even if we went beyond "equal opportunity" and allocated resources disproportionately to schools whose students now do worst on tests and are least likely to acquire credentials, this would not improve these students' prospects very much.

The evidence does not tell us why school quality has so little effect on test scores. Three possible explanations come to mind. First, children seem to be more influenced by what happens at home than by what happens in school. They may also be more influenced by what happens on the streets and by what they see on television. Second, administrators have very little control over those aspects of school life that do affect children. Reallocating resources, reassigning pupils, and rewriting the curriculum seldom change the way teachers and students actually treat each other minute by minute. Third, even when the schools exert an unusual influence on children, the resulting changes are not likely to persist into adulthood. It takes a huge change in elementary school test scores, for example, to alter adult income by a significant amount.

Equal Opportunity and Unequal Results

The evidence we have reviewed, taken all together, suggests that equalizing opportunity cannot take us very far toward eliminating inequality. The simplest way of demonstrating this is to compare the economic prospects of brothers raised in the same home. Even the most egalitarian society could not hope to make opportunities for all children appreciably more equal than the opportunities now available to brothers from the same family. Looking at society at large, if we compare random pairs of individuals, the difference between their occupational statuses averages fully 2 points on the Duncan "status scale" (the scale runs from 0 to 96 points). The difference between brothers' occupational statuses averages fully 23 points on this same scale. If we compare men's incomes, the difference between random pairs averaged about $6,200 in 1968. The difference between brothers' incomes, according to our best estimate, probably averaged about $5,700. These estimates mean that people who start off equal end up almost as unequal as everyone else. Inequality is not mostly inherited: It is created anew in each generation.

We can take this line of argument a step further by comparing people who not only start off in similar families but who also have the same I.Q. scores and get the same amount of schooling. Such people's occupational statuses differ by an average of 21 points, compared to 28 points for random individuals. If we compare their incomes, making the additional assumption that the men have the same occupational status, we find that they differ by an average of about $5,300, compared to $6,200 for men chosen at random.

These comparisons suggest that adult success must depend on a lot of things besides family background, schooling, and the cognitive skills measured by standardized tests. We have no idea what these factors are. To some extent, no doubt, specialized varieties of competence, such as the ability to hit a ball thrown at high speed or the ability to persuade a customer that he wants a larger car than he thought he wanted, play a major role. Income also depends on luck: the range of jobs available when you are job hunting, the amount of overtime work in your plant, good or bad weather for your strawberry crop, and a hundred other unpredictable accidents.

Equalizing opportunity will not, then, do much to reduce economic inequality in America. If poverty is relative rather than absolute, equalizing opportunity will not do much to reduce poverty, either.

Implications for Educational Policy

These findings imply that school reform is never likely to have any significant effect on the degree of inequality among adults. This suggests that the prevalent "factory" model, in which schools are seen as places that "produce" alumni, probably ought to be abandoned. It is true that schools have "inputs" and "outputs," and that one of their nominal purposes is to take human "raw material" (*i.e.*, children) and convert it into something more "useful" (*i.e.*, employable adults). Our research suggests, however, that the character of a school's output depends largely on a single input, the characteristics of the entering children. Everything else—the school budget, its policies, the characteristics of the teachers—is either secondary or completely irrelevant, at least so long as the range of variation among schools is as narrow as it seems to be in America.

These findings have convinced us that the long-term effects of schooling are relatively uniform. The day-to-day internal life of the schools, in contrast, is highly variable. It follows that *the primary basis for evaluating a school should be whether the students and teachers find it a satisfying place to be.* This does not mean we think schools should be like mediocre summer camps, in which children are kept out of trouble but not taught anything. We doubt that a school can be enjoyable for either adults or children unless the children keep learning new things. We value ideas and the life of the mind, and we think that a school that does not value these things is a poor place for children. But a school that values ideas because they enrich the lives of children is quite different from a school that values high reading scores because reading scores are important for adult success.

Our concern with making schools satisfying places for teachers and children has led us to a concern for diversity and choice. People have widely different notions of what a "satisfying" place is, and we believe they ought to be able to put these values into practice. As we have noted, our research suggests that none of the programs or structural arrangements in common use today has consistently different long-term effects from any other. Since the character of a child's schooling has few long-term effects, and since these effects are quite unpredictable, society has little reason to constrain the choices available to parents and children. If a "good school" is one the students and staff find satisfying, no one school will be best for everyone. Since there is no evidence that professional educators know appreciably more than parents about what is good for children, it seems reasonable to let parents decide what kind of education their children should have while they are young and to let the children decide as they get older.

Short-term considerations also seem decisive in determining whether to spend more money on schooling or to spend it on busing children to schools outside their neighborhoods. If extra resources make school life pleasanter and more interesting, they are worthwhile. But we should not try to justify school expenditures on the grounds that they boost adult earnings. Likewise, busing ought to be justified in political and moral terms rather than in terms of presumed long-term effects on the children who are bused. If we want an integrated society, we ought to have integrated schools, which make people feel they have a stake in the well-being of other races. If we want a society in which people are free to segregate themselves, then we should apply that principle to our schools. There is, however, no compelling reason to treat schools differently from other social arrangements, including neighborhoods. Personally, we believe in both open housing and open schools. If parents or students want to take buses to schools in other neighborhoods, school boards ought to provide the buses, expand the relevant schools, and ensure that the students are welcome in the schools they want to attend. This is the least we can do to offset the effects of residential segregation. But we do not believe that forced busing can be justified on the grounds of its long-term benefits for students.

This leads to our last conclusion about educational reform. Reformers are always getting trapped into claiming too much for what they propose. They may want a particular reform—like open classrooms, or desegregation, or vouchers—because they think these reforms will make schools more satisfying places to work. Yet they feel obliged to claim that these reforms will also reduce the number of nonreaders, increase racial understanding, or strengthen family life. A wise reformer ought to be more modest, claiming only that a particular reform will not harm adult society and that it will make life pleasanter for parents, teachers, and students in the short run.

This plea for modesty in school reform will, we fear, fall on deaf ears. Ivan Illich is right in seeing schools as secular churches, through which we seek to improve not ourselves but our descendants. That this process should be disagreeable seems inevitable; one cannot abolish original sin through self-indulgence. That it should be immodest seems equally inevitable; a religion that promises anything less than salvation wins few converts. In school, as in church, we present the world as we wish it were. We try to inspire children with the ideals we ourselves have failed to live up to. We assume, for example, that we cannot make adults live in desegregated neighborhoods, so we devise schemes for busing children from one neighborhood to another in order to desegregate the schools. We all prefer conducting our moral experiments on other people. Nonetheless, so long as we confine our experiments to children, we will not have much effect on adult life.

Implications for Social Reform

Then how *are* we to affect adult life? Our findings tell us that different kinds of inequality are only loosely related to one another. This can be either encouraging or discouraging, depending on how you look at it. On the discouraging side, it means that eliminating inequality in one area will not eliminate it in other areas. On the encouraging side, it means that inequality in one area does not dictate inequality in other areas.

To begin with, genetic inequality is not a major obstacle to economic equality. It is true that genetic diversity almost inevitably means considerable variation in people's scores on standardized tests. But this kind of cognitive inequality need not imply anything like the present degree of economic inequality. We estimate, for example, that if the only sources of income inequality in America were differences in people's genes, the top fifth of the population would earn only about 1.4 times as much as the bottom fifth. In actuality, the top fifth earns seven times as much as the bottom fifth.

Second, our findings suggest that psychological and cultural differences between families are not an irrevocable barrier to adult equality. Family background has more influence than genes on an individual's educational attainment, occupational status, and income. Nonetheless, if family background were the only source of economic inequality in America, the top fifth would earn only about twice as much as the bottom fifth.

Our findings show, then, that inequality is not determined at birth. But they also suggest that economic equality cannot be achieved by indirect efforts to manipulate the environments in which people grow up. We have already discussed the minuscule effects of equalizing school quality. Equalizing the amount of schooling people get would not work much better. Income inequality among men with similar amounts of schooling is only 5-10 percent less than among men in general. The effect is even less if we include women.

If we want to eliminate economic inequality, we must make this an explicit objective of public policy rather than deluding ourselves into thinking that we can do it by giving everyone equal opportunity to succeed or fail. If we want an occupational structure which is less hierarchical and in which the social distance between the top and the bottom is reduced, we will have to make deliberate efforts to reorganize work and redistribute power within organizations. We will probably also have to rotate jobs, so that no individual held power very long.

If we want an income distribution that is more equal, we can constrain employers, either by tax incentives or direct legislation, to reduce wage disparities between their best- and worst-paid workers. We can make taxes more progressive, and we can provide income supplements to those who do not make an adequate living from wages alone. We can also provide free public services for those who cannot afford to buy adequate services in the private sector. Pursued with vigor, such a strategy can make "poverty" (*i.e.*, having a living standard less than half the national average) virtually impossible. Such a strategy would also make economic "success," in the sense of having, say, a living standard more than twice the national average, far less common than it now is. The net effect would be to make those with the most competence and luck subsidize those with the least competence and luck to a far greater extent than they do today. Unless we are prepared to do this, poverty and inequality will remain with us indefinitely.

This strategy was rejected during the 1960s for the simple reason that it commanded relatively little popular support. The required legislation could not have passed Congress, nor could it pass today. That does not mean that it is the wrong strategy. It simply means that, until we change the political and moral premises on which most Americans now operate, poverty and inequality will persist at pretty much their present level. Intervention in market processes, for example, means restricting the "right" of individuals to use their natural advantages for private gain. Economic equality requires social and legal sanctions—analogous to those that now exist against capricious firing of employees—against inequality within work settings. It also requires that wage rates, which Americans have traditionally viewed as a "private" question to be adjudicated by negotiation between (unequal) individuals or groups, must become a "public" question subject to political control and solution.

In America, as elsewhere, the long-term drift over the past 200 years has been toward equality. In America, however, the contribution of public policy to this drift has been slight. As long as egalitarians assume that public policy cannot contribute to equality directly but must proceed by ingenious manipulations of marginal institutions like the schools, this pattern will continue. If we want to move beyond this tradition, we must establish political control over the economic institutions that shape our society. What we will need, in short, is what other countries call socialism. Anything less will end in the same disappointment as the reforms of the 1960s.

Reference

Bane, Mary Jo; Cohen, David; Gintis, Herbert; Heyns, Barbara; Jencks, Christopher; Michelson, Stephan; and Smith, Marshall. *Inequality: A Reassessment of the Effect of Family and Schooling in America*. New York: Basic Books, 1972.

2

The
Changing World
of Work
Report of
the Forty-Third
American Assembly

Preface

The American world of work. Despite civil rights legislation and equal employment actions, minorities continue to experience handicaps in both employment and advancement. Young workers are influenced by rising levels of education and higher expectations. Women's lib is pressing for equal employment. Growing demands for early retirement reveal disenchantment. Turnovers, absenteeism, grievances, union unrest and strikes all reflect varying degrees of job dissatisfaction.

How can these problems be reduced by the introduction of change in the nature of work and working relationships? What should be done to improve the quality of working life to optimize individual efforts and increase productivity? And in all of this what is the role of business, labor and government?

These major questions, among others, were addressed by the Forty-third American Assembly—*The Changing World of Work*—at Arden House, Harriman, New York, November 1-4, 1973.

The Assembly consisted of 80 persons from 16 states and the District of Columbia who represented varying pursuits and viewpoints. After discussion in depth for three days the participants reviewed in plenary session the report which follows.

Background for the discussions consisted of chapters prepared under the editorship of Jerome M. Rosow of Exxon Corporation as follows:

Daniel Yankelovich	*The Meaning of Work*
Eli Ginzberg	*The Changing American Economy and Labor Force*
George Strauss	*Workers: Attitudes and Adjustments*
Agis Salpukas	*Unions: A New Role?*
Peter Henle	*Economic Effects: Reviewing the Evidence*
Richard E. Walton	*Innovative Restructuring of Work*
Sam Zagoria	*Policy Implications and Future Agenda*

By its nature and articles of incorporation, The American Assembly, a private educational forum in public affairs, takes no stand on the matters it presents for discussion; and no one should establish a link between the recommendations herein and an official position of The American Assembly. It must also be said that The Ford Foundation, whose generous underwriting made this program possible, is not to be associated with any of the views on these pages.

CLIFFORD C. NELSON
President
The American Assembly

Final Report
of the
Forty-Third American Assembly

At the close of their discussions the participants in the Forty-third American Assembly, on *The Changing World of Work*, at Arden House, Harriman, New York, November 1-4, 1973, reviewed as a group the following statement. The statement represents general agreement; however no one was asked to sign it. Furthermore it should not be assumed that every participant subscribes to every recommendation.

The world of work is caught up in the cross currents of rapid change. Problems of the work place including job satisfaction demand immediate attention and action.

Three distinct forces are involved: the institutions and the jobs they provide, the society at large, and the individual worker. Each is changing at different rates of speed and with different degrees of responsiveness. The individual worker and the society are changing much faster than the institutions and the quality of the jobs they provide.

Disaffection and discontent are a reflection of increasing education and rising aspirations rather than of alienation. Worker disaffection also mirrors the problems of society generally. It is a symptom of a dynamic society that is questioning itself in order to achieve a better society.

The society must take a larger view of work and examine how it relates to increased or decreased satisfaction with life, both on and off the job. The issue is made clear by focusing on the expectations workers bring to the job and on the distinction between economic and psychological work satisfaction. While the employer is primarily motivated to create and maintain a productive work place, this is not incompatible with a high quality of working life, provided there is a balanced relationship among human, technical, and economic factors.

Worker reactions also reflect a conflict between changing employee attitudes and organization inertia. Employees want challenge and personal growth, but work tends to be simplified and over-specialized. Employees want to be involved in patterns of mutual influence, but organizations are characterized by decision-making concentrated at the top. Employees want careers and self-development, but organizations design rigid career paths that sometimes impede fulfillment of these goals. Employees want more opportunity to achieve self-esteem, but many organizations emphasize impersonality.

Some have argued that the press and the professors have created a straw man on the issue of worker discontent. The Assembly does not agree. The problem exists at many levels in both private and public employment. It affects white-collar, blue-collar, professional, and service employees.

Our lives are organized around our jobs. The work ethic is deeply imbedded in our cultural values. For Americans, it means a commitment to productive labor, involving security, independence, self-esteem, and dignity.

Yet the work ethic is often thwarted. The inefficiencies and impersonality at many work places, decision-making which excludes participation by individual workers, and insufficient recognition or reward to workers for high-quality output—all contribute to increasing consumer complaints about the quality of goods and services. Increasingly, workers question both employer decisions and the concept of work for work's sake alone. But the desire to accomplish something and to do so effectively remains.

New cultural trends are transforming the work ethic. These include: the changing definition of success, reduced fears of economic security, a new sharing of labor between the sexes, and a spreading disillusionment with a narrow definition of efficiency.

As the economic needs of workers are met, there will be increasing demands for improvement in the quality of working life. These demands will not substitute for the need for basic economic reward and security. Neither can we ignore the fact that millions of workers are still struggling to achieve a modicum of economic security and an opportunity to earn an adequate income. They are often obliged to sacrifice considerations of improvements in the quality of working life in their struggle to survive.

Big organizations often provide greater financial reward for workers than small organizations but are sometimes a breeding place for worker discontent. The individual can be diminished in these giant organizations, where special attention needs to be given to the quality of working life.

Unions have contributed significantly to the improvement in wages, hours, working conditions, the quality of work life, and the advancement of the interests of all workers. Union leaders, for their part, are concerned about the talk of "job enrichment." Many suspect it is a code word for speedup or a device to undermine unionism. The challenge now is for labor and management to work at resolving the issues of the work place in a nonadversary atmosphere, with a goal of improving the quality of working life.

Finally, it is recognized that needed changes must be sought within the context of rising international economic competition and other economic pressures.

Redesign of Work

Employers should place the same emphasis toward the design of human work that they have long placed upon the design of the physical plant. In the long-range interests of the enterprise, they should be as innovative and concerned about the needs and feelings of the workers as they are with their profits. A broad spectrum of experiments should include: basic changes in the production process; improving health and safety conditions; more attractive surroundings; reduction of special privileges and greater equity in amenities; consideration of more flexible work schedules; use of work teams; and more decentralized decision-making. New designs in the work place can more nearly satisfy the needs of workers while they enhance overall vitality of the organization.

Many workers want and should have more of a voice in the world of work. Work is so critical and vital to their lives that to continue to exclude them from participation in decision-making is to remain out of step with the rest of society. At the same time, it is recognized that not every worker wants to be consulted regarding his or her job. While authority is an integral factor in the operation of our society, the bases of authority should be competence and contribution, not just arbitrary rank.

The work place cannot remain authoritarian within an open society. Increasing organizational democracy will contribute to an increasingly free society.

EMPLOYERS

Management has the capacity for initiating changes in the work place and some have successfully done so. The record of successful experiments, while small, is encouraging. This Assembly believes that significant social and economic gains can be made if more experiments are introduced to improve the quality of the working life. A restructuring of work and work organizations holds promise of more effective development of employees while adding to their work satisfaction without adverse effect on the companies' costs and with potential gains in productivity.

To advance such experiments top management must recognize and seek to allay the insecurities of their middle managers, foremen, and workers. Middle managers and employees often resist any reduction of their power and authority since this may be viewed as a threat not only to their authority but to their jobs.

Too often managers underestimate the capabilities of their employees. If authority were reasonably decentralized or released, management could gain substantially. Therefore improvements in the quality of working life and increased participation in development of human talent will benefit the organization just as it serves individual aspirations.

UNIONS

Unions have since their inception been seeking to "humanize" work. The current ideas of improving the quality of working life are basically an extension of this long-range goal. Unions have primarily sought and have achieved significant economic gains and substantially increased job security. This should not obscure their long-term struggle for improvement in the quality of working life. Unions properly resent the view that they are not concerned over this issue.

Unions rightly fear that some management people will attempt to use "job enrichment" as a guise for speedup. Yet this fear should not be a bar to the possibilities of genuine improvement in jobs. Improved quality in work life may increase productivity, and often will, but this should not be the only factor considered. Unions will probably be reluctant to participate in experiments to change work unless there are rewards to the worker. This is legitimate.

Unions should continue to move ahead, cooperating and in some cases spurring management to induce change. Unions should participate in experiments and play a larger role. There are new and encouraging precedent-setting breakthroughs in recent union-management initiatives in the case of the steel and auto workers. Relations between management and labor unions have improved perceptibly over the past two decades. Thus new opportunities exist in their mutual interest to improve the quality of working life.

GOVERNMENT

The issue of human dignity at work is an important national goal. It must be high on the national agenda. Government at all levels has long recognized a commitment to enhance the work place environment. But to these commitments it should establish a new national policy that improvement in the quality of working life for all workers is desirable to raise standards of living, protect mental and physical health and welfare, and advance individual fulfillment.

Government should conduct surveys aimed at establishing and tracking levels of job dissatisfaction and factors associated with job dissatisfaction. It should identify the extent of the problem for a wide variety of organizations, and provide information for different segments of the working population. Government should encourage research and development in work design, fund experiments, convene national conferences, support worker exchange programs, distribute literature, stimulate and perhaps subsidize these efforts.

It should not be overlooked that governments at all levels employ 18 percent of the nation's labor force. Many of the recommendations for improving quality of work life in other sections of this report apply to federal, state, and local governments.

Advantage should be taken of the well-documented military manpower program (which exceeds $40 billion annually), and use should be made of these continuing studies to establish models on social issues pertaining to youth, minorities, and women.

INNOVATION AND DISSEMINATION

Improvements in the quality of working life will benefit from the discovery and application of effective methods of redesigning jobs and other changes. The present level of information and know-how is inadequate. We need new institutional arrangements to accelerate change. We need talent and organizations on the shop floor and in the office to deal with and advance the quality of working life. These concepts can be applied to both union and nonunion situations.

Agencies for Change: There is a need to establish nonprofit institutes to further the improvement of the quality of working life. These should be funded jointly from private and public sources. Funds should be contributed by government, foundations, management, and unions so that all are involved and all have a stake in the outcome. These institutes would stimulate and assist management and labor in developing experiments and programs and in the measurement of the full range of their effects. They should serve not only as a stimulus for experimentation but should reflect changes around the world. They should develop professional talent equipped to facilitate change.

In addition, universities and other established educational institutions should continue to conduct research into and evaluation of experiments on improving the quality of working life and to distribute their findings. Moreover, schools of business, engineering, law, labor relations, and other disciplines training people directly involved in designing and managing work must include in their curricula greater consideration of factors affecting the quality of working life.

Work issues should also become the concern of civic, religious, educational, neighborhood, and other organizations to increase the linkage between the work place and the community and to achieve new approaches to workers' needs in the broadest possible framework.

Adapting to Change

While the nature of work is central to discussion of the quality of work life, other aspects of work frequently cause strong and specific worker discontent. Improving only job tasks may not be sufficient to improve worker satisfaction unless these other factors also are improved.

(The following recommendations presuppose the development and maintenance of a high level of employment, without which they cannot be fully implemented.)

Flexibility and Mobility: Rigid rules and restrictive customs regarding work should be reexamined. Acceptable programs are needed to enhance mobility, develop the use of human resources, fulfill human potential, and advance economic welfare. Many employees want job mobility and more options in their fringe benefits, pensions, and other deferred payments.

The barriers to job change presented by economics, geography, invalid credential requirements, and other factors should be reduced or eliminated.

Part-time Employment: More and better part-time jobs would greatly increase the opportunities and choices for all workers, particularly women, youth, handicapped, and older workers who seek such opportunities. Such jobs are more easily harmonized with new life styles combining work, education, home, and family. Current wage and benefit practices which discriminate against part-time workers must be changed so as to increase opportunity and ease labor shortages in particular occupations or industries.

Transitions Involving the Home, the School, and the Work Place: Many young people are poorly prepared for the world of work. Schools, in cooperation with government, business, unions and parents, should improve methods for career development. Career education and co-operative education programs should become an integral part of the school system. Provisions must be made for the financial commitment and job redesign which such programs require. Moreover, all people must have access to education throughout their lives with minimal financial and occupational disruption. Continuing education upgrades existing careers, advances second careers, and generally enriches lives.

Discrimination: Despite progress, ethnic and racial minorities, women, youth, and older workers still suffer severe discrimination in public and private employment. Our progress is significant only in contrast to where we were a decade ago. We must develop a more effective national effort to achieve opportunity for full participation in the work force at all levels of employment. The Equal Employment Opportunity Commission (EEOC) must be sustained and strengthened. The handicapped also need more opportunity to enter the world of work and establish their full place in society.

This effort would help give these groups access to employment and begin to meet their most basic aspirations for decent jobs, income security, and a sense of self-worth. The continuing discrimination against ethnic and racial minorities resists change and must be eliminated. A full employment economy will accelerate the achievement of these objectives.

Women: Women represent the single largest sector of the population that has been blocked from access to meaningful jobs and careers. To improve the opportunities of those who seek work out of the home requires that they have access to financial aid for educational opportunities, preferably prior to or at the time they are ready to enter or reenter the work force.

It also requires employers and trade unions to remove all barriers to equal employment, compensation, training, and promotion. Women must receive equal pay for equal work. Greater flexibility in hours should be provided by employers so that both husbands and wives can arrange their schedules with greater ease. A substantial expansion in educational day care and after school care centers will further improve opportunities for meaningful working careers for women and should be undertaken by employers, unions, and government. And where applicable, fee schedules should be geared to family income.

Middle-Aged and Older Workers: Options for older workers are often severely limited. Not only is their age an artificial handicap to other employment but deferred benefits are tied to their jobs and lost if they leave. Moreover, there are few opportunities for them to find additional education or training. The labor market itself is a frightening place.

Increased mobility and second career chances are needed. They also strengthen the institutions where work is performed since organizations often carry employees who are marginal performers, blocked, frustrated, and relatively unable to make a worthwhile contribution. Continuing education with income support would broaden the options available to workers. More funds are required from both public and private sectors.

Pension Plan Reform: It has been assumed and accepted that both employers' and employees' interests were served by establishing pension plans which put a high premium on staying with one firm. This philosophy is incompatible with the need for flexibility, mobility, and individual freedom in our society. Nor does it serve the best interests of the firm. In too many enterprises, executives, middle managers, and rank and file workers have left the firm mentally but will not leave physically until they retire.

Pensions represent the single most important deferred benefit of American workers. Private retirement plans now cover nearly 50 percent of the private work force, more than double the proportion for 1950. However, it has been estimated that more than half of all the workers covered by these plans will draw few, if any, benefits under present law. In addition, half of the American labor force is without *any* private pension plan coverage.

We must therefore expand pension coverage and endorse comprehensive federal pension reform legislation, especially provisions for early vesting and adequate funding.

Conclusion

Something, clearly, is stirring. In part, we are witnessing changes in personal values that are seen and felt not only in the United States but around the world. In part, we are experiencing the latest chapter in the continuing story of the quest for fulfilling American goals and aspirations: a fair and equitable society; an opportunity for each citizen to participate in the forces that affect his life; a confirmation that the democratic process does, indeed, work for all. Now that challenge is emerging at the most basic level of work itself. The questions have come down to society's responsibility to provide a higher quality of working life and increasing opportunities for those millions on the fringe who for so long have endured the reality of a life in which all our fine talk about job enrichment and job humanization is meaningless. We believe that the changes we advocate can help us work toward a more democratic and more productive society. They will not solve all the problems; they are a beginning.

Our view is pragmatic: improving the place, the organization, and the nature of work can lead to better work performance and a better quality of life in the society. A crisis, though it may not presently exist, could confront us if business, labor, educational institutions, community leadership, and government fail to respond. If we are lulled by our successes of the past, if we presume they inevitably will carry over into our future, we are mistaken. They will not. While we differ on specific points and proposals, we are united in one belief—these questions are vital. The time has now come to put our words and proposals into action.

PARTICIPANTS

The Forty-Third American Assembly

RICHARD AULT
Coordinator of Consulting Services
Organization Research &
 Development
General Motors Corporation
Detroit

SALLY HILLSMAN BAKER
Assistant Professor of Sociology
Queens College

MSGR. GENO BARONI
Director
National Center for Urban
 Ethnic Affairs
Washington, D.C.

°°HARRY BERNSTEIN
Labor Editor
Los Angeles *Times*

°°Rapporteur

ARTHUR C. BOYDEN
Executive Director
Staff Manufacturing
3M Company
St. Paul

WILLIAM W. BROOM
Washington Bureau Chief
Ridder Publications
Washington, D.C.

MICHAEL J. BROWER
Heller School
Brandeis University

COURTNEY C. BROWN
Columbia University

WILLIAM CAMPBELL
Superintendent, Industrial Relations
Monsanto Textile Company
Pensacola

RUTH C. CHANCE
Executive Director
Rosenberg Foundation
San Francisco

ELY CHINOY
Professor of Sociology
Smith College

HENRY COHEN
Dean
Center for New York City Affairs
New School for Social Research

JEAN J. COUTURIER
Executive Director
National Civil Service League
Washington, D.C.

GEORGE DAOUST
Deputy Assistant Secretary
  of Defense (Manpower
  Research & Utilization)
Washington, D.C.

LOUIS E. DAVIS
Professor of Organizational Sciences
University of California
Los Angeles

VIRGIL B. DAY
Vice President
General Electric Co.
New York

JOSE deVARON
Counsel
The First National Bank of Boston

RT. REV. ROBERT L. DeWITT
Bishop of Pennsylvania
Philadelphia

°Discussion leader

PETER S. diCICCO
President
IUE New England District
Lynnfield, Mass.

JOHN DIEBOLD
President
The Diebold Group, Inc.
New York

THOMAS R. DONAHUE
Executive Assistant to the President
AFL-CIO
Washington, D.C.

ELMO ELLIS
Vice President
Cox Broadcasting Corporation
Atlanta

THOMAS P. FAHY
Vice President
Perkin-Elmer Corporation
Norwalk, Conn.

WILFRED FEINBERG
Circuit Judge
United States Court of Appeals
New York

BEN FISCHER
Director
Contract Administration Dept.
United Steel Workers of America
Pittsburgh

ROBERT N. FORD
Director, Work Organization
  Research
American Telephone & Telegraph Co.
New York

ROBERT FOSTER
Chief, Social Psychology Group
Office of Research & Development
U.S. Dept. of Labor
Washington, D.C.

ROBERT M. FRAME
Director, Organization Development
Northern Natural Gas Co.
Omaha

°ELI GINZBERG
Hepburn Professor of Economics
Graduate School of Business
Columbia University

°°JUDSON GOODING
Urban Research Corporation
Chicago

SHEILA GORDON
Associate Dean
Division of Cooperative Education
La Guardia Community College
New York

°°Rapporteur

49727

PETER HENLE
Senior Specialist (Labor)
Congressional Research Service
Washington, D.C.

JOHN HERLING
Herling's Labor Letter
National Newspaper Syndicate
Washington, D.C.

JUDITH HERMAN
Coordinator
National Project on Ethnic America
American Jewish Committee
New York

KIRBY HICKS
Interstate Steel Company
Chicago

JAMES HODGSON
Senior Vice President
Corporate Relations
Lockheed Aircraft Corp.
Burbank, California

SETH M. HUFSTEDLER
Attorney at Law
Los Angeles

°°HAYNES JOHNSON
Assistant Managing Editor
Washington *Post*

JACOB J. KAUFMAN
Director
Institute for Research on
  Human Resources
The Pennsylvania State University

LYMAN KETCHUM
Manager
Organizational Development
General Foods Corporation
White Plains

IRVING M. LEVINE
Director
National Project on Ethnic America
American Jewish Committee
New York

SAR A. LEVITAN
Director
Center for Manpower Policy Studies
George Washington University

LANCE LIEBMAN
Assistant Professor of Law
Harvard University

°Discussion leader
°°Rapporteur
°°°Delivered formal address

ELLIOT LIEBOW
Chief
Center for Studies of
  Metropolitan Problems
National Institute of Mental Health
Rockville, Maryland

°°°ROBERT D. LILLEY
President
American Telephone &
  Telegraph Co.
New York

°FREDERICK R. LIVINGSTON
Attorney at Law
New York

JOHN P. LYNN
President & Chief Executive Officer
The American Welding & Mfg. Co.
Warren, Ohio

EDWIN S. MILLS
Director
Quality of Work Program
National Commission on Productivity
Washington, D.C.

FRANCIS A. O'CONNELL
Vice President, Employee Relations
Olin Corporation
Stamford, Connecticut

JAMES O'TOOLE
Graduate School of Business
University of Southern California

°°°CHARLES H. PERCY
United States Senator from Illinois

PRISCILLA PERRY
Assistant Director
Center for Urban and
  Regional Studies
University of Miami

HARRY POLLAND
Labor Economist
San Francisco

A. H. RASKIN
Assistant Editor, Editorial Page
New York *Times*

J. W. REYNOLDS
Director, Industrial Relations
B. F. Goodrich Company
Akron

JEROME M. ROSOW
Public Affairs Planning Manager
Exxon Corporation
New York

STANLEY H. RUTTENBERG
President
Stanley Ruttenberg and Associates
Washington, D.C.

AGIS SALPUKAS
New York *Times*
Detroit

FRANK W. SCHIFF
Vice President & Chief Economist
Committee for Economic
    Development
Washington, D.C.

ROBERT SCHRANK
Social Development Office
The Ford Foundation
New York

STANLEY E. SEASHORE
Research Coordinator
Institute for Social Research
Ann Arbor, Michigan

JOSEPH SHANE
Director, Labor Relations
State of Maryland
Annapolis

°°HARVEY D. SHAPIRO
Russell Sage Foundation
New York

JACOB SHEINKMAN
Secretary-Treasurer
Amalgamated Clothing Workers
    of America
New York

WALTER M. SMITH
Installer-Repairman
Chesapeake & Potomac Phone Co.
Falls Church, Virginia

WILLIAM A. STEIGER
Representative from Wisconsin
Congress of the United States

BEN S. STEPHANSKY
Associate Director
W. E. Upjohn Institute for
    Employment Research
Washington, D.C.

GEORGE STRAUSS
Professor of Business Administration
University of California
Berkeley

°Discussion leader
°°Rapporteur
°°°Delivered formal address

MITCHELL SVIRIDOFF
Vice President
The Ford Foundation
New York

ELEANOR TILSON
Security Plan Director
United Store Workers Union
New York

ROY W. WALTERS
President
Roy W. Walters Associates
Glen Rock, N.J.

RICHARD E. WALTON
Professor of Business
Harvard University

JUDSON C. WARD
Executive Vice President
Emory University

WALTER WERNICK
Professor of Education
Northern Illinois University

°BASIL WHITING
Program Officer—Social Development
The Ford Foundation
New York

WILLIAM W. WINPISINGER
General Vice President
International Association of
    Machinists & Aerospace Workers
Washington, D.C.

WILLARD WIRTZ
President
The Manpower Institute
Washington, D.C.

°°°LEONARD WOODCOCK
President
United Auto Workers
Detroit

DANIEL YANKELOVICH
President
Yankelovich Corporation
New York

°SAM ZAGORIA
Director
Labor-Management Relations
Service of the National League
    of Cities, U.S. Conference of
    Mayors and National
    Association of Counties
Washington, D.C.

About the American Assembly

The American Assembly was established by Dwight D. Eisenhower at Columbia University in 1950. It holds nonpartisan meetings and publishes authoritative books to illuminate issues of United States policy.

An affiliate of Columbia, with offices in the Graduate School of Business, the Assembly is a national, educational institution incorporated in the State of New York.

The Assembly seeks to provide information, stimulate discussion, and evoke independent conclusions in matters of vital public interest.

AMERICAN ASSEMBLY SESSIONS

At least two national programs are initiated each year. Authorities are retained to write background papers presenting essential data and defining the main issues in each subject.

About 60 men and women representing a broad range of experience, competence, and American leadership meet for several days to discuss the Assembly topic and consider alternatives for national policy.

All Assemblies follow the same procedure. The background papers are sent to participants in advance of the Assembly. The Assembly meets in small groups for four or five lengthy periods. All groups use the same agenda. At the close of these informal sessions participants adopt in plenary session a final report of findings and recommendations.

Regional, state, and local Assemblies are held following the national session at Arden House. Assemblies have also been held in England, Switzerland, Malaysia, Canada, the Caribbean, South America, Central America, the Philippines, and Japan. Over one hundred institutions have cosponsored one or more Assemblies.

ARDEN HOUSE

Home of The American Assembly and scene of the national sessions is Arden House, which was given to Columbia University in 1950 by W. Averell Harriman. E. Roland Harriman joined his brother in contributing toward adaptation of the property for conference purposes. The buildings and surrounding land, known as the Harriman Campus of Columbia University, are 50 miles north of New York City.

Arden House is a distinguished conference center. It is self-supporting and operates throughout the year for use by organizations with educational objectives. The American Assembly is a tenant of this Columbia University facility only during Assembly sessions.

The American Assembly

3

The Four-Day Work Week and Its Educational Prospects*

Raymond L. Cravens

A poem alluding to "Blue Tuesday" and a cliché, "Thank God for Thursday", are portents of the revolutionary four-day working schedule which is already a reality for thousands of American workers. One marvels at laborers accepting the four-day, forty-hour week when it is more often than not the idea of management which envisions new production efficiency growing out of increased flexibility in production schedules, less absenteeism, reduced monotony of certain jobs, and greater worker morale.

It is perhaps ironic that labor's dream of the four-day week would gain impetus from management's concern for solutions to behavioral and production problems. But then it may follow that some of these advantages are short-term—avoiding the worst rush of the afternoon traffic jam can be enjoyed only so long as most other workers stay on the traditional work schedule; Women's Lib may approve of the concept of a shorter week but not of a long day with its adverse effects on home and family obligations; a worker who "moonlights" by taking a second job on weekends may be too tired to be efficient on the regular job; "weekend widows" may find their husbands away for an additional day; and a worker is likely to experience frustration if his weekend freedom is limited by his child's five-day school week.

*Reprinted by permission from *Adult Leadership*, March 1973, pp. 278-281.

33

The recent Congressional legislation requiring the observance of five national Holidays on Monday already places a high percentage of the national labor force on a four-day work week for approximately ten percent of the year. While these five official three-day weekends result in a great increase in travel, special events, and certain peculiar social problems, general acceptance of the four-day week should normalize the utilization of this lengthened free time. Undoubtedly, the typical three-day weekend will include expanded educational and cultural as well as recreational activities, but it may follow that less time will be available for such concerns during the regular work week.

Opinions about the rapidity with which business and industry will move to the four-day week vary from predictions of its inappropriateness for large manufacturing concerns to a forecast by Mrs. Riva Poor, a management consultant in Massachusetts, that the next five years will see 80% of industry converting to this or some flexible work schedule,[1] while business executives are issuing warnings that business and industry should not rush into a four-day week until a better analysis of its advantages and disadvantages can be made. It is fairly certain that this trend will catch on much faster than the change from the six-day to the five-day week, which became standard only in 1945 after over 37 years of evolution.

If the claims for increased productivity for the four-day week are borne out, this innovation could contribute to our competitive ability in international commerce. Some progress is already being made in this regard since several companies have reduced the work week to four-days, thirty-six hours in recognition of production gains already realized under the new schedule. Parenthetically, it is interesting to note that the U.S.S.R. has only recently granted the five-day week to its workers and that much of Europe is still on a six-day week. Historians recall that a French representative to the Versailles Peace Conference in 1918 somewhat facetiously proposed that German workers be required to sleep an hour longer each morning to accommodate the less-disciplined French workers. Only experience will reveal whether the four-day week can contribute positively to productive capabilities of American workers and thus to the national balance of payments.

Some educators may prefer to wait until experience with communities of workers on this new schedule can provide some direction for education. It is apparent that should the four-day school week follow the four-day work week, basic educational changes would result. A move to a four-day week for elementary and high schools would probably either be accompanied by a proportionate lengthening of the school day or the school year. New types of utilization of school and college facilities on the weekends for continuing education and special programs would undoubtedly follow, and research in many subject fields on the impact of the new work week will provide scholars a new area of study in the years just ahead.

By lengthening the school day one to one-and-one-half hours, the school may be able to accomplish the same amount of instruction as during the traditional five days. Advantages which could follow such a move might include the removal of many extracurricular activities, athletic contests, band days, field trips, and club meetings to Friday. An accompanying increase in efficiency and instructional utilization during the four-day class week might improve the academic climate in some schools. At least two schools in New Jersey have adopted the four-day schedule and one in Massachusetts and another in New Jersey are considering such a change.[2]

The lengthening of the school year, which could be considered as another alternative in a shift to a four-day school week, might facilitate the scheduling of classes on a year-round basis. The Warren, Michigan Education Association has requested a four-day week as a way of achieving a year-round school and schedule and credit flexibility.[3] Based upon 180 days of classes, a school term runs for 36 weeks. On a four-day week without the lengthening of the class day, 45 weeks would be required to accomplish the 180 days of instruction. The school system could then schedule a four-week summer vacation, a two-week Christmas vacation and a one-week spring vacation during the calendar year.

In either type of revised school calendar, there will undoubtedly be increased demands for the utilization of school classrooms and facilities for continuing education and community purposes during the three-day weekend. Conversely, it might be anticipated that the utilization of the facilities during the evenings may decline during the regular four-day week. This prediction is based upon the assumption that a worker's participation in scheduled evening events, meetings, and continuing education classes will decline because of the extra time he is spending on his regular job at least so long as forty hours are compressed into four days. This may necessitate the concentration of more of these activities into weekend periods which, it would seem, constitutes another pressure upon the school system to also place its regular class schedule on the four-day week.

An analysis might reveal that certain significant economies could be realized by operating a school system on a four-day week by extending the class schedule to accomplish the same amount of instruction as on the five-day plan. These economies would come in such areas as bus transportation, where a 20% reduction in the number of trips would be possible, in the cost of utilities, food services, and janitorial work. Such savings might more than pay for the expanded use of the school plant for other types of educational programs including adult education and enrichment activities during the three-day weekend.

The professional development of teachers should be enhanced and encouraged by the availability of the long weekend wherein graduate work, individual study, course of study revision, and research could take place. The scheduling of periodic in-service activities could also be facilitated if Fridays could be used for this purpose.

As new patterns of class scheduling emerge and are brought into harmony with the general work schedule in the community, it should logically follow that colleges and universities will find it relatively easy to gain approval for the institution of a four-day class week. This will be justified by some other type of instructional utilization for facilities during the weekend periods.

The use of the three-day weekend period for special types of graduate and continuing education should help employed adults accelerate their studies. For example, it would be feasible for an employed adult to be a one-half or three-quarters time graduate student by pursuing classes scheduled on Fridays and Saturdays. With the additional time that would be available for reading and laboratory work, the quality of such courses for part-time students might be increased considerably. Classes would undoubtedly be scheduled both on campus and off campus with an increase in the independent-type study involving direct conferences between the student and the faculty member. Current trends toward external-type degree programs may also be encouraged. The fact that many of the students enrolled in such programs would be available for special seminars and other kinds of concentrated study during a lengthened weekend should reduce the time required for the completion of such degrees.

Students and professors alike would be expected to readily concur in such a schedule innovation. In fact, many students and some professors are already well-accustomed to a three- or four-day week to which they are privileged by the vagaries of the college class scheduling system. Students generally have not been known to seriously object to abbreviations in the process of receiving their education. They usually applaud the dismissal of classes and staunchly defend their inalienable right to be absent. A four-day week will be compatible with the temperaments and industry of many students.

Johnson and Wales College, Providence, Rhode Island, has already instituted a Monday through Thursday, four-day, trimester schedule, and a number of other colleges schedule one day, usually Wednesday, as a free class day utilizing it for laboratories, field trips, and other special purposes. Theological seminaries often have Mondays or Fridays free to facilitate the part-time pastoral work in which a high percentage of their students are engaged. C. W. Post College in New York has already begun an instructional program called "weekend college" designed for students who are unable to attend regular day or evening classes.

Many other questions concerning the use patterns of facilities, libraries, laboratories, cafeterias, etc. and the schedule patterns for special events on college campuses will certainly arise out of the consideration of the four-day college week. Increasingly, colleges and universities find it quite difficult to attract students to remain on the campus during weekends. The ubiquitous automobile and the ease of movement on the interstate highway system attracts students away from the campus on free days. Even when students are several hundred miles from home, they are tempted to travel to where the girls or boys are when classes are out. The attendance at traditional Saturday athletic contests, weekend concerts, dramatic performances, and other similar events may be adversely affected.

Perhaps one of the most important questions of resource utilization will be that of the college professors who may be asked to assume additional instructional and consultative activities during the weekend. The possibility of increased inservice graduate education for school teachers has already been mentioned. Its corollary for business and management personnel would undoubtedly follow with special courses, conferences, and planning sessions requiring the participation of college and university subject specialists.

The in-house educational opportunities for business and industry under the four-day week would at first glance appear to be considerable. By using the fifth day for training and planning activities, considerable dividends might accrue to an industry or business. Obviously this type of educational effort might in effect lengthen the work week for management.

In passing, the question should be posed, "If business, industry, and education adopts the four-day work week, can government be far behind?" Bureaucrats are already pondering this question especially in regard to the apparent need to extend office hours into the weekend period. A move to a four-day shift system coupled with an extended office schedule may be a future trend. And then there are the military services—how about a well-paid volunteer army on a four-day week?

Another educational consideration is the potential for research, scholarly investigation and conjecture which is presented by this social revolution. At a time when some fields of knowledge are becoming staid or victims of a morass of minutia, the advent of this new work week may offer broad new intellectual challenges.

Sociological practitioners such as those who conducted the spring, 1971 Gallup Poll on the four-day week have already sampled the research possibilities. For example, this Gallup Poll found that while 45% of all men polled favored the four-day week, two-thirds of all women were against it. The women cited reduced time for housework as a principal reason, but also indicated that they considered the ten-hour day to be too hard on their husbands. Sociologists and psychologists will not be long satisfied with these tentative conclusions.

Philosophers and theologians may be led to debate the relationship of this change in the work week to the basic question of the nature of man and the purpose of his existence. For example, the work ethic on which so many adults have been reared will have to face squarely the Aristotelian proposition that the end of all human action is leisure. Political scientists will join in the conjecture as to whether Aristotle's highly limited concept of citizenship, presupposing adequate leisure for the assumption of civic responsibilities, may find its democratic fulfillment facilitated by the four-day week.

Economists must decide whether they agree with Paul A. Samuelson that the gross national product should include leisure as one of its factors in output.[4] Obviously, physical educators and recreation specialists will find special educational challenges in the new social phenomenon. If, as Professor Samuelson has suggested, the four-day week is a "momentous social invention" and if its impact is anywhere near that which can be anticipated at this time, scholars will be hard-pressed to complete the investigations which will be necessary for an adequate understanding of this basic change in the work patterns of Americans.[5]

Judgments concerning this significant shift will be as varied as the positions from which they are viewed. This was true when the present five-day week was evolving in the 1920's and 1930's when such men as John E. Edgerton, president of the National Association of Manufacturers, argued that the five-day week was in direct contradiction to the work laws decreed in the Bible.[6] Contrary to Mr. Edgerton's contention, it is not difficult to argue a theological position supporting the four-day-week as fulfilling the God-given right of all men to a maximum amount of leisure. Domestic communists might view the four-day week as a victory of the working class over the class of capitalists, and equally well, Christians may view the three-day weekend as an extended Sabbath offering new possibilities for religious service.

From most any viewpoint, this change in the work schedule has far-reaching implications, and these thoughts and projections can serve only to illustrate some possible implications of this development. Whether the four-day week in its present form becomes the standard in American industry and business only time can tell. If, as some predict, the novelty of the four-day week wears off, it may still have been the precursor of the four-day, thirty-two hour week which has been the objective of organized labor for many years.

In the long run, the effects of either type of four-day week should be similar on the educational scene and only certain short-term adjustment problems in schedules for continuing education and public events should differentiate the two. It is not too soon to speculate about and to consider this, perhaps inevitable, shift in the working patterns of our citizens. Certainly, education must be ready to respond to this revolution.

Notes

1. "The Sabbath Day Grows Longer", *Iron Age*, 28 January 1971.
2. Riva Poor, *Poor's Workweek Letter*, 15 March 1972, p. 6.
3. Ibid.
4. Poor, *Four Days, Forty Hours;* Foreword by Paul A. Samuelson (Cambridge, Mass.: Bursk and Poor Publishing Company, 1970), p. 7.
5. Ibid., p. 9.
6. "Coming: The Four-Day Work Week", *Nation*, 30 November 1970.

4

Career Education: Every Student Headed for a Goal*

Sidney P. Marland, Jr.

Reduced to its least common denominator, the goal of vocational and technical education is wonderfully simple. It is to educate students for specific types of work.

There is a wonderfully simple way to measure the success of these programs. You find out how many, or what percentage, of the graduates actually get jobs for which they are trained, and whether or not they work at them successfully as well-developed citizens.

Academic programs in high schools also have a simple goal when reduced to least common denominators: to prepare students to enter institutions of higher learning. The success measurement? The percentage of students who are accepted for higher education and who undertake such study with some degree of success. These would be basic and admittedly oversimplified measures that could be refined and elaborated in many ways.

But because a proposition is simple, almost to the point of being taken for granted by society, it does not mean that it is not profound. Most profound ideas in our civilization can be fairly simply stated. In our urgent concern over education's success or failure, we tend to oversimplify the profound meanings of our goals and our measures.

*Reprinted by permission from *American Vocational Journal*, March 1972, pp. 34-38.

Elementary and secondary education is a field marked by hard-working, dedicated individuals who are currently undertaking serious self-examination in an effort to discover how closely their work approaches the real national needs and the individual needs of the pupils. In the past decade or so, through the impetus of federal funding, an enormous amount of research has been done to improve teaching, to provide new instruments for educating the young, and to obtain accurate evaluations of programs.

In two areas of education we do fairly well if we are working with youngsters who have a reasonable amount of self-discipline and motivation. These areas are the ones I have just described, vocational and technical education on the one hand, and college preparatory education on the other. But the majority of students are not touched by these areas.

Failing Curriculum. The majority of students do not prepare for particular jobs requiring skill training and they are not truly and systematically preparing for higher education, though some may drift in that direction. They are the students in the courses we customarily label "general education."

If we examine by any measure we care to use the accomplishment records of the schools of the nation, we find that the most severe failings can be found in the general education courses and with the young people who are enrolled in them.

Without undertaking a detailed discussion here of its nature and record, we can, nevertheless, say that the general curriculum's failings are self-evident. On paper, the students may or may not fail; in reality, the program fails. While passing grades may be awarded the general education student, his failure resides in his emphasis upon graduation.

We can say with confidence that the program fails because it has no real goals. It doesn't prepare students for a job nor does it prepare them for higher education; therefore we can't use the measures we use for the vocational education and college preparatory programs.

The fact is, no one knows what it is that should be measured in the general curriculum. It seems to be, in some vague way, education for its own sake—or even more euphemistically, "because it's the law." And yet we know that education, as a joint process of teaching and learning, works only when it is conducted for a purpose on the part of the learner, as well as the teacher.

The general curriculum, which engages the largest number of our students and which returns the worst record of failure, lacks the clear purpose which marks the other two areas of reasonable success.

First, a Clear Purpose. I believe that all education must have a defined, stated purpose and I think we can agree on a statement of purpose for our system of formal elementary and secondary education. The purpose can be stated simply, but again this does not mean that it will be easy to reach:

The purpose of elementary and secondary education in the United States is to prepare all students as well-developed people to enter successfully either a job or some form of post-secondary education, whichever they choose, as soon as they leave the elementary-secondary educational system.

This is one way to state briefly the overall goal—to develop citizens who function well in society. However, we educate in an imperfect society and under imperfect conditions. Young people, for very legitimate reasons although mostly unfortunate ones, frequently leave school before they are graduated.

I think our goal must include those who, for whatever reason, choose to leave the formal system at any point. In other words, the stated goal is to prepare each student to enter a job or advanced study, successfully, regardless of when he leaves our system.

Entry Ticket for the Dropout. This is not unrealistic. Perhaps we are unrealistic at present to think we can prescribe a "school-leaving age" in universal application. We could be most helpful, while drop-outs are a widespread national phenomenon, if we could reduce the crushing effect that dropping out now creates.

If a pupil successfully completes ten grades say, at age 16, and drops out, he is often as ill-equipped to function in society as if he had never gone to school at all, according to present social expectations.

Those ten grades should be meaningful and should represent a level of success that is one grade higher than nine grades of education and one grade lower than eleven grades of education. This should mean an automatic entry ticket to a great many jobs. At present, of course, completion of only ten grades represents failure in our society's stereotype, and it is not an entry ticket to very much at all.

High Priority at USOE. Can we actually set as a national goal for education the preparation of each and every pupil for meaningful work or meaningful higher education lending itself to ultimate career entry and personal fulfillment? Can we keep the options open for *all* young people, so they do not have to choose unalterably at any age between the world of work and the world of continuing education?

Yes, we can, and we have done so. I have proposed, and the U.S. Office of Education has undertaken as a high priority activity, a direct and total confrontation with this concern for purposeful education. We call this new concept "career education."

We are deep into working out the details of how to meet this stated goal. As U.S. Commissioner of Education, I have spent a good deal of time around the nation speaking to groups of people with a specific role to play in this new effort. These groups include secondary school administrators, vocational and technical education specialists, school counselors, business and industrial leaders, state school officials, and labor representatives.

The response is encouraging because education is a deep concern of people interested in our national development. A feeling of need for substantial change in our educational system pervades much of our profession and our citizenry. They see career education as a rational direction of change.

In the context of this encouragement we are supporting research and the implementation of model programs. These programs and the specifics of their operation remain local, as is all of our elementary and secondary education. The federal role is that of supplying financial support and technical assistance and advice. I will describe some broad ideas that have been put forth, and the stage of development of career education.

Must Be All-Encompassing. In the first place, if career education is to work in terms of the goal I stated, it must encompass the entire school program from kindergarten through secondary school completion. In addition, it should include the post-secondary level and adult and continuing education. This will involve changes in the curriculum as well as in teaching approaches. What we are doing is applying a wholly new concept to the entire system; change, therefore, will be substantial.

Besides encompassing every school year, career education will include all students. They will learn about the wide range of career possibilities in our technologically advanced society. They will learn what is involved in getting a job and holding it. They will receive sound guidance and counseling to help them consider their interests and abilities in relation to potential careers. They will learn of the occupational needs of the nation, as projected.

They will be helped to develop career decision-making skills. They will learn specific job skills. And they will get actual help in finding a job, because if career education is to succeed it cannot merely deliver its graduates to the labor market. There is a destructive gap between school and job, and the way to eliminate it is to bridge it ourselves as teachers.

Fifteen Clusters. To accomplish these things, we think that the curriculum should be built around jobs and work. Experts have identified more than 20,000 distinct jobs that people fill. We have had a team of specialists codify these jobs into 15 major groupings which we call career clusters. Some examples are health, marketing and distribution, public service, fine arts and humanities, and manufacturing.

Pupils in the first six grades would become familiar with all of these career clusters through instructional materials and field trips and the kinds of teaching approaches now used to complement courses in basic language, social studies, science, and mathematics.

In Grades 7 and 8, pupils would begin to explore those clusters that most interested them individually. In Grades 9 and 10, a pupil could explore a single cluster of his choice in depth and receive practical experience, even start to develop some specific skills in particular jobs.

In Grades 11 and 12, the student would pursue a selected career area more intensely with three options open to him: he could acquire enough skill to get employment as soon as he left school; he could get a combination of academic and job training courses in preparation for further occupational training at a post-secondary institution; or he could follow a program directed towards enrollment in higher education for a professional degree.

An important aspect of career education would be that opting back into school would be as easy as opting out. Maturity, changing interests, higher aspirations, and increased economic security are among the reasons for returning, and the schools and colleges would be receptive to such re-enrollments.

Out-of-School Models. In order to provide alternative choices, apart from the formal system, three out-of-school models are being developed for career education.

A home-based program would make extensive use of television, correspondence courses, and possibly, tutors. It would combine adult education with vocational education to open career opportunities to adults who have little hope of advancement at present. Women required to be at home would be a special target of this approach, as would handicapped persons.

An employer-based model would rely on industrial firms, businesses, labor, and government agencies to operate work-training programs related to their own varied employment needs. This program, providing basic academic learning along with skill training, would serve students still in school as well as those who might find the alternative more meaningful on a full-time basis.

A rural-residential model would serve entire families who would train together for better employment opportunities. One program based on this model is underway near Glasgow, Montana. It will serve a six-state region.

Main Thrust in the Schools. I believe, however, that it is in the established school system and colleges that the greatest number of individuals will be reached, and this is where we will be making our greatest effort. Teachers of all subjects will be encouraged to learn new techniques in relating their work to career education purposes.

Classes in basic academic subjects will use career-oriented materials. There will be a far stronger role for guidance and counseling than now prevails.

The initial costs will be considerable; we must face this fact. There will be new expenses for planning, for curriculum revision, for training supervisors, counselors, and teachers, and for acquiring new instructional materials.

The best estimates I have indicate that after the "turn-around" costs of the first two or three years, the annual costs of operating such a program would still be slightly higher than current costs. But we would be accomplishing far more than we are at present in terms of developing productive and fulfilled human beings.

Why Career Education? One may ask what motivates the Office of Education to move vigorously toward career education as agent of substantial change in our schools. Some statistics help in illustrating the large problems that confront us as a nation.

Of every ten students in high school, two receive occupational training of some sort and three go to college (although one of these drops out). This means that more than one-half of all students now in high school—1,500,000—ought to have opportunities, counseling, and attractive options in occupational training. The system, and the attitudes of young people and their parents, foreclose these conditions in most schools.

Here is another way of looking at the problem. In the 1970-71 school year there were 850,000 elementary and secondary school dropouts. There were 750,000 general education students who graduated from high school but who did not attend college and were not prepared for entering a job. There were 850,000 high school students who entered college (in 1967) but dropped out in 1970.

These three groups comprise an estimated total of 2,450,000 young people who should have had the opportunities for realistic education in career development but did not. Education is now the nation's largest enterprise, costing $85 billion a year, a figure surpassing the defense budget. Those 2,450,000 pupils cost us about $28 billion, which is almost one-third of the entire educational expenditure for the nation.

Getting More Realistic. For years our secondary schools have been so strongly college-oriented that most of the effort, planning, and aspirations have been directed toward the academic program. And yet the Department of Labor tells us that for now and the foreseeable future, 80 percent of the nation's jobs will be handled by employees with less than a baccalaureate degree.

In some ways we are starting to be more realistic. In fiscal year 1970, one million more secondary school students were enrolled in vocational education courses than the year before, representing a 25 percent increase. Post-secondary vocational and technical education enrollments in fiscal 1970 exceeded one million, an increase of more than 40 percent over 1969.

Local and state governments, exceeding the requirements for matching funds, are spending five dollars on vocational education for every one dollar spent by the federal government.

We have been doing a good job in vocational education and training, and in vocational counseling, but only 12 to 14 percent of all high school students enter these programs. We have attached such emphasis to the baccalaureate degree that we have by implication downgraded other equally worthy options.

Career education would embrace vocational and technical education and go farther and wider. It would help direct every student toward a career goal, including those aiming for professions.

It would, I believe, greatly enhance the quality of learning in the academic subjects as a result of more realistic motivation. And it would enhance the vocational-technical training programs by attaching prestige and attention to the arena that they now occupy alone. That arena is where education is engaged in for a purpose and where a student can see for himself the relevance and usefulness of his efforts.

Catching On. Career education seems already to have the beginnings of a national movement. We have not consciously sought this degree of consensus, believing more time is needed for development and debating the concept among all concerned, especially teachers.

In examining the need for systematic progress, we have, besides developing models, asked each state to undertake plans (with federal funds) for one or more career education projects of its own. Even before this, many states had outstanding local programs in operation—Delaware, Georgia, Mississippi, New Jersey, North Dakota, and Wyoming, for example.

Several cities, such as Dallas and San Diego, are using the concept of career education for their basic design. In connection with its model-building efforts, the Office of Education is sponsoring six pilot projects in the public schools of Atlanta; Los Angeles; Hackensack, New Jersey; Pontiac, Michigan; Mesa, Arizona; and Jefferson County, Colorado.

Interim Strategy. Exemplary vocational education programs funded by the Office of Education in many states have resulted in findings that are being incorporated into emerging career education curricula for trial and demonstration.

The Leadership Development Awards established by the Office of Education, which went to 160 experienced vocational educators for full-time doctoral work, will be helpful in filling the professional staff requirements in the home states of these candidates after their training.

Until we are ready for a whole new system based on career education we can proceed under an interim strategy that must include four major actions: (1) Changes in the $500 million-a-year vocational education program of the Office of Education in line with career education goals, particularly in moves toward career preparation in many high-demand occupations which we have not dealt with; (2) more flexible options for high school graduates to continue on to higher education or to enter work, instead of being locked into choices they made when they were 14; (3) bringing business, industry, and organized labor into closer collaboration with the schools; (4) attracting new leadership and commitments to career education at federal, state, and local levels.

A Focus for All Efforts. This is a time of great ferment and change in education; there is a tremendous amount of sound activity directed toward a great number of goals—universal literacy, raising levels of self-esteem, compensatory programs of all sorts to overcome physical, social, emotional, and cultural handicaps of youngsters in schools. They all have a special concern, and a specific population to be reached. Career education is viewed as a new form for all young people in school. It can embrace within itself the special concerns and special needs of nearly all educational objectives.

We can bring these concerns and all of our extra, and very often separate, efforts together in a meaningful way if we have the wisdom, the courage, and the will to find a large new consensus on what the schools might be. Career education can be that goal.

5

The Claim for
Occupational Man
on the Curriculum*

*Arthur R. King, Jr.,
and John A. Brownell*

The answer to the question, "What is man?" has often been "farmer," "lawyer," "plumber," "teacher," "doctor," "carpenter." The deeper significance of such responses should not be lost. A persistent belief exists that the good life is defined by the quantitative and material forms of human "goods," by the autonomy and security which money provides, in short, by economic success. Since the prestigious kinds of work are those which yield social approval, wealth, power, and success, persons tend to be judged by their occupations. The hierarchy of occupational prestige is frequently turned into a hierarchical scale of human worth, with stereotypes of manners, general culture, influence, and intelligence. Since occupational success looms in importance, every means for its achievement is mobilized. It becomes the school's task to train for something "practical," which for most means to give marketable skills. The importance of utility as the purpose for study leads schools and teachers to defend even liberal studies with the same argument.

Such a view conflicts with the tradition of democratic morality, wherein work is everyone's responsibility and is morally and intrinsically good. Idleness, even for the wealthy, is considered evil. (It may be noted that this image of the dignity of work is restricted to those who work with things and people; those who "work" with ideas are frequently suspect.) Closely related to the tradition of universal work is the Christian notion of "vocation"; it, too, is at odds with the "success society." A vocation is the call for dedication to any task for which one is fitted and through which one gains self-fulfillment. A vocation is not merely a means for making a living, but a way of using one's life, a way of ennobling even the lowest task.

The survival of the concept of "vocation" during this period of rapid technological change and subsequent job obsolescence is doubtful. Furthermore, the perspective of occupational man is further clouded by the fact that many who are successful by economic measures are dissatisfied and unfulfilled; many change occupations.

We have used the heading of *occupational man* to gather the claims on the content of the curriculum which place man, the worker, first. We use the words *occupational training* to stand for professional, vocational, technical, agricultural, commercial, business, distributive, industrial, and homemaking "education," for training signifies education narrowly rather than liberally and making people qualified and proficient in a specific task or occupation.

In evaluating the persistency of the claim of occupational training, other than for the professions of law, medicine, and theology, on the content of the curriculum, we must recognize that it has been considered a demand on schools only in recent times. For example, Plato treats education extensively in *The Republic, The Laches,* and *The Laws,* regarding it as one of "the grandest and most beautiful subjects," and "the first and fairest things that the best of men can ever have," yet no mention is made of public education of the industrial class nor is there any proposed system of schooling for occupations. True preparation and training for crafts, occupations, and vocations has always been provided somehow—through systems of apprenticeship primarily. But with industrialization in the nineteenth century, enormous pressures from management and labor brought public schools clearly into the occupational training process. Today probably all public secondary schools and colleges have some courses or curricula which are directed toward the development of marketable knowledge and skills. A number of such institutions are formed almost entirely for this end. In recent decades the public elementary schools, with the possible exception of grades seven and eight, have lost their earlier occupational training function. Probably only in a few independent secondary schools and colleges is the curriculum entirely devoted to liberal studies.

With the advent of universal elementary and secondary education the function of shops, vocational programs, homemaking, and business courses frequently became that of handling casualties of the academic program. A persistent argument for occupational training says that some students are not fit either by capability or seemliness for liberal education and that, with universal schooling, occupational training is their only alternative. This argument has been challenged in recent years by a number of experimental programs which are based on the assumption that nearly all persons are fit for liberal education when liberal studies are properly conceived, programmed, and taught.

Occupational training programs as substitutes for extensive liberal education draw most heavily on students from ethnic and racial minorities and from poorer families. Dr. James B. Conant contends in his book *Slums and Suburbs* that these students "fit" occupational training programs. He argues that schooling for jobs is the answer to the plight of minorities, the poor, and the slow learner. "The lesson is that to a considerable degree what a school should do and can do is determined by the status and ambitions of the families being served." He does not relate this prescription to the generally recognized waste of talent among the economically, politically, and culturally submerged of the United States and other countries. Nor does Conant honor the traditional right and opportunity of the individual to transcend the humble circumstances of his family.

The potency of the occupational training claim for priority in the high school, college, and university curriculum is best exemplified by another statement of Conant: "I submit that in a heavily urbanized and industrialized free society the educational experiences of youth should fit their subsequent employment." The appropriateness of this notion for a "free society" is not clear; indeed it has characterized totalitarian societies. If man's most important goal is to be worker, if his worth lies in his work, then logically any society which so defines the nature of man would find the statement appropriate. How students and their counselors determine "subsequent employment" in advance also raises an interesting question. Such an assumption implies a fairly static society with a marked degree of determinism based on family background and a stable occupational structure. The democratic ideal of vertical mobility seems at odds with Dr. Conant. His ideas about the kind of occupational training suited to the young can be seen in this statement:

Practically all of these practical skills are of such a nature that a degree of mastery can be obtained in high school sufficient to enable the youth to get a job at once on the basis of skill. They are in this sense skills marketable immediately on graduation from high school.

Many citizens and educators agree with Dr. Conant. To all of like mind we ask this question: "To what kind of job, in what kind of occupation or industry, with what kind of future do these immediately marketable skills lead?"

Let us analyze the claim for priority of occupational training further. The delayed entry of youth into the job market until age eighteen or older is a fact supported by both legislation and labor-management practices. This trend for rising age of employment appears irreversible for the present. Already there are certain technical industries which have no jobs, other than janitorial ones, for males with only high school diplomas; such industries require completion of junior college or other post-high school technical programs. Occupational training for any person tends to be centered in those years immediately before leaving school; as the average number of years of schooling for all has increased, occupational preparation has occurred later. The later the occupational training starts in the student's total program, the more sophisticated this training is likely to be. Increasingly, adult education programs provide both liberal education for persons already in the occupations as well as occupational training for those seeking new positions or more sophisticated skills.

With the advance of automated technology, the phenomenon of job obsolescence seems endemic and malignant. Too often the specifics of occupational curricula have been built on occupational patterns which have either disappeared or are rapidly disappearing. What suits the immediate labor market may be highly inappropriate for the future. Even with later, more technical, more cognitive occupational preparation, it is not clear how such training can be related harmoniously to the changing job market. Engineering, medical, and teacher preparation faces the same difficulty.

Businesses, industries, and the armed services have assumed more and more responsibilities for occupational training in recent years. Few are bold enough to estimate the amount spent formally and informally by American industry for in-service occupational training. Rough estimates range upward into the billions of dollars each year. Armed forces expenditures for basic and special schooling in 1959 exceeded 3.4 billion dollars. The costs of the continuous training programs on complex military hardware would probably far exceed this figure. Only in the immediate job contexts are specific training programs practicable. If this trend toward delay in vocational preparation continues, the efforts of secondary schools, perhaps colleges, in industrial, business, and vocational preparation may well become more and more general, more theoretical, and less and less immediately marketable.

This trend may be short-lived if the emphasis on vocational education contained in a number of the newer specialized government programs, such as "antipoverty" and "job corps," should be passed along to the public schools. Such an action would probably bring demands for reduction in liberal education for those youth who are already by environment and association most severely curtailed.

An almost ironic twist emerges with respect to occupational training in the schools. The more such training an individual has at the expense of liberal education the poorer is his prognosis with regard to income, advancement, social position, and opportunity for contributions to society. If training starts early, it limits theoretic insight; the individual is locked into entry jobs, is denied opportunity for advancement and leadership, and is marked for job obsolescence. Radical retraining programs for the unemployed, which consist of substantial academic study, must be designed to remedy these deficiencies.

We cannot leave the subject without noting that early occupational training tends to limit the accumulation of liberally educated individuals necessary for trade and professional leadership. Without more extensive liberal education, labor management, and the professions will not carry out their most responsible roles in society. In short, when occupational and professional training short-circuits liberal education, the education of the person *qua person* is reduced; his ultimate worth is denied.

For the right persons at the right time occupational training is a significant and worthy venture. Premises governing the placement of pre-service, as contrasted with in-service, training include the following:

1. The logic of occupational training is the logic of the industrial or commercial process to be served.

2. Occupational training, because of job obsolescence, is most practical immediately preceding or accompanying, through apprenticeship, entry to the job. Such training should be specific, intensive, and short-term.

3. Occupational training should be built on optimal prior liberal studies, for the greater the intellectual background the wider the range of vocational options open to the individual.

When occupational training is the priority claim on the content of the curriculum, certain pedagogical characteristics follow. As Phillip Phenix says, the vocational orientation imports "into the whole educational system the patterns of prestige and power that characterize the acquisitive culture." Occupational training emphasizes the acquisitive motive, the case value for studies, and downgrades the intrinsic values in learning, in preparation for the good life, and in opportunities to engage in useful and interesting work.

A general reinterpretation of studies and courses follows. Business English, commercial geography, shop mathematics, applied physics, household chemistry, business arithmetic, and the like are established and substituted for liberal studies. Utility becomes the primary defense for any course or study. By this reasoning English is important because it helps one in his occupation. The skill elements of reading, writing, spelling, and speaking expand; the aesthetic elements of literature recede; knowledge about literary conventions, modes, genre, rhetorical devices, linguistic geography, and the history of the language fades. Courses and studies aimed at liberating the young from cultural impoverishment, from aspirationless families, from suffering and boredom may decline or draw students only from those homes which already have the most potent educational resources.

As noted above, there is an almost irresistible tendency to consign the slow, the poor, and the difficult students as well as those from certain ethnic groups to programs of occupational preparation. A clear-eyed view of the biases and assumptions behind such practices seems essential.

Some curricular designs have used preparation for occupations as their organizing principle. Here, the assumption is made that the student "emerges" from occupational studies to liberal studies, in a way more compatible to his "interests" and "needs." The success of such plans has never been documented; the theoretical justification has been obscure.

When the claim for occupational man is made prime, the control and definition of the curriculum move inevitably to the consumers of manpower—the industries, the military, the government, and the professional school. The economic establishment becomes the pied piper, the schools the beguiled children.

6

Career Education: Earning a Living or Living a Life?*

*Robert J. Nash
and Russell M. Agne*

The U.S. Office of Education is currently advancing a case for career education that will affect schooling at all levels. HEW Assistant Secretary for Education Sidney P. Marland talks about a "school-based" model of career training that will expose all children to a full range of career opportunities. Every subject in the public school curriculum will be "refocused" to help students narrow their occupational choices. When a student has selected a career he will be provided with intensive training to achieve "marketable, salable" skills. The USOE plans to spend $168 million in 1973 on career education experiments; Marland has even stated that the "central" mission of all community colleges (with a projected 1975 enrollment of 3.3 million) will be to equip students with the skills guaranteeing them "useful" employment.[1]

Obviously, there is much that is positive in the career education concept. To provide people with the training to enter and succeed in a career whenever they decide to leave the formal educational process is a humane way to ensure each person a modicum of economic independence and a personal sense of worth. Also, the desire to relate abstract academic experiences to actual field work can only be salutary.

*Reprinted by permission from the authors and *Phi Delta Kappan*, Vol. 54, pp. 373-376.

For example, teachers in Mesa, Arizona, and Pontiac, Michigan, are requiring that course work in social studies and science be related directly to on-site experiences in journalism, social work, x-ray technology, and oceanography.[2] Finally, career education has the potential of obliterating forever the myth that only a college degree signifies personal worth; by shifting the emphasis from gaining a career through academic certificate to gaining a career through performance, there is the chance that involuntary attendance at colleges will disappear and that work will begin to take on the important function of helping a young person to develop personal meaning.

In spite of the above, what disturbs us most about the career education movement is the number of key assumptions left unexamined. Nowhere in an exhaustive review of the literature have we discovered a single word of caution or criticism concerning the possible misuses of the career education concept. Nowhere have we found an analysis of the ideological premises underlying career education proposals. Instead, we observe that the literature accepts as an unchallenged good the continued existence of a corporate social order and a concept of human behavior which is achievement-motivated. As a result, much of the pleading for educational reform toward a career perspective is a thinly disguised politics.[3] Also, the literature on career education conveys a theory of learning which is at least open to question. Not once, however, have we encountered an explicit discussion of the learning theory peculiar to career education, let alone an in-depth analysis of its possible limitations. And, finally, in spite of the frequent references to career education as a program designed to effect "radical" educational change, there is practically nothing in the literature that recognizes any weakness in contemporary American schooling other than its poor performance as a feeder of skilled workers into the occupational world. Therefore, because of its excessive claims and the absence of significant self-criticism, we believe that the career education prospectus must undergo careful, constructive examination.

The Corporate Reality Principle

At the heart of the career education movement is an ideological commitment to a corporate social order. In his writings, Marland stresses his belief that American society is moving inevitably toward a social order that developing industry and technology will transform substantially from the one we now know. No longer will people be trained for one lifetime job. Instead, because society is becoming increasingly "organizational" and "technical," each person will have to learn new skills throughout his life if he is to enter and reenter the different careers which will emerge and disappear in the future. In one article Marland maintains that America's expanding corporate society will necessitate such sweeping "pragmatic, theoretical, and moral" changes in education and the business-industrial world that people will become "obsolete" unless they can learn new attitudes and work skills.[4]

What is disturbing about all this is that American educators are being urged to accept, as an unquestioned social ideal, a type of corporate reality principle emphasizing high productivity; spiraling wages; automation; increasing economic growth; accelerating rates of social change; systematic administration; complex, large-scale organizations; and a technical approach to the resolution of human problems. Because Marland and others rarely challenge the direction toward which the corporate reality principle is pulling education in America, many career education programs are being constructed without the possibility of students' being exposed to alternative societal models. For example, in Pontiac, Michigan, career training begins in kindergarten; children are taught that their education is important only if it prepares them for "the varied world of employment." From kindergarten on, students are helped to perceive themselves as "productive workers"; third-graders are visited by leaders in industry; sixth-graders are interviewed by an employment agency for jobs in the cafeteria and library; preschoolers are taught that their parents' jobs are "of indispensable importance" in maintaining the family unit.[5] Nowhere in the Pontiac model, however, is a student allowed to speculate about such "utopian" possibilities as a society where a person's worth is not dependent on his being a productive worker who contributes throughout a lifetime to an expanding economy.

A reader searches the career education literature in vain for the slightest sign that its advocates have read any of the social or political critiques of the corporate reality principle—critiques that have been on the upswing in recent years.[6] The critics have shown that corporate life often has a bogus quality that overvalues expertise and performance. They warn that technique and bureaucratic manipulation must never substitute for risk-taking personal expression. Also, some of the more political critics have demonstrated that American schools traditionally have rewarded students who exhibit the characteristics of compliant, passive workers. These students learn to subordinate emotional modes of personal cognition to modes which are cerebral and achievement-oriented. What these critics emphasize most, however, is that the tracking structure of formal education in the United States tends to reflect the structure of industrial production: Just as students cede control over their activities to career educators, so too are workers stratified within the industrial system. What results is a worker who can be motivated only by the promise of external rewards and status-enhancement.[7]

Another tendency on the part of some career spokesmen is to conceal their corporate biases beneath a gloss of "futuristic" prediction. For example, the editors of a national journal assume that because technological growth is inevitable, given current trend indices, then such growth is ipso facto desirable.[8] Underlying their injunction to prepare students for the "new technological realities" is the assumption that corporate systems of business, production, and technology, with their ever-expanding growth potential, will be (ought to be) *decisive* in shaping human behavior and values and in determining the best possible future of American culture. Not once in their proposals do the editors build into programs for vocational education a unit detailing the present evidence of systemic failures that the corporate growth principle has left all over the world. The editors have virtually ignored the imminent danger (as a consequence of unfettered technological growth) that the world's minerals will soon be exhausted and the biosphere enveloped in the pollution.[9]

Marland assumes that career education is "a way of combatting apathy" because such a perspective teaches "the skills, the knowledge, and the attitudes necessary for our citizens to adapt to change . . . so that our society will continue not only to survive but to *flourish.*"[10] What he overlooks is the burgeoning group of young people who are questioning the moral validity of learning skills which continue only to perpetuate a laissez-faire, expansionist economy with the GNP as its central index of achievement. Many youths are resisting attempts to be siphoned off into careers, because their educational experiences do not allow them to challenge the whole structure of corporate capitalism. These youths believe that earning a living is always secondary to living a life; by implication, career education programs must begin to contest the long-held assumption that in order to secure material well-being man's energies have to be channeled into the making of money.[11]

An economist, Frank Riessman, points out that the possibility of qualitative growth in the human services is minimized because the GNP as an evaluative economic norm legitimizes industrial-technological growth while devaluing growth in the "people services."[12] Much of the literature on career education conveys the impression that only through continuous industrial-technological growth, and through the new careers created as a spinoff, will economic growth continue to flourish in the United States. A representative of the Pontiac Division of General Motors has extolled the concept of career education because it "presents the free enterprise system and its opportunities so that students can prepare themselves." He has offered to send several General Motors executives into the Pontiac, Michigan, schools to explain, among other things, the automobile industry's contributions to the GNP.[13]

Where such an approach is deficient is in its one-sided view of contemporary social reality. Industrial-technological growth is resource-depleting and capital-intensive; such growth is resulting in widespread unemployment, underutilization of people's talents, and the steady deterioration of the world's natural resources. Meanwhile, there is a dearth of people who have the career skills necessary to resolve the crushing personal and social problems of drug abuse, alcoholism, estrangement, human despair and malaise, and pathological violence. The single greatest failure of career education programs would be to push people into the corporate (industrial-technological) growth sector, with its status and financial attractions, while underplaying the value of careers in the human services.

Achievement-Driven Man

Joseph Cosand, assistant commissioner of higher education, bases his prescriptions for career education reform in colleges and universities on the following:

> It seems obvious that if you begin making students aware in kindergarten of all the career opportunities that lie before them, you are going to have students who are motivated — alive, alert, and working students — by the time they enter college. They are going to college with a purpose, with goals to *achieve*.[14]

Marland subscribes to a similar concept of human motivation; he has gently scolded young people who reject "conventional economic motivations" in favor of "an avocational interest more attractive to them at the moment." In spite of his comment that he understands young people's alienation from the achievement ethic of Western culture, Marland nevertheless considers youth's real needs to be achievement-based.[15]

Much of the program development in career education is rooted in a belief that people's economic needs are pre-potent. For example, the Sonoma County public schools in California have developed a career curriculum which integrates subject matter at all levels. In the junior high schools, math and English teachers have designed a collaborative program to relate their subjects to students' "real interests"—an examination of occupations in the banking industry. Activities include visiting a local bank, buying a car, writing a contract for a loan, computing monthly interest, writing a play about the "banking and auto sales industry," and taking slides of a typical day's activities at the bank.[16]

What is open to question about the above is *not* the attempt to relate academic material to real-life situations, but the obvious effort to fuel the achievement drives of students by appealing directly to their acquisitive needs. Another questionable assumption is one that educators often make: Students will respond enthusiastically to subject matter only when it is reduced to occupational relevance. A social scientist, David McClelland, has made the classical defense of the achievement motive as the most forceful drive in contemporary man. He maintains that leaders can exploit this achievement drive in order to accelerate economic growth. Among his suggestions, he urges the introduction of "ideological conversions" emphasizing individualistic achievements; reorganizing people's fantasy lives so that they can begin to daydream about what they have to achieve; and encouraging the emergence of a corporate class characterized by a vigorous drive for economic achievement.[17]

Almost daily, events demonstrate that the Sonoma school system's image of human motivation, like McClelland's, is splintered. Contrary to McClelland's hypothesis, young people need more than "conventional economic motivations" to feel fully human. Recently, in Detroit, assembly-line workers disrupted the automobile factories because of their conviction that they are becoming "nothing better than machines to turn out profits." Although highly skilled and salaried, they have turned to alcoholism, drugs, and high absenteeism to express their resentment toward numbing, unfulfilling work.[18] Similarly, a social scientist, Daniel Yankelovich, found in a study of college students' personal and political attitudes on 50 campuses that young people are becoming increasingly skeptical of economic well-being and achievement striving as an exclusive prescription for personal happiness. Instead, students value friendship, privacy, freedom of opinion and emotional expression, the family, and nature.[19]

To view human behavior as predominantly achievement-driven, and then to develop curricula based on such a belief, is to risk a total misunderstanding of contemporary social realities in America. For example, it is at best a dubious assumption that members of minority groups after being socialized to consume in middle-class ways, and after being given the training in skills to pursue the white, middle-class, corporate careers, will actually be allowed equal opportunity to achieve those careers. Even more questionable, however, is the assumption that any young person ought to strive for a career at all. Because of the instability of the economy, careers go in and out of fashion, and an occupation that seems so attractive and permanent in 1972 might be nonexistent in 1978.[20] What is especially unsettling, however, is the inability of so many career educators to understand that the more a person achieves, the greater his need for further achievement. Achievement, like acquisition, is rarely self-limiting; to promise a person total economic satisfaction because he has developed "marketable" skills is to provoke intense personal disillusionment. Personal happiness based on economic success is a chimerical formula; the ultimate social consequence is to convert each person's need for potency into a sense of impotence, generating an estrangement so severe that the society itself is brought to the breaking point.

Learning Fallacies in Career Ed

In Marland's basic rationale for all career education programs, he also advances an implicit theory of learning. He believes:

> A major component of the reform we seek must be increased productivity — finding ways of getting more out of each dollar invested by turning away from obsolescent cottage-industry methods through a major reordering of our principal resources, including teaching talent, and wider reliance on technology, which is our principal hope for the effective development and implementation of high-quality, lower unit-cost learning.[21]

In his review of how a "school-based model" of career education will work, Marland specifies that throughout the first six grades a student will be made aware of the various clusters of occupations available to him. These include "business and office occupations," "marketing and distribution occupations," and "media and manufacturing occupations." As in high school and college, academic subjects will be "refocused" so "that these classes are presented in terms of the student's career interests."[22]

One educator recommends the use of Occupacs, "multimedia packages of materials that can be used for presenting kindergarten through ninth-grade career-development activities." These modules help students study specific occupations via cassette recorders or simulated work experiences "for the purpose of learning vocabularies and skills." For example, the Secretary Occupac module enables children to code letters alphabetically and prepare masters.[23] Another educator recommends a curriculum including such activities as "role playing," "coloring, drawing, and pasting types of occupations," "vocabulary lessons," "discussions concerning attitudes and feelings about certain careers," and "requirements for success in various occupations." One of the objectives in these activities is to understand "the characteristics of good students and workers."[24]

In grades 7-10, a student will select a "job cluster" to explore in great depth. One New Jersey middle school model, the Introduction to Vocations Program, involves a study of local industry, employment trends, and professional opportunities, via field trips, visits to classrooms by successful professionals, and television and film productions.[25] Grades 11 and 12 will enable the student "to acquire the skills" to take a job immediately after graduation, "or prepare himself for entering a post-secondary institution that would train him as a technician."[26] For example, August Martin High School in New York offers students a comprehensive program in airline occupations including pre-pilot and pre-stewardess training, air-traffic control, ticket sales, and management.[27] Finally, higher education will provide students with "training ... in technical careers," in order to become "more alert to the changing realities of the job market."[28]

Career programs like the above assume a theory of learning based on four interrelated fallacies. What follows is a brief examination of the false assumptions and our own generalized suggestions for redirecting present career education programs.

Specialism—Whenever educators create a perspective of knowledge that is exclusively functional—i.e., ideas are relevant only when they can be used to promote success in a career—then the educational experience is reduced to a kind of specialized training or programming. Knowledge gets filed into a series of "pragmatic" activities, distributed in clusters and modules, so that students can cultivate one narrow sector of their abilities in order to achieve occupational competence.

What is most disconcerting about collapsing the learning experience into such specialized boxes as "occupational clusters" is that educators sell their souls for a view of life superficially utilitarian. This view is fragmented because students gain insight only into the nature of outer reality; they neglect their inner nature—the intuitive and emotional life dependent for its sustenance on the arts, humanities, and religion. Unfortunately, there is an inexorable logic to specialized education: When persons are locked into one mode of thought or specialty, they become impervious to new ideas and experience. Vance Packard has shown the dismal consequence of career specialization: People become "strangers," driven from job to job, often under terrible stress, impelled chiefly by the external goals of status, promotion, and financial power.[29]

As long as career education remains highly specialized, human beings will continue to be separated from the totality of their experiences. In the future, career educators will have to construct programs more sensitive to young people's needs to absorb and integrate all kinds of knowledge (liberal, spiritual, instrumental, sexual, expressive, political, scientific). This entails placing far less emphasis on restrictive vocational goals and specialized work skills, and helping young people instead to assess the potential of a career to develop the total self.

Sequentialism—Eli Ginzberg has a developmental scheme demonstrating that occupational choice is a slow, sequential process, and not the result of a single, isolated event.[30] Unfortunately, one gets the impression that often the emphasis on levels and progression is self-authenticating. An administrator decides that career education will become the mission of schooling in a local community. Therefore, as an operational convenience, training gets meted out in stages, over specifically planned periods of time. And because a "major component" of career education is "increased productivity" and the "development of lower unit-cost learning," it follows that career training is efficient—and concerned with performance criteria, precise measurement methods, and the behavioral evidence that signals the student to move from one level to another.[31]

Rigid sequencing, in conjunction with performance objectives, can be a devastating learning block for some students. To train all children in an inflexible age and grade sequence is to risk swamping the special tempo and style of each person's unique rhythm for learning. According to recent research in group theory and human potential studies, learning can occur as the result of exposure to new experiences, active discovery, and a restless searching and questioning. As students who have interrupted their formal education often demonstrate, it is possible to grow through a variety of informal learning situations. Some students gather in urban collectives, some in rural communes; others staff free schools, travel, become migrant laborers, and work in day-care centers.[32]

These activities grant the individual the sovereignty to develop his skills and interests at his own pace, whenever the need to disengage from established structures strikes him. When career educators can resist the tendency to schedule every moment of a student's time

for occupational awareness and technical training, then human beings
may be able to frame their own purposes and create their own satisfactions; they may even become more competent, satisfied workers.
First, however, educators will have to free students from the suffocat-
ing sequential modes in which they have traditionally been trained.

Fundamentalism—The current emphasis on vocabulary, mathematical, and attitudinal competencies in curricular packages is incom-
plete and shortsighted. It is becoming exceedingly difficult to designate any body of knowledge or behaviors as "fundamental" for *all* students, because workers in the world of the future will need a diversity
of skills and attitudes—some of which are still unknown. For example,
one social scientist has predicted that in the future people will require
a greater variety of human services than at present. In addition to
health, education, and welfare services, people will need help in becoming more artistic, religious, philosophical, and interpersonal.[33]

To counteract the current preoccupation with marketable skills
typical of many career programs, educators will have to consider the
value of skills which may be probing, questioning, noninstrumental,
and confrontative. This might mean that teachers will have to become
human relations leaders, helping students to explore, discover, and
test a number of personal competencies usually suppressed in formal
educational settings. For example, many students will need competencies in becoming political clarifiers and activists; they will have to
develop skills to clarify their own purposes and values and the ability
to relate these insights to systematic political participation. These
nonoccupational skills will necessitate a curriculum that helps students to think about issues and problems, aids them in clarifying their
value confusions, and urges them to consider and act upon workable
alternatives to the corporate system as it is.

Credentialism—Mr. Marland has stated that entrance to the professions, trades, and unions should be based exclusively on a person's performance, not on whether he has accumulated formal credentials.[34]
While Marland's inclinations are praiseworthy, career educators have
yet to show how they can avoid converting a performance-based
model of education to one that is exactly the opposite—namely, the
selection, training, and certifying of workers for the corporate state.
Students will be quick to see that when performance criteria are
product-oriented, system-serving, and adult-imposed, then they are
indistinguishable from the tyranny of a credential.

In the future, a performance-based curriculum must include more
than functional career training. The most "useful" learning, like play,

is intrinsic, spontaneous, and leisurely—subordinating technical competence to growth in personal, physical, aesthetic, social, and political awareness.[35] Consequently, career educators will have to learn how to designate performance criteria for expressive learning as effectively as they do for "marketable skill" learning. This type of learning confers superior career advantages on a person because it is evocative and heuristic: A student learns to discover for himself the worth and meaning of an experience, the methods for arriving at and assessing that experience, and the implications an experience has for his private and public worlds. Evocative education prepares students, *not* merely to make a living, but to live a full life, free from boredom and excessive striving after meretricious credentials.

Earning a Living *and* Living a Life

We suggest that, in the future, career educators will have to ask three kinds of questions concerning the purposes of their programs:

1. *To what extent is career education enhancing the principle of maximum possibilities in occupations?*

Educators must begin to move their curricula away from the unilateral provisioning of skilled careerists for the corporate state and toward the enhancement of human possibilities. Careers will have to increase personal joy and hope; this will mean preparing persons to live comfortably and enthusiastically with the inevitability of multiple occupations during a lifetime. One approach might be to prepare people to experiment with diversification in their work. For example, the quality of a person's daily living could be intensified if he had shorter work periods, broken up by other forms of work, such as teaching, gardening, counseling, wood chopping, poetry writing, or machine tinkering. In the future career educators will have to resist the temptation to rely on such subtle incentives as human greed and status climbing to motivate students to choose careers. Students will have to be helped to select careers on the basis of whether a profession promises them *human* enhancement, rather than enhancement through power, profit, or prestige. The type of career to be avoided will be the one where a credentialed hierarchy imposes restrictions on occupational diversity because it wants to maintain its special privileges.

2. *How can career education obliterate the distinction between work and leisure?*

Career educators must help each individual find meaning and hope in a profession by pointing out its possibilities for being a sphere of consequential leisurely activity. This might mean helping people to evaluate a career according to the opportunities it offers for contentment, joy, challenge, and excitement—experiences people ordinarily seek *away* from their work. Perhaps this will necessitate a kind of "personal worth index" where an occupation is assessed, *not* on the corporate terms of the wealth it produces or the mobility it generates, but on the total impact a job has on human life. One function of the "index" will be to blur the false distinction we have created between work and leisure, and to enable persons to pursue competence and personal meaning in their careers as well as in their avocational activities.

3. How can career education be more concerned with human services?

Educators will have to develop and emphasize innovative, labor-intensive "human service clusters" while minimizing capital-intensive clusters (such as "marketing and distribution," and "construction and manufacturing") grounded in an infinitely expanding technological base. We urgently require persons trained in helping us to improve the quality of our education, health services, food, leisure-time activities, air, and water. Likewise, we need people with the skills to help us expand our appreciation for the artistic, recreational, spiritual, aesthetic, philosophic, political, and experimental facets of contemporary living. Until career educators build programs committed to maximizing each person's fully lived experiences, his sense of personal and professional competence, and his affiliative relationships; and until each person is included as a decision maker in the human service process, then the corporate state will continue to exacerbate the destruction of the earth's nonrestorable commodities and the deterioration of human hope and vitality.

Notes

1. Sidney P. Marland, Jr., "Education for More Than One Career," *World,* 7 June 1972, pp. 46-49.

2. John C. Rogers, "Where Job Training Starts in Kindergarten," *Parade,* 9 April 1972, pp. 18-19.

3. For example, see "Nixon Sees U.S. Work Ethic Reaffirmed," *Boston Globe,* 7 September 1971, p. 9.

4. Sidney P. Marland, Jr., "Career Education 300 Days Later," *American Vocational Journal,* February 1972, pp. 14-17.

5. Rogers, op. cit.

6. For example, see Philip Slater, *The Pursuit of Loneliness: American Culture at the Breaking Point* (Boston: Beacon Press, 1970).

7. Joel H. Spring, *Education and the Rise of the Corporate State* (Boston: Beacon Press, 1972).

8. "Tooling Up the System from Kindergarten Through Community College," *Nation's Schools*, December 1971, pp. 36-38.

9. See Donnella H. Meadows, Dennis L. Meadows, Jorgen Randers, William W. Behrens III, *The Limits to Growth* (New York: Universe Books, 1972).

10. Joseph Cosand, "OE on Career Education," *Change*, June 1972, pp. 7, 60, 61.

11. See Richard Flacks, *Youth and Social Change* (Chicago: Markham, 1971).

7

Schooled
Vocational Experiences:
Some Modest Proposals*

Ronald A. Palmer

T hat the schools have done and continue to do a less than adequate job in the whole area of vocational education is no secret. The very same hoax perpetrated on earlier generations under the name vocational education still flourishes. Only the names and faces have changed. The outmoded, the irrelevant and the mundane are still words which best characterize so-called programs of vocational education at all levels of public schooling. The fact that schooled vocational experiences bear little or no relationship to the real world of work somehow goes unnoticed.

Let me not mince words. Anything less than a major overhaul of existing vocational education programs would be a total waste. Successive generations have watched continued tinkering with courses, credits, and time allowances, realizing these efforts were truly only cosmetic at best. Wood shops continue to crank out more bookends and checkerboards (yes, checkerboards are still in). A semester in metal shop grudgingly yields a crumbtray, if that. Home Economics courses generate aprons and evidently a disdain for the culinary arts. Now I ask any literate man this question: Are the above described vocational experiences of the kinds or quality one needs to compete successfully in the ever-changing world of today?

*Reprinted by permission of the author. First published in *Clearing House*, 1974.

The schools' task of providing worthwhile vocational experiences over the last several decades has grown immensely more difficult. The new technology has placed at the disposal of our children many more sophisticated tools for learning. Today's learner is literally bombarded by a flood of electric media. Most school age children see a score of technology toys pass through their lives. Think of the twelve year old boy who makes clay pinch pots while in school only to come home later in the day to tune-up his mini-bike or snowmobile. Herein lies one of the greatest dilemmas of the public schooling. The environment outside the schools has grown far richer in experiences than the environment the schools can possibly provide within four walls.[1] Could it be that schools might well be a place where children come to learn to be stupid?

Such a notion has broad implications for vocational programs provided by the schools. As Toffler has suggested, if the schools are to remain viable institutions they must shift into the future tense.[2] When it comes to vocational efforts of the schools, may I humbly suggest a giant leap forward to the present tense.

How It Is

The numbers of students participating in skill-producing vocational programs has been and continues to be remarkably small. A recent figure shows that only about 12 percent of our high school students have traditionally been exposed to some kind of skill-producing training.[3]

Not much is really new in schooled vocational experiences. Vocational educators go on fighting the blue-college image and their programs remain largely repositories for potential school dropouts. Newness of program is usually disguised under new names such as technical education or occupational awareness. Unfortunately, the title of the program is too often the only thing that has been altered. Call these programs what you will—they all fall under the umbrella of vocational education.

Let's look closer at the vocational doings of the schools at various levels. It might be well to begin at the high school level where the majority of schooled vocational experiences take place. It seems logical that the ultimate question after graduation from the secondary schools should be this one. What skills do the products of the schooling process (the students) possess? Can you tie two pieces of pipe together so they don't leak, or can't you? Can you effectively use a typewriter or can't you? Can you solder a wire or can't you? Can you sew a dress or can't you? Can you assemble words in a literate form or can't you?

Too often the answer to these and similar questions is No. Yet, if one looks at the student's evaluative record one would find a fantastic collection of remarkably high grades. This absence of a relationship between grades earned and skills possessed is the ultimate mockery. For it becomes clear that students trudge their way through the schools collecting courses, instead of practical utilitarian vocational skills. So rampant is this educational malpractice that hiring persons in industry speak of the schools' graduates as persons "well educated to do nothing." Beneath the window dressing of the educational establishment (behavioral objectives, courses, credits, grades, etc.) lies the ultimate accountability harshly revealed by the real world—What can you do my friend?

While my words on the efforts of the secondary schools are less than kind, I find myself less impressed by the efforts of the junior high school. While one is occasionally able to locate programs and projects of real substance in the high schools, one is hard pressed to find anything resembling a program in the junior high schools. By and large efforts are directed at generating small scale mementos whose final resting place is the trash can. This is probably in keeping with the established American practice of throwing most things away.

It is a simple matter to discuss vocational experiences provided in the elementary school for little or nothing is being done. If any vocational notions are gained they clearly accrue through chance rather than by planned learning experiences. I have noticed the emergence of the term occupational awareness in the elementary schools and applaud its arrival. Evidently man is coming to realize that children as early as grade one start to exclude certain occupations. More than a decade ago Lifton was concerned about the absence of realistic literature concerning occupations at the elementary level. After contacting publishers he was informed that they do not plan to publish books of this type because "children are not interested in vocations."[4]

It seems almost a pity that the occupational doings of men have never enjoyed their rightful place at the center of the curriculum at all levels of schooling. How could man distort curriculum priorities to the absurd? How could vocational education programs be relegated to mere decoration on the curriculum tree?

Some Modest Proposals

That's the state of affairs in schooled vocational experiences as I see it. The next question is what to do about it. I dare not suggest an extension of present curricular offerings in the way of new courses. For this is a simplistic way to merely magnify the existing hoax. So rather than extending or patching up what now exists I would propose that vocational programs that are truly outmoded or irrelevant be dismantled. Such programs run rampant across the land.

You heard right. My proposal is to "hang up your hammer." I assure the reader my proposal is really a modest one. For if present vocational programs exist in name only and bear only a superficial relationship to the working world I ask, What is there to be lost? It is my thesis that present tinkering is not in any stretch of the imagination vocational education. It is rather more of the "assembly line" efforts of public schooling whose main mission it is to distribute certificates of literacy. Whether or not graduates of the schools are ill equipped to "plug in" to the world with substantive skills seems to matter little.

That we need to seek alternate paths for providing worthwhile vocational experiences can be vividly illustrated by a simple episode involving this writer. A young married high school graduate invited me to view his newly purchased Spanish inspired dining room set. He was quick to point out the intricate wood carvings which highlighted this set. Somehow he was really surprised when I informed him that the delicate wood carvings were nothing more than molded plastic inserts neatly disguised. I suspect such naivety on the part of a consumer could be minimized if his schooling experiences had included experiences at the lumber mill, the lumber yard, the furniture manufacturer and maybe even a furniture retailer. You see it is one thing to build a bird house in a conventional woodshop class. It is another to be an intelligent buyer in an economy which can hardly afford many more illiterate consumers.

So now that the jig saws are silenced, I would urge the schools to provide vocational experiences in a new fashion. I would suggest that the new programs would have as their goal an intensive study of life styles and occupational alternates that the world has to offer. Studies in the area of vocational theory, occupational analysis, job satisfaction and job entry exemplify the kinds of experiences I would direct the schools' energies toward. By study I do not mean more lifeless book learning exercises supplemented by musty vocational literature from the 1950's distributed by guidance counselors. Rather, I am suggesting that all vocational experiences take place in the field, in shopping centers, in wholesale outlets, in business and industry of all sizes, shapes and kinds. And here's the best part. Uncountable man hours will be saved as the curriculum has been neatly indexed for educators by the local telephone company. (See the yellow pages.)

Do not construe my proposal as being more trips to the local museums where the most persistent exercise for students is to keep their "fingers off the glass." I have in mind strategically planned and executed experiences that would expose school-age children to a host of occupational options available. Such exposure would give students an opportunity to see, hear, smell, and feel alternate working environs. More totally vicarious classroom experiences won't do.

A New Consciousness

It's time all men look inward and start asking the right kinds of questions concerning their future work. It is with hesitation that I even use the term work. For in the great society the notion of work has attached to it a host of negative connotations. Reich states that for most Americans, work is mindless, exhausting, boring, servile, and hateful, something to be endured.[5] When men find themselves in their chosen occupation and perceive the experience to be sheer drudgery the consequences can only be disastrous. A man alienated from his life's work is a hollow man.

Could this negativism toward work be fostered in the schools. No doubt a disdain for work is a learned response. One can only speculate on the influence of schooling on such attitudes. But certain outdated myths are very definitely perpetuated by the schools. The very words vocational education still evoke notions of blue collar, academic incompetence, and low socio-economic status. To a large degree such an association is no longer accurate and is one of the unpleasant remainders of an earlier technological era. Nevertheless, the very institution charged with the responsibility of educating the young with wholesome experiences and attitudes toward life appears to be doing just the opposite.

We need to build a new consciousness on the part of students. They must be urged to be introspective and develop some realistic notion of self. Human beings must look inward periodically to appraise their interests and capabilities in terms of the working world. Such an exercise would place students in a better position to make rational vocational decisions. We cannot allow many more generations to make occupational decisions solely on the basis of chance. For every phase of their adult existence will be directly effected by these earlier decisions. In the words of Ginzberg, "Since occupational choice involves the balancing of a series of subjective elements with the opportunities and limitations of reality, the crystallization of occupational choice inevitably has the quality of a compromise."[6] It is my fear that for many occupational choice involves a simple compromise between happenstance and cumulative ignorance.

A Call for Change

My proposal would not fit nice and neat with the present model of public schooling. Teachers could not be inhibited by bells or study hall assignments. The only restraint would be that of the teacher's imagination. My proposed changes clearly call for a new role for vocational educators. In place of their present role as "shopkeeper" teachers would act as managers of a broad spectrum of learning experiences. In this new capacity as manager teachers would find themselves making phone calls, setting up field experiences, and lugging around a portable video tape package. The teacher's domain would shift from a 40 by 60 foot rectangle to new dimensions measured in terms of miles. Risk taking on the part of teacher and learner would be the new imperative.

While I urge a new role and extended responsibilities for teachers of vocational education, I can only sympathize with their present situation. Certainly, one cannot place sole blame on vocational educators for the decrepit state of affairs. For they find themselves hopelessly trapped in an outdated factory-oriented system which sometimes marches hundreds of students past them each day at convenient forty-five or fifty minute intervals. Under such "assembly line" conditions teachers aspire to survive one day at a time. One is hardly surprised to find visible signs of despair. I can see vividly the sign in a woodshop neatly masked to the side of the table saw which reads "NO students —For teachers use ONLY!" Some teachers even go beyond signs as they personally dismantle machinery for survival purposes. It is difficult to cut off a thumb on a table saw with no blade. It is equally difficult to cut a board.

I recognize my proposal for change is less than new. To the contrary it has probably been advocated by scores of others. Yet, the public is still willing to send its children to schools to learn the skills of a bygone era. Maybe it is easier to be schooled in a world of what was instead of a world of what is or what will be.

Every decade or so vocational education seems to undergo a rebirth. Now that vocational education programs are back in popularity it would appear the time is right to initiate far-reaching changes. More tinkering with existing programs won't do. Such narrow superficial approaches have been tried and failed over repeated generations. Nothing short of a major overhaul is in order. The public, the teachers, and even the students are aware of the big put-on in vocational education. How much longer they will endure the fraud is a matter for debate.

Continuous Change! The two words which best describe our culture have somehow eluded the vocational doings of the schools. But the choice is a simple one. Change or be changed.

Notes

1. See James S. Coleman, "The Children Have Outgrown The Schools," *Psychology Today,* February 1972, pp. 72-75.

2. Alvin Toffler, *Future Shock* (New York: Random House, 1970), p. 427.

3. Sidney P. Marland, Jr., "Educating for the Real World," *Business Education Forum,* November 1971, p. 4.

4. Walter M. Lifton, "Vocational Guidance in the Elementary School," *Vocational Guidance Quarterly,* Winter 1959, pp. 79-81.

5. Charles A. Reich, *The Greening of America* (New York: Random House, 1970), p. 7.

6. E. Ginzberg, S. W. Ginzburg, S. Axelrad, and J. L. Herma, *Occupational Choice: An Approach to a General Theory* (New York: Columbia University Press, 1951).

8

Getting at the Attitudes Problem: Career Development and the Affective Domain*

Bruce W. Tuckman

H ow often one hears a potential employer say (though perhaps not in these exact words): "Give me an individual with the proper attitudes and suitable motivation, and I will give him the rest."

Yet schools, for a variety of reasons, have chosen to concentrate on the "rest" and have left attitudes almost entirely out of the career development process, satisfied to focus their efforts on occupational exploration and the dissemination of occupational information.

Occupational exploration has typically taken the form of giving students smatterings of experience or exposure to various occupational activities. Information dissemination has included the distribution of printed information—made accessible by computer—and the opportunity to ask questions and receive answers.

These two components of career development cannot be considered sufficient when judged against the role the school can play in the career development process. The value of occupational information depends on the ability of the student to ask the right questions and get answers that are helpful to him. The short span and unrealistic nature

*Reprinted by permission from *American Vocational Journal*, January 1973, pp. 47-48.

of the occupational exploration experience, as typically given, tends to limit its usefulness as a trial opportunity.

Matching Up Process

R. A. Katzell conceived of career development as a matching of self to the occupation in terms of interests, aptitudes and attitudes. Development, according to this concept, occurs as the student becomes more aware of his own capabilities and interests, more aware of the characteristics and requirements of a variety of jobs and, insofar as possible, begins to adjust each to the other.

The opportunity for adjusting the self to meet the requirements of the world of work has received minimal attention in educational attempts to provide for career development. Schools have concentrated on a cognitive approach.

Cognitions represent knowledge and information that students can gain about the world of work through field visits, formal presentations, question-and-answer periods, and occupational libraries. An equally important but often neglected area of human functioning is the affective domain which includes attitudes, feelings, and motives.

The approach I am advocating in this paper is to broaden the concept of career development to include an affective component, namely the development of motives, attitudes and feelings toward oneself and one's environment. The assumption is that suitable emotional or affective states not only lead to a satisfactory work experience but also contribute to the worker's total pattern of growth.

What is proposed specifically is the development of a curriculum guide, methods course, course of study, or set of lesson plans that can be used for training classroom teachers in procedures intended to facilitate the career development process vis-a-vis the affective domain.

This approach does not require that teachers so trained teach separate career development classes or provide experiences devoted exclusively to career development. Instead, it presumes that career development in the affective domain can and should occur in all classrooms, be they English or social studies, shop or art, and that all teachers should be trained to use techniques appropriate to this goal.

In each classroom, the teacher occupies a role in relation to the student similar to that of an employer in relation to an employee. Many of the dynamic tensions in play between student and teacher operate between employee and employer. Given this parallel between classroom reality (a compelling reality to the student) and the work-a-day world (a compelling reality to the employed adult), teachers can make good use of a set of procedures that enable them to employ this reality and their relationship to students as a basis for career development in the affective domain.

Rather than limiting itself to a design or program exclusively for students, this approach recommends a program that can be used with teachers and thus multiply the potential for influencing the career development process in students. Once the teacher is trained, he can adapt many of the activities so designed for his own classroom purposes.

Stages in the Affective Domain

In an earlier study, I characterized the affective domain as including the following four stages: (1) introspection/experiencing, (2) orienting, (3) valuing, and (4) integrating.

In the introspection/experiencing stage, students begin to explore their own feelings, attitudes and motives in order to determine what their internal life is like. Typically, this does not come about in systematic fashion, nor should the teacher attempt to use this stage as a part of career development or any other process. According to Katzell's formulation, however, students must be aware of their own inner states before they can choose or pursue an occupation that will bring maximum satisfaction.

Therefore, the first set of exercises recommended for the proposed manual or methods course will provide teachers with techniques to help students explore and become more fully aware of their inner life. Fantasy, role playing and other related procedures can be used for this purpose.

The second stage, orienting, refers to the manner in which our inner states affect our reaction to, or our readiness to react to, external situations. This stage plays a large part in selecting an occupation, relating to an employer, relating to peers, and so on. Our ability to control our emotional states, and when appropriate, to express our feelings is related to the process of orienting.

Emotional orientation to the work-a-day world should be included in the teacher training program. In many ways, the classroom can serve as a model in which emotional orientation toward one's environment can be explored. For the student, school is his job; the teacher his boss.

He is confronted by the authority of the teacher, the demands of the job, and his own needs for achievement, affiliation, dominance, and so on. He orients himself to his classroom and thus sets his tone for reacting to his teacher and his school work in terms of his internal state.

To use the classroom as the model for exploration in the orientation stage will not only be advantageous in respect to career development; it will also be helpful in enabling students to deal with their conflicting feelings toward school.

Arriving at a Value System

In the third stage, valuing, students establish and reinforce values, motives, attitudes, and feelings toward a variety of objects, other people, and themselves. It is during this stage that the self-concept, much theorized about by Super and others, comes to the fore.

Activities should be planned that will enable teachers to help students arrive at attitudes and motives which will be conducive to life success.

Attempts should be made to help students develop the desire for achievement—which has been found to be an important motivator for occupational success. Other needs and values related to working with other people and dealing with authority and one's own dependency needs should be dealt with at this stage. Raths, Harmin, and Simon provide a number of suggestions that teachers can use to help students clarify their values.

The fourth stage is integrating. It is here that individual values, attitudes, motives, and feelings become more closely welded to provide a value system which affects an individual's external and internal behavior.

Through the use of simulation and other small group activity, attempts can be made to provide the kinds of experiences that encourage the integration of these inner states into well-defined value systems.

Firm Ground for Decisions

It is my contention in this article that the four stages delineated are important aspects of the career development process. Insofar as activities appropriate to these stages occur in haphazard manner, internal states which negatively affect the selection and pursuit of careers may result.

Choosing and pursuing a career require more than information, a cognitive grasp of possibilities, and thinking about which career to follow. Young people must be prepared to sustain their decisions by strong inner states of motivation, values, attitudes, and feelings. Parents and other significant influences in a young person's life can affect this process in only a limited way.

Heretofore no systematic opportunities for the development of affective states—beyond an intensive counseling experience, which is usually available to only a limited few—have been available to the young person. By bringing the affective element of career development into the classroom and providing teachers with the skills and background to use it, we can increase the likelihood of producing workers with the attitudes and motivation that employers constantly look for.

References

Katzell, R. A. "Personal Values, Job Satisfaction, and Job Behavior." *Man in a World at Work.* Edited by Henry Borow. Boston: Houghton Mifflin, 1964. Pp. 341-63.

Raths, L. E., Harmon, M., and Simon, S. B. *Values and Teaching.* Columbus, Ohio: Chas. E. Merrill, 1966.

Super, D. E. *The Psychology of Careers.* New York: Harper and Row, 1957.

Tuckman, B. W. *A Study of Curriculums for Occupational Preparation and Education* (SCOPE Program). Final Report. New Brunswick, N.J.: Rutgers University (USOE Project No. 8-0334), 1970.

9

What about Career Education for Girls?*

Edna Mitchell

C areer Education" is the new terminology applied to programs designed to develop an early awareness of varied and related vocational opportunities. Spanning the total school years, kindergarten through high school graduation, career education attempts to provide for greater vocational flexibility in a world of rapid vocational change.

However, the new efforts have not recognized the seriousness of the vocational miseducation of girls. They focus largely upon the idea of work, and its multiple and related forms, without indicating an awareness that sexist prejudices still pervade the entire curriculum and are subtly reflected in the attitudes of the school personnel.

Admitting a girl to a high school shop or drafting course does not constitute a realistic career program which increases aspirations of women. High school is already too late to attempt to break stereotypes drawn from sex roles. From a feminist point of view, effective career education for girls would have to be remedial even in the elementary school. Attitudes limiting women's career opportunities are rooted deep in early childhood. If there is to be an effective change in future vocational roles for women, there must be a concerted effort directed toward parents of preschool children, and elementary teachers, as well as high school counselors and teachers.

Steps have recently been taken to open doors to women in corporations, government, and university faculties. While these steps may be viewed as tokenism on the one hand, they could be useful opportunities to improve the status of women. The irony is that women cannot be offered jobs at these levels until routes leading to such positions are more accessible to them. There are relatively few women who have "made it" to a highly qualified level, and many of those who have done so are nonetheless caught in the internal conflict and guilt precipitated by an uncertain identity.

The professional level in graduate school is a bitter place to unlock the doors to a woman when she has been socially brainwashed against her own development. The system must be opened up from the preschool through the entire educational system and finally out into an open society.

Sex Stereotypes Begin in the Crib

It is not necessary to document the pervasive social attitude which favors the birth of a boy baby over the birth of a girl. One may protest the truth of such a statement, and yet it is more customary to sympathize with families who have only daughters than to commiserate with a man who has all sons.

Children become aware of differences in sex roles, and learn which roles are appropriate for them, long before they start to school. Many sex-role patterns have been established by the time a child is two years old. Some important differences between the sexes may very well be biological.[1] Behaviors which seem to be innate, however, need to be carefully interpreted in order to avoid the error of reinforcing old myths based on unexamined folk wisdom.

It is scientifically important to learn in what ways male and female are innately different. Such studies are valuable in learning more about humankind in general. However, the sex differences which emerge do not provide evidence supporting the subordinate, inferior, and dependent role which women in our society have been assigned.

Even Girls Think Boys Are Best

Not only are parents' attitudes apparent in a "sex-set" before the baby's birth, but as soon as the child is born its sex influences the way in which it will be treated. Baby boys generally are handled more roughly than baby girls; baby girls are talked to and cooed to more gently; baby boys are encouraged to be independent and energetic explorers while the passive side of girl babies is reinforced.[2]

We take for granted sexual distinctions in color choices (pink and blue), in clothing, and in early toys. Even the toy manufacturers, when informed that girls like Tonka trucks too, refused to change their slogan "You can't raise boys without Tonka Toys," telling one mother, ". . . there is a psychological factor involved in that little boys don't want toys that girls can also play with."[3]

Adult attitudes expressed about the importance of the sex of the child during infancy are continued throughout the pre-school years, resulting in the development of negative attitudes by both boys and girls toward what is considered to be female. Several studies have shown that femininity and being female are devalued by both sexes. Boys readily identify with male figures and activities, but girls are less likely to make the same sort of identification with female stereotypes. In fact, women have so internalized the contempt for being female that they may be the worst offenders in subverting their own growth.[4] The self-hate which is characteristic of groups which feel impotent or powerless finds expression in women's contempt for other women.

Examples of this contempt are easily cited. Recent ferment among women employees at the United Nations placed blame on women, rather than on men, for indifference about women's rights.[5] Studies have repeatedly shown that both men and women (but particularly women) rated men as more worthwhile than women, or found that with increasing age both boys and girls had a better opinion of boys and a lower opinion of girls.[6] Women's rejection of the capabilities of their sex was demonstrated further by Goldberg, who had a group of women rate the scholarship in an essay which was signed John McKay and Joan McKay, alternately. Women generally judged the article by John to be more scholarly than Joan's, although the articles were identical.[7]

Sex stereotypes which begin early are not simply a matter of role differentiation by sex, but they repeatedly show antipathy toward activities or objects viewed as female. Boys learn quickly that to be labeled "sissy" is highly derogatory, but to tell a girl she is a tomboy or "almost as good as a guy" is considered a backhanded compliment. Further, girls who have been tomboys are found to be much more likely to be successful as creative self-reliant women.[8]

However, even girls who are successful tomboys learn self-defeating attitudes early. Baumrind makes the following assessment:

> It is common in the public school setting for boys from about age 6 to
> 13 to put girls down, and each other for playing with girls. Few girls pro-

test, believing that this is how it has to be. Teachers almost never interfere or present an opposing viewpoint. Beginning readers show girls and boys playing with different toys, and men working while women stay at home. Physical education is segregated by sex, although in the early elementary school years much overlap exists between boys and girls in athletic skills. Somewhat later boys are offered woodworking and machine shop classes, while girls are offered child care, sewing, and cooking classes. Thus the traditional division of labor by sex, reinforced by textbooks, teachers, and counselors, is as discriminatory as a similar division by ethnic group.[9]

Parents are clear in their expectations of higher achievement for boys than for girls. By adolescence girls have learned to equate intellectual achievement with loss of femininity.[10] Academic success, intellectual superiority in competition with men are often sources of guilt for the adolescent girl who may be achievement motivated but who also wants to be sexually attractive.

Girls learn to rely almost solely on *expressive competence* and are incompetent in *instrumental skills* or those skills considered essential for achievement in our society.[11] Instrumental skills which are valued and nurtured in the male, and which have survival value for either sex, are assertiveness, rationality, and independence.

Recommendations for Career Education

Solutions to the miseducation of girls which can be implemented through new career curricula in the schools should include some, if not all, of the following strategies:

1. A plan should be developed and implemented in each school for examining the nature of the school experience in order to identify the subtle ways in which girls are being restricted in their achievements specifically by sex stereotypes. All teaching materials should be examined for possible sex discrimination and appropriate steps should be taken to eliminate the discriminatory impact of that material.

In the case of textbooks and reading materials, children can be alerted to the narrow interpretation of roles offered in such books. At the same time, schools should make efforts to eradicate feminine stereotypes from school textbooks. In the case of toys and manipulative materials, both sexes can learn to use materials traditionally designed for boys or just for girls. If this cannot be done, the material should be eliminated from the classroom.

2. Workshops and in-service training sessions for teachers should be designed to focus attention on the pervasiveness of sex stereotyping. Deliberate steps should be presented to sensitize teachers and enable them to avoid repetition of the old patterns of expectancies set for both males and females.

3. Change within the curriculum itself should include two aspects: (a) sections about the changing status of women and material from women's studies should be incorporated in the social science curriculum; and (b) deliberate techniques should be taught to enable teachers to help girls develop instrumental competency.

More attention should be given to girls' use of thought, logic, and problem-solving techniques, and less reinforcement should be given to rote memorization and verbal facility. Perhaps girls should be deliberately exposed to experiences which try to raise their abilities to tolerate frustration, anxiety, and criticism. Discussion techniques should be explored in classroom groups which could expose girls to verbal conflict, disagreement, and even hostility in a way which would help them learn how to face difficult interpersonal relationships without resorting to traditional feminine behaviors of withdrawal, acquiescence, passive submission, or emotional irrelevancies.

4. Special efforts should be made in the elementary school to draw into the school women who have achieved in various fields. Women in science, politics, medicine, and business, for example, could be invited as leaders in workshops, seminars, or as resident scholars. Whenever possible, these women should be representative of those who are combining serious careers with the roles of wife and mother.

5. Parent education, focusing on the issue of improving opportunities for the full development of girls' potential, should be sponsored by the school as early as the kindergarten.

6. Finally, high school counselors should be given special professional training for the elimination of discrimination against girls in vocational and educational counseling. This writer's own research on the aspirations of high school seniors dramatically indicated the depressed level of aspiration in general among girls regardless of class rank, socioeconomic status, or academic ability.[12] We look not only to the schools to aid in the liberation of women but also to the government for legal support, to society for social awareness, and to women themselves for sustained effort. However, it is through education that we expect the greatest impact. Pat Minuchin expressed it well when she wrote:

> . . . It seems evident that the nature of schooling, from the earliest years on, shapes the capacities and strengths of the growing female. If we are to understand such forces, we shall probably have to look at schools in all their complexity, as small societies and total educational environments, rather than at specific pieces of curriculum for teaching one point or another. And if we are to implement on any sizable scale a kind of educational experience that equips young women to choose, fight for, and carry out personally meaningful life patterns, we may need to make dra-

matic changes in the prevailing organization of many schools: the values
they represent, the relationship they foster, and the form and control of
the learning experiences they offer.[13]

Notes

1. Jerome Kagan, *Change and Continuity in Infancy* (New York:
John Wiley and Sons, 1971); idem, "The Emergence of Sex Differences," *School Review* 80 (1972): 217-27; G.D. Mitchell, "Attachment
Differences in Male and Female Infant Monkeys," *Child Development*
39 (1968): 611-20; Eleanor E. Maccoby, "Sex Differences in Intellectual Functioning," *The Development of Sex Differences* (Stanford,
Calif.: Stanford University Press, 1966), pp. 27-28.

2. Florence Howe, "Sexual Stereotypes Start Early," *Saturday
Review*, 16 October 1971, p. 76; Michael Lewis, "Parents and Children: Sex Role Developments, " *School Review* 80 (1972): 229-40.

3. Judith Hole and Ellen Levine, *Rebirth of Feminism* (New York:
Quadrangle Books, 1971).

4. Philip Goldberg, "Are Women Prejudiced Against Women?"
Transaction 5 (April 1968): 28-30; E. Keniston, "An American Anach-
ronism: The Image of Women and Work," *American Scholar* 33
(1964): 255-75.

5. Kathleen Teltsch, "At the U.N., Polite Feminism," *New York
Times,* 25 April 1972, p. 48.

6. S. Smith, "Age and Sex Differences in Children's Opinion Concerning Sex Differences," *Journal of Genetic Psychology* 54 (1939):
17-35.

7. Goldberg, op. cit., p. 30.

8. Ravenna Helson, "Childhood Interests Related to Creativity in
Women," *Journal of Consulting Psychology* 29 (1965): 352-61.

9. Diana Baumrind, "From Each According to Her Ability,"
School Review 80 (1972): 166.

10. Ibid., p. 165.

11. Ibid., pp. 161-97.

12. Daniel Levine, Edna Mitchell, and Robert Havighurst, *Op-
portunities for Higher Education in a Metropolitan Area: A Study of
High School Seniors in Kansas City 1967* (Bloomington, Ind.: Phi Delta
Kappa Press, 1971).

13. Patricia Minuchin, "The Schooling of Tomorrow's Women,"
School Review 80 (1972): 207.

10

Basic Content: People*

*Janet K. Whealon
and Norma Meyer*

Career education is the refocusing of the curriculum on people—using people and their activities to teach basic skills. This instructional focus is being used in many classrooms and is demonstrating that learning experiences are most meaningful when they come from primary sources and when they involve the active doing of something.[1]

Fifty years ago, children did not need to rely upon their teachers to provide them with experiences with adults. Kids followed their parents around as they did their work, and thus were frequently in contact with the adult world and with the work activities that took place there. When schools were established, they became "information givers," being responsible for providing the types of information which were not readily available to the child in his home environment. Today, however, television and other forms of mass media in the home provide abundant informational content—and often provide it more effectively than schools could hope to—but the structures of our society no longer give children the opportunity to watch their fathers, mothers, uncles, etc., perform their work activities. Children are unable to be involved with or to inquire from these significant resource people. The circumstances of our time suggest that the school

*Reprinted by permission from the authors.

should now shift its emphasis toward providing this contact and giving children the opportunity to inquire from primary sources—i.e. people.

Putting children in contact with adults who do things can make classroom instruction more relevant and meaningful. Children can see more clearly the need for developing a proficiency in certain skill areas because they will be in touch with real people who actually are employing the knowledge. Instead of insisting that the students work page seventy-five in the blue mathematics textbook, a teacher can initiate projects which involve parents or other adults as resource people—but which also will involve learning and using the concepts outlined in the blue textbook on page seventy-five. Such concepts learned in a meaningful context are not only more permanent, but also more transferable to other related contexts.

Because the teacher's imagination is the key instrument for instruction, effective career education programs will be focused on the teacher. The teacher—a person utilizing professional skills—considers the needs, interests, and abilities of the students, as well as school policies, community concerns, and community resources; from all of this comes an *idea* in the teacher's mind. This idea can be the nucleus around which an exciting but workable teaching plan can be built. The "organizing center concept" is an instrument for such planning that is currently being used by hundreds of teachers in elementary schools in Illinois and in Kentucky—helping them to use human resources more effectively.[2] These teachers are focusing not on occupations but on the people within occupations.

Using the person-in-the-occupation as an organizing center for the teaching plan enables the teacher to introduce the academic skills without being subject-oriented. Teachers are discovering that mathematics, art, science, history, language arts, and other skills can be incorporated very naturally into projects for discovering what people do in food-related occupations, or in banking, in a greenhouse, in a telephone company, etc. Teachers can use "people" to keep content relevant and timely and to make academic work more interesting to the students, thus motivating them to learn. Career education allows for the integration of the curriculum so that the pupils can see a correlation between content areas. Learning can be more natural and more meaningful.

When invited to serve as resource persons, parents can become involved in the education of their children in a positive way. They can share their own experience within the work-world (in one of their various roles—parent, provider, volunteer worker, board member) and benefit from knowing that schools are interested in what they do.

Parents can "show and tell" what they do and how they do it; and they can respond to students' questions in an interview situation, questions such as the following: "What do you like best about your job?" "What do you like least?" "What caused you to choose this job?" "How is your job important to the community?" Such contributions not only make classroom learning more relevant for the children, but at the same time the parent can learn first-hand information about the school, the classroom, the interests of the students, the role of the teacher, and perhaps even his own work attitudes. A situation is provided where everyone—teacher, student, parent—can learn.

By using resource persons as the vehicle for learning, teachers can better equip children to make intelligent occupational choices when the time comes. Too many people spend their entire lives unaware of the varied job opportunities that are available to them. As a result, they choose an occupation which is unsuitable for them, but from which they cannot escape. With effective career education—based upon the teacher as the creative agent, focused upon people rather than things, and backed up by the school's various support systems —perhaps today's students will find themselves better equipped to make career decisions than were many of their unhappy predecessors.

Notes

1. Two cities where instructional focus upon people is being implemented system-wide are Peoria, Illinois, and Bowling Green, Kentucky.

2. The "organizing center," as an instructional tool, was originated and developed by ABLE Model Program, directed by Dr. Walter Wernick and headquartered at Northern Illinois University, DeKalb, Illinois 60115. A more detailed account of the organizing center concept and the ABLE Model for Career Education is available by writing to ABLE Headquarters for *Career Education Activities through World of Work Resources* (160 pp., $3.00).

11

Career Development: A New Focus*

*Earl J. Moore
and Norman C. Gysbers*

C areer development as a new focus for education has the potential to restructure substantially the processes and activities of education, modify the values and attitudes of educators, and maximize the opportunities for student involvement and responsibility. Career development can become the lens through which educators view and understand students. Career development concepts can become the organizer for the total curriculum.

In traditional education, students tend to be viewed as objects to be brought up to grade level in basic content areas at the end of the school year. The career development perspective, however, puts a premium on students as persons—on personalizing education to make it meaningful. Career development, defined in this context, is self-development over the life span through education, work, and leisure. It is a way of describing and understanding total human development.

Value of Career Development

To illustrate the value of the career development orientation, Figures 1, 2, and 3 contrast the traditional education orientation with

*Reprinted with permission of Association for Supervision and Curriculum Development and Earl J. Moore and Norman C. Gysbers, Authors. Copyright © December 1972 by the Association for Supervision and Curriculum Development.

the career development orientation in three different school contexts: educational processes and activities; values and attitudes of educators; and student involvement and responsibility.

Relating the school and its curriculum to the outside world is a necessary first step in establishing career education in a school system. Instead of talking about the outside world in the abstract, the outside world can be used as a major vehicle for instruction. Teachers can use the career world outside the school as a teaching medium for transmitting basic education knowledge and skills.

Figure 11.1. Educational Processes and Activities

Elements	Traditional Education	Career Development
Instructional process	Book contained	Experiential centered
Learning activities	Abstract rich/Action poor	Action-Abstract balance
Content emphasis	Past	Here and now/Future
Reinforcement	Abstracting ability	Doing/Abstracting abilities
Evaluation	Group norms	Individual performance

Figure 11.2. Values and Attitudes of Educators

Elements	Traditional Education	Career Development
Teacher focus	Content departure	Person departure
Learning goals	Autocratic	Shared responsibility
Teacher stress	Imperfections/Failure	Worthiness/Success
School climate	Closed	Open
School staff	Specialty oriented	Interrelated

Figure 11.3. Student Involvement and Responsibility

Elements	Traditional Education	Career Development
Student—Task	Encourages dependency	Encourages responsibility
Student—Motivation	Apathetic	Involved/Creative
Student—Peers	Self-centered	Interdependent
Student—Teacher	Power struggles	Cooperative
Student—Self-image	Distorted/Shallow	Positive/Realistic

THE THREE R'S

The career world can be brought into the school by resource personnel, parents, and the students themselves. Action oriented, learn-by-doing processes should be used. For example, a teacher in Cobb County, Georgia, has used the banking business as one of the career worlds through which a wide variety of basic education objectives can be incorporated.[1] The traditional content area skills and knowledges in this instance are correlated and related to the banking business. The restaurant business, the construction industry, and other work settings can be used in a similar manner.

While a content-oriented teacher may recognize the potential careers as a medium for teaching traditional content knowledge and skills, the career-oriented teacher will appreciate the medium for the opportunities it affords students to develop a personal sense of how to relate present worth to future worth. Nelson notes that through guided career exploration it is possible for a student to develop an awareness of his own potential and worthwhileness in the present and thus project this in the future as a participant in a greater world.[2] Through career exploration, he will have an opportunity to observe what it takes to be a responsible contributor within the adult world around him.

A MEASURE OF SUCCESS

Exploring career worlds will help students develop a feeling of how adults achieve their place in society. Through career exploration, students can examine the meanings of work and leisure and their relationships to personal life styles. Also, since career exploration is a personal endeavor and not a competitive venture, each student can explore at his own pace in his own unique fashion and thus be assured of a measure of success.

As Glasser contended in *Schools Without Failure*, self-worth and willingness to assume responsibility for one's own learning are built on a foundation of encouragement.[3] The student active in career exploration can be reinforced whether or not he possesses abstract scholastic skills. This does not imply that basic competencies are not important, but simply that content-oriented group achievement tests are not the only way of providing feedback to students about their self-worth.

School Superintendent Alton B. Crews of Cobb County, Georgia, noted, "Perhaps the most important part of Career Development is the humane way it helps each child develop. The poorest reader in third grade might be the best with a hammer, and he will get esteem from his peers."[4] Students with competence in basic education will find that career exploration can be enriching and rewarding and can be pursued without waiting for other students to reach their level.

INDIVIDUALIZED EDUCATION

Career exploration as a point of departure for education has the potential of individualizing education, a subject that has been talked about for decades but has rarely been accomplished. Traditional strategies to individualize education have focused on matching student learning styles with abstract content-oriented tasks which occur only in the classroom. Little attention has been given to the learning style of students as these relate to the broader world outside the classroom.

Students have difficulty achieving self-identity because they are treated as objects and are placed in competitive situations where they can only compare themselves with others involved with the same task. The career exploration view, on the other hand, can stimulate learning which will provide individualized feedback to students concerning their self-identities.

ASSUMING RESPONSIBILITY

Many teachers not only determine all instructional goals but also assume total responsibility for seeing to it that students attain minimal content competency. Career development-oriented thinking, however, encourages individual student planning and self-accountability. In Santa Rosa, California, teams of students organized a worker visitation unit and made visits to workers in the community. Using recorded interviews of workers talking about their jobs and pictures taken of these workers on the job, they prepared several narrated slide presentations which they shared with other class members and their parents.[5]

A career development-oriented school atmosphere has the potential of being a democratic school atmosphere. While a content-oriented school tends to create a passive, dependent student who may be apathetic, irresponsible, or rebellious, the career development-oriented school offers the opportunity for all students to achieve and become competent. Instead of fostering grade competitiveness, students can be encouraged to be helpful to one another. Each person, if he feels of equal worth, will aid others in achieving their individual goals. Bruner has suggested that a learning community can be a powerful force for effective learning and thus mutual learning and instruction can occur, with a sense of compassion and responsibility for members.[6] The work world models this relationship for the student. A worker not only recognizes his individual responsibility, but appreciates the need for interdependency with fellow workers.

Who Is Responsible?

Who is responsible for career development programs in the school? The answer is that all members of the school community have a shared responsibility. At the present time, however, little is being done to assume such responsibility on a systematic basis. Many classroom teachers are concerned only with imparting knowledge, concentrating on grade level content, and manipulating the classroom environment for that purpose. Counselors and students may discuss future plans, but do so usually in the confines of the counselor's office. Parents and employers expect the schools to impart knowledge to students without understanding that the home and community can be a laboratory to help students relate subject content to the outside world.

Career development as a unifying construct in education provides the opportunity for all members of the school community to cooperate and to be responsible. Unfortunately, however, many programs that are now being organized around career development concepts are really traditional education programs in disguise. Typically, such programs emphasize only the world of work in the abstract; students are taught about occupations.

Even when these activities are done in the context of the work world, the emphasis is still teacher centered and product oriented rather than student centered and worker life style oriented. Other programs rely heavily on "commercial publishers who market a fantastic collection of occupational encyclopedias, file cases of job descriptions, films and filmstrips, and more recently slide-tape programs, microfilm systems, and computerized occupational information systems—all under the guise of teaching individuals about the world of work."[7] Such materials unfortunately are seen as ends in themselves.

The Future Begins Now

To take advantage of the current and future emphasis on career development as a way of making education relevant, we need to begin now. Teachers, counselors, and administrators should examine their current practices and techniques from a career development perspective.[8] School-age youth at all levels must have the opportunity continuously and systematically to explore, from an internal frame of reference, their interests, aptitudes, attitudes, and values in relation to the wide range of educational and career opportunities which may be available to them, in order to avoid premature educational and occupational foreclosures.

Following are some cooperative efforts that a career development approach will require:

1. Teachers and students should:

a. Take responsibility to sample the career world and share their findings

b. Make classroom decisions and plan activities in a manner similar to the ways it is done in various work settings.

2. Teachers and administrators should:

a. Establish procedures and provide resources to enable students to explore the career world

b. Provide for the use of media, worker role models, and appropriate support personnel.

3. Teachers and counselors should:

a. Attend to and plan for each student's unique career needs

b. Plan cooperatively to take advantage of the expertise each has to offer.

4. Elementary and secondary teachers should:

a. Develop sequential programs of career development

b. Establish and maintain accountability procedures for career development programs.

5. Parents and business and industry personnel should:

a. Establish advisory groups

b. Serve as resource persons to school career development programs.

When the school builds upon the inherent interest of the child in activity and exploration, enriching his learning through appropriate experiences which help him to see what he is about and to consider what is most important to him in relation to the adult world, we then begin to have the elements of a career development program. With such a program, each member of the school staff has a stake in the child's career development; each teacher, and indeed each parent and businessman, carries some responsibility.[9]

Notes

1. J. Smith, Project Director, Cobb County Occupational and Career Development Program, Marietta, Ga. Personal Communication, 1971.

2. R. Nelson, "Opening New Vistas to Children Through Career Exploration," *Needed Concepts in Elementary Guidance* (Report of the Eighth Annual All Ohio Elementary School Guidance Conference, State Department of Education, Columbus, Ohio).

3. William Glasser, *Schools Without Failure* (New York: Harper and Row, 1969).

4. Alton B. Crews, as quoted in Eleanor Clift, "Careers for Kindergartners," *McCall*, January 1972.

5. C. Cunningham. (Presentation at a career development workshop of the Sonoma County Office of Education, Santa Rosa, Calif. October 22-23, 1971).

6. J. Bruner, "The Process of Education Revisited," in *Dare To Care/Dare To Act*, ed. Robert L. Leeper (Washington, D.C.: Association for Supervision and Curriculum Development, 1971).

7. William H. Van Rooy and Larry J. Bailey, "A Conceptual Model of the World of Work" (Career Development for Children Project, Department of Occupational Education, Southern Illinois University at Carbondale, 1972).

8. Norman C. Gysbers and Earl J. Moore, "Career Development in the Schools," in *Contemporary Concepts in Vocational Education,* ed. G. Law, Yearbook of the American Vocational Association (Washington, D.C., December 1971).

9. W. Wesley Tennyson, "Career Development: Who's Responsible?" *American Vocational Journal* 46 (March 1971):56.

12

An Educational Strategy for Professional Career Change*

*James A. Farmer, Jr.,
and Robert G. Williams*

As long as relatively few professionals were changing careers, it could be assumed that vocational choice, having once been made, would be pursued for the rest of the professional's working life. Such an assumption is no longer tenable. There is increasing evidence that sizeable numbers of 30, 40, and even 50 year-old persons in a variety of professions, voluntarily or of necessity, are becoming involved in the professional career changing process.

Involuntary Career Change

Thousands of high-salaried engineers and other professionals in the aerospace industry have entered the ranks of the unemployed. They have been joined by many whose professions are related to the stock market. The *Manpower Report of the President* for 1970 indicates that the percentage of professional and technical workers that are unemployed has gradually risen from 3% in 1958 to 5.1% in 1969.[1] When the statistics of the current period are reported, they are likely to show a higher percentage.

Voluntary Career Change

While some of the unemployed professionals are desperately

*Reprinted by permission from *Adult Leadership*, April 1971, pp. 318-320.

searching for work related to their fields, many others are seeking to change careers. In this desire for career change, they are joined by other professionals who wish to change for different reasons. The observation has been made in the *Wall Street Journal*[2] that on the professional, managerial level "radical, voluntary switches have become almost commonplace." A variety of reasons why professionals choose to change careers in mid-stream have been noted. Drucker has observed: "Not everyone makes the right career choice the first time, and even if they do, they're likely to get stale after doing the same thing for 15 years or so."[3] Some seek to switch from professions in which they feel trapped to ones in which, as they perceive it, there will be a greater opportunity for personal satisfactions and personal need fulfillment. According to Hahn[4], for such persons, "work has become a dull, deadly affair and the feeling persists that one is being pushed, not pulled; the future has lost its glitter." The resulting need for successful career change may be virtually as pressing and immediate as the need generated by loss of employment.

Career Change Is Difficult

Even though professional career change has become more commonplace, to make such a change in one's 30's, 40's or 50's is nonetheless generally difficult. Where once the professional may have known some degree of success and stability, now he must struggle with only hopes of what may be. He may feel lonely and uprooted, as friendships are affected by his new intentions. His responsibilities—family and financial—may not allow him much time to change careers. It is likely, therefore, that the enormity of the tasks facing the career-changer may engulf, frustrate, and depress him.

Despite the difficulties, many faced with the need for career change receive little or no supportive help in this potentially disorganizing process. According to 24 counselors of adults in business, industry, universities, colleges, community colleges, and public adult education schools interviewed during the past year[5], insufficient practical attention has been given to the professional mid-career changer.[6] Often he has been treated as an oddity or a nonentity. Counselors in business, industry, and education alike attested to having given little or no assistance to professional career changers. Many counselors of adults who were interviewed indicated that, at the present time, reliable information on the resources which are available and relevant to the professional career changer's needs, including adult education, is either non-existent or hard to locate. So, for the most part, the professional career changer is left to ferret on his own. The resulting adaptive behavior can range from frantic trial and error attempts to find a suitable occupation to various forms of withdrawal.

Educative and Assistance Seeking Coping Behaviors

More beneficial to most professional career changers, it would seem, would be assistance seeking behaviors and/or educative coping behaviors. According to Knox[7], seeking assistance is characterized by making a request of another person or of an agency to arrange or at least help plan the necessary adaptation tasks. Educative coping behavior is characterized by active efforts to alter one's own competence as a means of adaptation. The unanticipated acceleration of professional career changing and the accompanying problems seem to have caught adult educators and counselors of adults for the most part unprepared to provide needed assistance, including adult education for professionals who are changing careers.

Potentially, adult education can play a major role in helping professionals change their careers. Developing ways to transform this often difficult and disorganizing process into a fruitful one presents a formidable challenge to adult educators and others seeking to provide assistance to professional career changers. The theoretical model provided below hopefully will be of assistance in meeting this challenge.

An Educative and Supportive Model

In 1960, Burkett[8] projected a hypothetical, comprehensive adult education program which could meet the changing educative needs of an adult throughout his life. He suggested that such education is "never a 'planned' program but always a 'planning' program adjusting to the dynamic needs of an individual in a dynamic culture." Burkett provided a projected program of life-long learning for the hypothetical Mr. Harry Garfield, an aeronautical engineer. The developmental tasks and the educational needs of Mr. Garfield were predicated on the assumption that he would have a single professional career, moving through the managerial and junior executive ranks in his 30's and 40's to become a top executive after the age of 55.

But what if Mr. Garfield's aeronautical engineering career were terminated voluntarily or by necessity at the age of 36, causing him to seek another career? Almost certainly he would need to accomplish or reaccomplish, in an abbreviated period of time, the developmental tasks, specified in Figure 1. According to Super[9], each of these developmental tasks typically constitute a life stage in an uninterrupted career.

At the time of professional career change, a series of planned

adult education and counseling experiences can assist the professional
to accomplish or reaccomplish each developmental task necessary for
successful change. The following "Career Change for a Professional"
model utilizes the same general form as Burkett's model with some

Figure 12.1. Developmental Tasks
in Life Stages Based on Super (6)

Developmental Tasks	Typical Stages In Which Tasks Occur In Uninterrupted Careers
1. Crystallizing a vocational preference.	14-18 years of age
2. Specifying a vocational preference.	18-21 years of age
3. Implementing a vocational preference.	18-25 years of age
4. Stabilizing in a vocation.	21-30 years of age
5. Consolidating status and advancing in a vocation.	30-45 years of age

variations necessitated by the nature of career change. It incorporates
need to accomplish tasks specified by Super. It shows the steps a theoretical person would take through adult education to reorient himself
after deciding on a career change.

A Projected Program for Career Change
for Mr. Harry Garfield

DESCRIPTION OF MR. GARFIELD:

Harry Garfield is a university graduate with a degree in aeronautical engineering. He has been employed by a large aircraft firm as
a project engineer and had hoped to advance in the company to a position in management. At the same time, he has had some doubts about
his own satisfaction with this vocation.

Harry has developed an interest in the study of American history,
in art and design, and in music appreciation. He has been taking adult
education courses in history and in design, as well as business administration. He is married and has three children; his wife is a registered
nurse.

Now at age 35, due to cancellation of government contracts,
Harry has been laid off and has been unable to find a new position. He
is contemplating a career change, but is uncertain of his direction or
how to proceed.

The following educational model assumes: (1) that, as a result of
counseling and testing, Mr. Garfield will seek a master's degree in
Business Administration and will plan to enter a firm in the computer
field; (2) that he will be able to procure an interim sales position in an
engineering firm, allowing time for his education program; and, (3)

Figure 12.2. Career Change
Educational Model for a Professional

Age	Developmental Tasks and Educational Needs	Adult Educational and Supplemental Experiences	Method Code°
35–40	Crystallizing a vocational preference.	Vocational counseling and testing	
	Redefinition of values	Career Changers Group	LF
	Specifying the vocational preference.	Counseling, Field Study	
	Mapping out a program.	Counseling	
	Re-establishing skills involved in the learning process.	Study-Skills Seminar	LF
	Learning how to relate to the family in a reversal of roles.	Role of the family in a time of change	SC
	Implementing the vocational preference.	Management Mathematics	CL
		Business Communications	CL
		Business Statistics	CL
		Business Finance	CL
	Possible changing of self-image and functional life-style.	Career Changers Group	LF
		Creative Family	SC
		Principles of Data Processing	CL
		Management Theory and Policy	CL
		Elements of Marketing	CL
		Computer Programming	CL
		Human Factors in Management	SC
		Business, Labor and Government	CL
		Problem Solving with Computers	CL
		Advanced Management Theory	CL
		Selected Topics in Data Processing	CL
		Business and Society	CL
		Advanced Computer Systems	CL
		Business Policy (M.B.A. awarded)	CL
	Stabilizing in the vocation.	In-company orientation	SC
	Consolidating status and advancing in the vocation.	Personnel Development	SC

°*Method Code*
CL—Class
SC—Short course or conference
LF—Study-discussion group

that Mrs. Garfield will be employed throughout this period as a registered nurse. We realize that all of the adult education experiences specified in the model may not be in existence at this time in any one locality.

Within such a program, the educative and counseling needs of a professional seeking to change his career may be met. In seeking to establish educational experiences which can effectively meet the challenge of the mid-career changer, adult educators in a wide variety of institutions can make it possible for professionals to change careers with a minimum of floundering. Through adult education and related, supportive services, professional career changing can be facilitated.

Notes

1. *Manpower Report of the President* (Washington, D.C.: U.S. Department of Labor, 1970), p. 232.

2. Dan Rottenberg, "A Way Out," *Wall Street Journal*, 18 February 1970, pp.1, 14.

3. Ibid.

4. Milton E. Hahan, "Planning Ahead After 40, Beverly Hills, California," Western Psychological Services, 1967.

5. Robert G. Williams, "The Interrupted Career: An Intermediate Model" (Master's thesis, University of California, 1970).

6. Ibid.

7. Alan B. Knox and Richard Videbeck, "Adult Education and Adult Development: Toward a Theory of Adult Development as a Basis for Adult Education Programming and Research." Unpublished paper, Teachers College, Columbia University, 1968, p. 13.

8. Jess Burkett, "Comprehensive Programming for Life-Long Learning," *Adult Education*, Winter 1960, 2: 116-121.

9. Donald Super et al., *Career Development: Self-Concept Theory* (New York: College Entrance Examination Board, 1963), p. 81.

Part 2

Career Education in the Elementary School

The emphasis on career education at the elementary level is a recent phenomenon. It has brought about many questions from educators concerning curricular emphasis and the role of the elementary school teacher. The first article in this section ("Four Big Questions Children Need to Ask and Ask and Ask") should give the reader an understanding of how career education fits into the development of a child's self-concept. It suggests some fundamental questions that should confront every child if growth in self-awareness is to be emphasized in the classroom. These same questions are basic to developing career awareness in the child.

The next series of articles gives examples of unique ways in which teachers have incorporated career education into the curriculum. The articles range from a teacher working with pre-school children to one working with middle school students. Their methods are by no means to be construed as "the way" to implement career education, but they offer food for thought on how one might go about his own classroom approach.

The final three articles are not written for specific grade levels. Ellis' article suggests how a teacher could plan a career education program geared to a child's cultural and economic background. "Occu-pacs for Hands on Learning" provides an example of how hardware and media can involve the child in the "real world" of career education without leaving the classroom. A teacher using techniques like these can give children a clearer understanding of the skills necessary for specific kinds of jobs. The last article, by Mary Stell, discusses the process that any teacher can apply to the learning environment when attempting to implement career education.

13

Four Big Questions Children Need to Ask and Ask and Ask*

Robert Sylvester
and Esther Mathews

I. What am I like?

To an adult, childhood behavior may seem random, even mosaic. It focuses on the trivial and the significant with equal enthusiasm; jumps from topic to topic with a refreshing lack of adult logic.

Through all this activity, children seek personal meaning to give order to bits and pieces of experience. As each piece falls into place a child begins to answer his own question, "What am I like?" And the answer to this question, which comes over a long period of time, is a necessary element of career exploration. Self-awareness and career awareness nourish each other.

During early childhood years, children need to explore many roles and make many decisions without being intimidated by any sense of finality in those decisions. For example, the child who announces quite seriously on Monday, "When I grow up I wanna be an airline pilot," should feel free on Tuesday to change his mind. Perhaps now he wants to be a doctor. But don't squelch his aspiration, enthusiasm, and imagination by reminding him of Monday's resolve. Rather, help him discover relationships he might not have considered—relation-

*Reprinted from *Instructor*, copyright © February 1972, The Instructor Publications, Inc., used by permission.

ships that may well trigger still another resolution on Wednesday. "That's interesting, Tommy. Pilots and doctors are more similar than you might think. Both must handle delicate instruments masterfully and both are responsible for the well-being of others. What other occupations demand the same skills and responsibilities?"

The school, as a work setting itself, is in an excellent position to assist in the positive development of a child's occupational awareness and self-image, simply because it brings together a wider range of values and experiences (which are at the very core of career exploration) than are typically found in the family environment.

But the school must consider the background and experiences each child brings from his home. Family values create a child's earliest, even strongest, attitudes toward work. In one family work may be approached with curiosity, eagerness, and a confident hope of reward and fulfillment. In another, it may be a painful struggle for survival. Such attitudes affect the child's early play and learning experiences too. Some children learn in an atmosphere of encouragement and even pleasurable excitement, while others sense anxiety and disapproval as they learn to walk, talk, manipulate objects, express themselves, and exert growing independence.

It is important that such early learning activities be encountered positively, because all subsequent work behavior and career development are in reality intricate expansions of these explorations. Significant changes will certainly take place as children encounter more experiences and move toward adult life, but the earlier they understand their own preferences and patterns of learning, the better able they will be to grasp career development concepts in later stages.

Teachers should, and can, expose children to an entire spectrum of positive and negative reactions to work. Through this exposure children will develop the necessary skills to visualize their career lives. Every day offers opportunities to promote skill development through perceptual activities which demand acute powers of observation, listening, contrasting, differentiating, and manipulating. By developing these skills in the lower elementary grades, teachers can prepare children for more advanced levels of exploration including field trips, visits and interviews with representatives of specific occupations, demonstrations, role playing, and familiarity with occupational terminology.

Growth and development are continuous; throughout, children need to ask, "Who am I? How am I different from other children? How am I both alike and different from my parents and other adults? Am I friendly? Do I like to spend time alone? Am I kind, happy? Do I like to help my classmates? What things do I value most? What qualities do I most admire in other people? How do I feel about myself and my actions? What special skills and talents do I have? How do these talents help me contribute to my family, school and community? What kind of person do I want to become? How can I use my talents to develop my own special way of living?" Children need to ask themselves these questions and answer them in the context of the moment. And answers will change because children change as they grow.

Each pupil is part of his own family and should know himself as part of this group. Yet he also exists apart from his family with unique qualities and values of his own. Use the classroom as a supportive setting in which he can explore this duality and accept it comfortably.

Perhaps the most important factor in guiding children toward self-discovery and occupational awareness is your acceptance of the tentativeness of their questions, statements and behavior. Through your acceptance, the child will learn to respect individual qualities of every other student and to recognize and respect his own uniqueness.

APPLICATION

Classroom activities should help children be aware of the influence of the family on occupational knowledge, work, attitudes, and self-awareness. To balance this, other activities should introduce work experiences, views, and values that differ from those students might already have.

• Get acquainted with the current occupational situation in your community and develop discussions about it. What industries or occupations dominate? What contributing factors made these influential? How do they affect community values? Discuss labor-management relations, job security, labor turnover, levels of unemployment. Have these factors influenced the values of your students' families? Do parental occupations enhance or diminish each student's perception of himself?

• Encourage students to talk with parents, family friends, and school staff members about the work they do. Have children write reports. Get them started with a lead such as "If I were _____ for a day, these are the things I would do."

• Through thoughtful readings of your students' accounts you will uncover basic attitudes and values. Do they define work in romantic, heroic, or mundane terms? Are their comments positive or negative? Do they show a good understanding of the work done by persons they know? Do children see occupational roles defined in terms of sex or race? Do they see them in ways that might limit their own occupational futures?

• Encourage children, through their writings, to share with classmates their attitudes toward work. Post reports on the bulletin board, or bind them in a folder for the reading table. When different points of view emerge, bring them out in open discussion.

• Writing and talking about family occupations will encourage inquiry and discussions about family values and work attitudes. Let children compare and contrast their attitudes with those of their parents. Discourage the use of such designations as good and bad, right and wrong. Emphasize respect for and acceptance of different values. Help children understand that bridges across the "generation gap" must be built from both sides! Caution: You must also permit children the option of not telling their feelings in this type of situation.

• As you learn more about your students, use your knowledge to plan and develop experiences appropriate to each one's particular needs. Develop self-enhancing activities through which each child can explore areas of interest in greater depth.

At first, use activities to which students can relate easily. Many home activities have occupational counterparts. For instance: sewing—dress design; flower arranging—floristry; cooking—hotel chef; gardening—horticulture and landscape architecture. How many occupations can your pupils name that parallel home living activities?

• Select one specific activity at a time and name as many related occupations as possible. For instance, how many occupations can children list which are related to sewing? (Home economics teacher, dress designer, fashion editor, tailor, shoe repairman, carpet binder, fabric-shop manager, needlecraft instructor, sewing-machine salesman, knitting-mill employee, bookbinder.) Invite several persons working in these occupations to talk to the class. Try to get a whole spectrum of attitudes toward particular kinds of work. Have children sewed at home? Perhaps children have mended their own clothes, made stuffed animals, designed their own costumes for a special party, helped their mothers with patchwork quilts, or mended sails for model boats. Again, encourage children to ask themselves, and to answer honestly, "What careers does this work suggest? Is this work I like? Is this work I would do well? Why?"

II. How am I changing?

Life is a process of change, growth, and development. And for children to understand the nature of work, they must learn to accept the interrelationship of these factors and to deal with the tentativeness each one brings to life experiences.

Children implicitly acknowledge change every day as they alternate between two interrelated worlds with surprising ease. One is a Here-and-Now world with neither past nor future; a world of random bicycle riding and curiosity-filled explorations of puddles, empty lots, and play with others. The other world is an indeterminate When-I-Grow Up future in which adult life is somehow perceived as a single unit of time. But in both worlds children focus on specific isolated points in time. You must help children explore the dimensions of these worlds, encourage the interpretation of them in terms of each child's life experiences, and guide children toward the concept of life as a dual process of being and becoming.

Even adults fix on and romanticize certain times in their lives such as anniversaries, weddings, and promotions. But the mature adults see these as illustrations of the transitory rather than the static nature of life. Children should understand this too.

Help them conceptualize the tentativeness of life experiences by exploring the dimensions of time—especially the difference between what may be called linear time and cyclical time.

Linear time measures life from birth to death; the story from page 1 to page 249. It suggests a one-time-only opportunity. A boy, for instance, is ten only once in his life. So he'd better make the most of it!

On the other hand, cyclical time emphasizes the recurrence of actions and decisions. Assembly-line workers, teachers, farmers, and incumbent congressmen all encounter cyclical time in their work. By repeatedly going through similar experiences, each perfects his ability to deal with his work.

The interplay of linear and cyclical time partly defines a person's vocational life. All occupations have linear and cyclical aspects. The advancement from apprentice to foreman to company president demonstrates both a straight line and a series of cyclical loops. But so does the life of a farmer who saw fifty harvests come and go. He repeated the crop sequence each year (cyclical) but he was able to improve and increase the product each time because of similar past experiences (linear).

Time, growth, change, and development are important interrelated concepts to explore with your students. Change is a continuous process. Typically, it is gradual. Children are growing, and growth means change. They must continually ask themselves, "In what ways am I changing? Am I getting taller? Are my interests changing? Am I changing in the same ways as my classmates? What will I be like next year? When I go to high school? When I grow up?" And you can help them think about these questions by providing them with a perspective on growth and change.

APPLICATION

Children need tangible evidence of time and the change, growth, and development which occur with its passing. To help youngsters visualize the effects of time, plant a fast-growing vine early in the school year.

• Train the vine up the wall and then start it around the room. Can your students get it to grow around the room before school ends? As a class, have students keep a growth chart, measuring the plant every two weeks. Children should research the care of their particular plant. How is it best protected from disease? How is growth increased or decreased? The vine will become increasingly important as children come to see it as a representation of their time in class. Use the vine as a springboard to activities dealing with time, change, growth, and development. What does it need for full growth?

• Prediction is an important process at this point. Children must be able to visualize and anticipate possible career futures in order to make choices in their present lives. Although a child's career ideas are always changing, awareness of present preferences, skills, and talents provides a sound basis for career-related activities. Encourage children to project themselves in many possible career roles, analyze these roles in terms of what they know about themselves, and relate findings to their present situations. What are the implications for them in terms of growth and change? Children should also be aware that while they are always changing, the world around them is changing too. They need to acquire the skills to project future needs, and consequently, the future occupations which may require these skills.

• Use the vine as a living time line and a class diary. Designate important classroom events (birthdays, holidays, the day everyone mastered the multiplication table) with small cards attached to the vine. Measure growth every two weeks. Let children observe and measure growth at regular intervals to distinguish a pattern. Based on this knowledge, can each child predict plant growth for a specified period of time? Where will the terminal bud be on his birthday; the next all-school holiday? Children may observe spurts and plateaus in the plant's growth. Can students draw any parallels with their own growth patterns? Monthly height and weight measurements offer an example. Are there parallel growth patterns not observable, measurable?

• Keep a more extensive room diary in a loose-leaf notebook or a large scrapbook. Appoint a different student each day (or week) to observe and record classroom events, thoughts about local and community events which affect people's lives, and significant news from the larger world beyond the community. The recorder can synthesize each day into one page-long entry; then read it aloud to the class. The diary should reflect each child's perceptive skills as much as it should reflect events affecting the class as a whole. Encourage children to re-

read entries during spare moments. This will impress upon them even more clearly the processes of change, growth, and development as they relate to time. Youngsters will better understand changes not only in their physical appearances, but changes in their attitudes and abilities to deal with other people and new situations as well. Use a class camera to include pictorial records of trips, classroom visitors, outstanding projects, and everyday events in the diary.

• As a class, have children make a map of their neighborhood. Identify houses and their occupants, stores, public buildings, and so on. Children should be alert to changes in their neighborhood such as new buildings, demolition of old buildings, houses bought and sold, new occupants. Color-code changes; then try to identify developing patterns. Based on these patterns, can students predict changes five or ten years from now? Thirty years from now?

• Let children also record changes in their school population on the wall map. From what areas do new children come? Where do children and their families move? Do occupational demands require some people to move more than others? What occupations might involve many family moves? Encourage children to talk about moves their families have made. Where did they live? What unusual experiences did they have? How did they feel about moving to a new town; making new friends?

• Now children should be ready to develop their own time lines. Give each a sheet of butcher paper. Ask each to draw a line down the middle of the paper; then create a time line of his entire life to date, and his future as he thinks it will, or he would like it to, unfold. Encourage imaginative prediction. What does he think will happen? When does he think it will occur? Cartoons, original drawings, interpretive paragraphs, and pictures should all be included. You'll gain new insights into each child's feelings about himself and help children become more interested in relating present situations to their future lives. If possible, ask older persons in the community to develop their own time lines; then show them to the class. Discuss these in groups or conduct a symposium.

• Ask pupils to block off their life lines in stages. Do this chronologically or by important events. Encourage children to produce puppet plays or write stories which use these stages as acts or chapters. Display their time lines. How do they compare with each other? Do pupils tend to agree on the timing of standard events such as marriage or first fulltime employment? How will their lives be similar in some ways, different in others? Have children identify linear and cyclical elements in their time lines.

• Use magazines as reflections of change. Select one magazine;

then collect back issues approximately five years apart working from the present back to the first publication date. How have they changed? Do children notice changes in design; in types of material presented? How is this medium an accurate mirror of change?

• Encourage individual and group investigations of topics that emphasize change. How were certain occupations different twenty years ago compared to the present? Will these occupations be important twenty years from now? How have computers and automation affected local occupations? Discuss implications of the four-day work week, the effect of new means of transportation. Talk with representatives of both management and labor. How do their views compare or conflict?

In each of their investigations children will have to talk with older people—an essential form of communication if children are to relate the passing of time to change, growth, and development. As each child talks about many experiences with many different role models, he will create a stronger link with the future.

III. What will I be like?

It isn't enough to ask, "What will I be like?" Just as the child is changing and growing, so is the world in which he lives. What will it be like in terms of career choices?

Is there really nothing new under the sun, as children are too frequently told? Are we only elaborating on the basic discoveries which have already been made? Of course not. In fact, we're deluged with unsolved problems awaiting new insights and new knowledge, new careers, and new energies.

In looking to the future, help children think positively. Don't join the doomsayers who predict disaster for man and his world. Destructive patterns can be dramatically reversed in the future if mankind so chooses. Some students may discover career possibilities in this challenge. Children are probably thinking about adult careers in terms of today's occupational situation. Increased understanding of the influence of change, growth, and development should alert children to the fact that changes will take place in occupational choice.

This is why it is important that children sharpen their skills, try to anticipate future needs, and develop flexibility in adapting skills to emerging opportunities.

Several occupational trends are evident. As an important example, there are significant changes in the ways people think about career opportunities for minority groups and for women. These roles will (and should) demand basic shifts in the social orientation of elementary school children. The civil rights movement of the past decade and the women's liberation movement have already helped to effect some changes which mean that interests and abilities, not race or sex, may more largely determine occupational choices. The curriculum must reflect these changes and help students prepare for and demand more open and more numerous career opportunities.

Automation and computerization, miniaturization, and mobility of equipment strongly suggest that in the future human labor will be less important in the production of goods. Since jobs requiring essentially repeated actions can best be done by machines, humans will in some measure be free to meet the increased need for occupations which render services, and to give time and attention to human decision making in matters relating to man and machine.

Another development will be the increase in hybrid occupations such as astromedicine and biochemistry. Engineers will work more closely with conservationists and communications experts with space scientists. Such occupations inter-relate and synthesize clusters of complex fields of knowledge. For this reason, subject-centered curriculums will need alteration to prepare for such specializing, especially, of course, in higher education. But even in the elementary schools, this trend will call for changes in curriculum practice. As teachers, you will have to deal with new curriculum patterns which synthesize knowledge rather than fragmentize it.

You'll need to redefine career categories in clusters of related occupations. For example, occupations involved in personal services might comprise one cluster, careers in the performing arts another, and those in clerical work still another. Defining occupations in this manner rather than by specific occupational titles will emphasize the multi-dimensional application of a set of marketable skills.

This suggests that tasks will frequently be carried out by teams of people rather than by individuals. Your children observed this team effort at a very sophisticated level during recent space flights. Not only did the space flights reflect the changing complexities of space science but they also emphasized the new applications possible in the communications field, and dramatically illustrated the concept of team effort.

As one tries to anticipate the future, it becomes increasingly important that a mood of tentativeness permeate classroom activities. Things will be different when your students enter the occupational world—no doubt about it. But nudge them gently into it with significant activities that focus on the transitory present while simultaneously giving them realistic glimpses of the future.

The changing world in which the growing child lives is the background. In the foreground is the child himself. How do we help him think—and act—wisely about "What will I be like?" The guidelines already suggested continue to be important. We need always to be sensitive to individual attitudes and feelings. We need always to be open and tentative. Within the climate of the relationships those guidelines suggest, you can help each child grow in the understanding of his interests and abilities, and help him explore a wide range of career possibilities. Some ways of doing so are described in the application section which follows.

APPLICATION

Focus on activities that demand student reaction to occupational life today, and use those activities as opportunities to encourage each child to continue developing self-awareness.

• Each child may write a short letter to his parents saying, "Right now I want to be a _____ when I grow up. What do you think of my idea?" Then discuss students' career choices and parental responses to them.

• Ask each student to use pictures and samples from magazines, catalogs, advertisements, posters, and so on, to create a collage reflecting his own feelings about adult occupational life. Display collages by career clusters and ask students whose choices fall in the same cluster to talk informally together about their choices. What general interests stand out in the entire collection? Discuss each child's collage with him. Ask him to talk about one or two others that interest him. Have children guess who made which collage. What were the reasons for their choices?

• Set out a box filled with occupational tags (carpenter, nurse, photojournalist, geologist, medical librarian, for example). Play games using these tags: (a) Ask a pupil to draw a tag and "act out" the occupation in charade fashion. (b) Select two tags at random. Tell how the two occupations might both be important in a community. Can they work together on one task? (c) Choose a tag and ask children to tell which qualities and training the occupation requires. (d) Draw a tag and carry out all the functions of that occupation required in the classroom (mailman: hand out papers; electrician: operate projectors, turn off lights). (e) Have two children each select one tag; then create a role-playing situation in which they might meet at work. Children should feel free to write their own occupational titles. Have them read about their selection, research it, then prepare oral or written reports. Encourage the choice of offbeat occupations, and careers which may develop in the future.

• It's important that as children ask themselves, "What will I be like?" they encounter many role models. Men and women may be invited to the classroom or meet during field trips. Parents may like to visit the classroom to talk about their occupations. Seek a wide range of age groups. Invite a woman lawyer, a black banker, a male nurse, to class. Pupils will come to understand that stereotyped occupational designations can and must be ignored if society is to make maximum use of its human resources.

• Evoke thoughts from your pupils on the TV viewing as it relates to occupational life. What careers are featured in TV shows? What differences are evident in the occupational roles portrayed? How accurately are occupational roles depicted? Do the programs give realistic information about the skills, knowledge, and training needed for these occupations?

• Find activities in school life that parallel adult occupational life (pupil writing at desk; pupils making predictions in the science class, weatherman predicting tomorrow's weather). Discuss these. Create displays in which pupils show how classroom activities lead to adult occupations.

• If possible, have each child spend part of a day with his father, mother, or another adult at work. Send a cassette tape recorder along. Ask him to record brief interviews, sounds, and impressions throughout the day. A sketch pad can add a fine visual dimension to the experience. Follow up with a class discussion the next day.

• Arrange days when children can spend time observing occupations that particularly interest them. Encourage them to observe carefully, ask questions, and take notes. Can they catch the essence of an occupation in twelve photographs? Do the pictures characterize that occupation during an eight-hour day?

Such activities will start your pupils thinking about their occupational future in realistic rather than romantic terms. And by grounding them in the present, you are helping to prepare them for the future.

IV. How will I affect others and how will they affect me?

As children ask themselves (and begin to answer) the first three questions, each may seriously wonder about his influence as one small person. "Can I really make a difference?" they might ask. They can, they should, and with your help, they will.

With each activity, children should not only extend and clarify their self-images, they should also realize that responsible individual action can influence their own development, deepen environmental awareness, and strengthen their personal relationships.

But right now, as children think about their occupational futures, they are caught between newly emerging life-styles and the traditional philosophy which holds that man will be economically rewarded for hard work and perseverance. There is some conflict here. The thrust of certain modern thinkers holds, in general, that human conditions of work are more important than monetary reward; that it is improper, even immoral, to work under de-humanizing conditions; that man must have some measure of control over where, when, and how he works; that personal satisfaction is just as important as economic security in selecting a career.

Personal labor as a meaningful experience is a major criterion for a growing number of young adults. For example, Peace Corps and VISTA volunteers are working around the world to help people help themselves. Is this work? Certainly, but with the same underlying social consciousness reflected in recent television programs such as "Mod Squad" and "The Bold Ones." Here young workers in law enforcement, medicine, social work, law, and teaching demonstrate that jobs, people, and human understanding are inextricably woven in the fabric of a life-style.

Modern films and television programs increasingly emphasize the turmoil and decision making which confront socially concerned young people. As children observe certain ethical, legal, medical, and human problems depicted on the screen, they identify with the players and their roles and take part in a very real and very necessary rehearsal for the future.

So how can you help your children use school experiences to grow toward useful, loving, human cooperation? Begin by helping them recognize and acknowledge every single instance of understanding, cooperation, encouragement, and enthusiasm in their daily experiences. Attention to this kind of behavior, and encouragement of it, will increase its incidence.

These everyday experiences of all human beings in your class as they interact with one another will help shape and direct the patterns of growth and skill development which merge to form a child's career commitment.

APPLICATION

In focusing on cooperative actions, children will recognize that in adult life (and that is the life toward which they are growing) they will each affect others as a total person—by the kind of persons they are, by how they relate to other persons, and by their work and the special abilities they bring to it.

• Concentrate on examples of cooperative effort in occupational life. There's a great deal of literature available on this topic from labor unions, chambers of commerce, professional organizations, trade associations, and governmental agencies. *The Educator's Guide to Free and Inexpensive Materials* and copies of trade association and labor union magazines are good beginning sources of information.

• Newspapers, magazines, and television programs constantly deal with cooperation and lack of cooperation in the world of work. Labor management and strike negotiations are obvious examples. Find materials for students to read; then discuss these situations. Talk about them in terms of local and national events. Encourage children to think about causes and effects. What are the contributing factors? Try to define the issues in particular examples. Go on to discussions of the complexity of the matter to develop awareness that there are no simple solutions; no absolute answers.

• Arrange for a class field trip to a nearby medical clinic. Why do specialists often practice together? How do they cooperate in the operation of the clinic? What problems arise? How do they solve them?

• Assign a small committee to observe a particular occupation for a day. Have them record the variety of people and needs one worker deals with during a day; then have them report their findings to the class. Children will discover that even a seemingly easy job involves complex human relations. For example, a service-station attendant may be called upon to give directions, pump air into bicycle tires, sell parts and make minor repairs in addition to his principal job of pumping gas as he deals with dozens of people every day.

• Is there a house or building under construction in your school neighborhood? If so, suggest that children observe the work closely. A volunteer committee could observe its progress for fifteen minutes every day from the beginning of the project until the day the new owners move in. Encourage children to talk with the succession of workers who are involved in the planning and construction of the building. Provide tape recorders and cameras to record progress. Ask the committee to prepare a large classroom display tracing the development of the project. Focus class discussion on the cooperative effort of the many individuals and companies that produce the goods and services needed. Why is such cooperation necessary? What specific examples of cooperative effort can children identify?

• Generally, children don't realize how many different occupations contribute to the development and use of a manufactured product. To help students understand the complexity of an industrial society and its interdependent occupations, place a familiar manufactured object (cereal box, claw hammer, magazine) and a pad of paper on a table or counter top. Ask students to study the object during spare moments; then list the different occupations they think are involved in the development and use of the object. Transfer each listed occupation to a small piece of paper. Ask a group of students to study these; then arrange them in sequence from the inception of the idea for the product to its final uses.

Encourage the group to add occupations which their classmates neglected to list. When the children complete the study, ask them to chart the development on the chalkboard or in a wall display.

The reports and discussions that evolve from such an activity will improve as your pupils explore different kinds of objects, research their production and uses and grow in their knowledge of the many workers who interact during the development of a manufactured object.

• As a class, have children discuss the school environment as a work setting, emphasizing the interdependence of school personnel; principal, bus driver, teacher, cafeteria worker, janitor, maintenance man. What attitudes do you communicate to them about these people? Do you talk about each role respectfully? Have the class list all the tasks required to keep the classroom going. After a week, have them divide the list into tasks they do and tasks that school personnel do for them. Are there ways they can cooperate better in the execution of their responsibilities and with those who do things for them? How well do children follow through?

Discourage selection of vocational patterns before each child has filtered as many choices as possible. There's still a lot of time for that. Instead, during the elementary years, expand children's experiences by providing a strong support for tentativeness, and by encouraging the development of a confident and realistic self-image, balanced by the security needed to anticipate and deal with change.

Now children are ready to ask themselves the four big questions over again. But this time they can do so with an informed awareness of future choices, and the decision-making skills to move toward an occupational commitment and an enduring life-style.

14

Of Careers and Little People*

Coreen Fuller

C areer education theory and concepts are put to good use in many preschool situations. In one way or another, and perhaps completely unaware of it, the preschools of yesterday, today, and tomorrow are involved in some form of career education. It may be called such things as "role-playing," "Pretending," "Make-believe," "acting out," "socio-drama," "dramatization," etc. In some cases, a whole unit on career education may be developed with a central theme such as "Community Helpers," "Our City," "The World we Live In," "What would you like to Be" "Occupations," "What Does your Daddy Do?", etc. Whatever the title or label, the ultimate goal is to expose the pre-school age child to the world of work and its role in our society. Accordingly, the pre-school setting is arranged to accommodate this goal. Even our most "freely" structured schools are equipped with materials and equipment that suggest career oriented activities. Add an uninhibited and fantasizing young mind to this setting and you will find an ideal opportunity for career education to flourish.

The Pre-School Setting

Rooms especially arranged for the education of the pre-schooler,

*Reprinted by permission from the author.

age three, four, and five, generally contain many and various items, among which the children may play freely. For instance, there may be a corner of the room reserved for any number and sizes of play blocks. This area may also contain several large wooden trucks, airplanes, wheel barrels, etc. Another area in the room might be called the Housekeeping Corner. Here children may find "dress-up" clothes, dishes, a stove, refrigerator, and dolls and dollbeds at their disposal. A climbing apparatus would most likely be in still another area, and close by, a climb-in teeter totter. In the same room or an adjoining room, other materials such as scissors, crayons, paper, paints, paste, books, paper dolls, trucks, and games are found.

Some assortment of the above are usually considered minimal equipment needs to stimulate activity in the pre-school youngster. But the relationship of the pre-school setting and equipment with career education becomes most evident when it is observed in action.

A Pre-School Day

If you have ever been fortunate enough to observe a child in an unstructured activity they were probably acting-out some sort of role. Pre-school children do this to emulate characters, situations, and careers with which they are familiar or that have recently made an impression upon them. Merely witness the children over in the block corner building a city of blocks. You hear one child remark to the other, "Hey, the road needs to be larger so that the gasoline truck can get by." Another child says that they then need more cement for the road. And yet another child becomes the cement truck driver. In the same area, two other children are using a model airplane to carry passengers across the ocean. Nearby, a child is delivering meat to the grocery store in a truck. These children are fully involved in career education activities which mirror things they see and hear about daily.

Seated at a nearby table, several children are using materials with which they hope to create a fire engine. Using scissors, they cut the red paper into a shape they feel looks like a fire truck. The scissors also shape some paper into wheels, a ladder, etc. Yarn might be used for the hose, and aluminum foil for the chrome and of course, paste puts it altogether. Finally, one of the children completes his fire engine and pretends to rush off to a fire.

Over in the housekeeping area three girls and a boy are busily at work playing house. They will have been assigned roles, either by themselves or by an especially eager youngster. Naturally, the boy is the daddy and he hurries off to work at the Police Station. (He is a detective, of course.) The sister needs to go to college because she wants to become a teacher. The big sister needs to be at the office very early today because she has a lot of work to do for the big boss. What does mother do? Well, most of the time she stays home, fixes dinner, talks on the telephone, and puts baby to sleep. But today mother needs to have plenty of help around the house. She is going to work too. Mother has decided to become a telephone operator.

Over on the climbing apparatus and teeter-totter, several children are taking trips, climbing mountains, and any number of things. Even the child sitting on the chair over there, seemingly uninvolved, is visually engrossed in one of the activities.

All of this activity would suggest that the children are using their surroundings to aid them in play related to careers. A good pre-school program will capitalize on these almost natural career tendencies of young children and integrate them into a viable career education program. Take the career of the fireman for example. What kinds of things could the teacher provide to make the career of the fireman even more meaningful to the preschooler? We have already observed several children constructing a firetruck with the art materials. To supplement this activity, special books dealing with the firehouse, firemen, and firefighting could be made available. A supervised table might be arranged for experimenting with fire.

"What happens if we put water on a flame?"

"What happens when a glass is put over the flame?"

"Does fire need air?" A discussion on the usefulness of fire, as well as the danger and damage caused by fire might be appropriate.

"How can we help the fireman?" We could learn some songs and poems about the fireman.

Firemen hats, boots, and coats could be brought to school, or better yet, why not ask the fireman to visit our school. He could give a personalized answer to some of the children's questions. And if possible, a visit to a firehouse would be a great way to see the special equipment and learn about all the things a fireman does. The climbing apparatus could be made into a "pretend" firehouse, the wood-block trucks into fire engines, and wood-block houses into burning buildings. Conceivably, all of the pre-school equipment and materials could be used to aid in understanding the career of the fireman. But this is only one career. There are many more.

At Day's End

The materials, resources, and activities of the pre-school setting can lend themselves to other careers equally as well. Often, however, an unstructured activity can generate career exploration as productively as activities designed specifically for a given career unit. For example, what would the children do with a bladeless razor and shaving cream? A box of curlers and a mirror? A typewriter or a hammer and nails? What would the children do with a big box? Could they pretend it is a post office, a grocery store, or even a rocket ship that is being readied for a trip to the moon? We can imagine all sorts of activities and see even more created as we think about career education in the preschool setting.

Usually, the pre-school child needs little motivation when presented with these kinds of materials. He will most likely become actively or passively involved in role playing activities. Through play, children will discover, reinforce, and question many things about careers and their importance in this environment. The pre-school educator can be instrumental in pre-school career education by recognizing these interests and encouraging endless career experiences in and beyond the classroom.

As the pre-schooler leaves his pre-school setting, his career education continues. Part or all of his school experiences might be shared with an adult in the car on the way home, with a peer seated next to him in the bus, or with another peer as he walks to his home. Again and again throughout the day, these experiences are thought of, perhaps verbalized, maybe reenacted, and most certainly built upon. Pre-school career education is happening!

15

Boutiques, Banks, and Bakeries*

Virginia Weston, Janet Whealon, and Terry Whealon

The concept of career education has become one of the most recent educational issues to receive vast attention from today's media. The federal government has added 55 million dollars to the federal education budget for fiscal 1973 to introduce the concept of career education. Michael J. Bakalis, the Superintendent of Public Instruction for the State of Illinois, has stated that by July of 1973, a system of financial support for career education must be developed which is consistent with other educational funding practices within the state and that by 1975, occupational information must be provided for elementary school pupils and career education for all students in high schools, post secondary schools, or four year institutions. Many journals have devoted entire issues to the implications of career education. Teacher training institutions are offering workshops in career education for teachers of all levels, and enrollments in these workshops are filled to capacity.

Sharing the spotlight with career education is the open classroom movement. Many authorities in the field of education advocate this method of learning. Inherent in developing an open classroom is the abandonment of the heavy emphasis on textbooks in favor of a more

*Reprinted by permission from *Illinois Career Educational Journal*, Winter 1973, pp. 22-24.

experiential approach to learning. This challenges the teacher to determine what meaningful experiences she can provide. In order for these experiences to be meaningful they must relate to the child's real world. Through the use of career education one finds a practical way in which the teacher can open her classroom. What is more relevant to the real world of the student than the study of man in his world of work?

Four first grade teachers in Willow Grove School in Buffalo Grove, Illinois, have involved their students in Career Education projects this past school year. They initiated learning experiences through utilization of local community resources. This related school experiences to life outside school and helped children to learn to make decisions. The following describes one of their cooperative ventures during February, 1972.

The Willow Grove teachers decided to have their children learn about people who sell things, store owners, and stores in general. The next few days were spent planning with the students, making lists of the different kinds of stores, and discussing the various types of jobs involved. As a result of this introduction, the children suggested they would like to operate a department store.

The teachers thought each first grade class could be responsible for one department within a large store, but did not go into detail about the financial aspects of the project. To help the children gather appropriate knowledge from primary sources and to help the children learn to interview adults, the teachers decided to invite members of the business community to their classrooms so that the children could inquire directly from them.[1]

The first visitor was a banker. He explained how his bank helps businessmen finance their stores. He brought slides and other handouts as well as mini-budget books for mini-allowances. Through their interviewing of the banker, the children discovered that banks are businesses that make money by handling money.

Once a few key financial concepts were explored, a district manager from a local department store was interviewed. He explained how, why, and where stores are located and how they select merchandise for each individual store. He also brought a supply of catalogues and showed the children how to use the order form.

Another department store manager visited and the children learned about promotions, sales items, cashiers, etc. To learn how stores got their products to sell, a factory representative from a food manufacturing concern explained his job in person. The children found out that a network of relationships existed behind every department store sale.

One of the most interesting interviews was with a wholesale salesman. The children were especially interested in the fact that a salesman is "his own boss," that he has no regular hours, that he has no office or place of employment where he is required to be each day. This led into a discussion of commissions and, interestingly enough, self-discipline.

Not all the people interviewed came to the school. All four classes visited a department store owned by one of the first-grader's father. The children were guided through the accounting, receiving, shipping and sales departments.

In addition, the children made trips after school to various stores such as a bakery, a pet store, a drug store, and a large department store. This was done in small groups after school under the supervision of volunteer mothers. The children wrote individual learning contracts before going, and then reported their findings to the class when they had fulfilled their contracts.

Direct experiencing built motivation for scholarly activity and social projects. The children were eager to open their own store. The children chose an area of special interest to them. They proceeded to form groups, plan their operations, and stock their areas of a classroom that had been designated as their store.

Four stores were put into operation—a boutique, a sweet shop, a toy shop, and "Take-Five Store." The "Take-Five Store" was a place where children could purchase two cookies and juice for five cents as well as rest while they were shopping. Many aspects of operating a store came into play—production of articles to be sold, planning the physical layout of the store, pricing, advertising, and selling.

Some of the children made decoupage plaques and necklaces with the help of two volunteer mothers to sell in the boutique; some made candy for the sweet shop; some made cookies for the "Take-Five Store"; some repaired toys which they brought from home to sell in the toy shop. Involvement in these activities produced tangible accomplishments in the academic areas of language arts, math, social studies, and science.

Oral language skills were developed through interviewing; written language skills through the writing of notes, reports, and thank-you letters to the people who visited; mathematical skills through measuring ingredients for the candy and cookies. Each child was involved in an educational activity that combined many dimensions of the child's work-play world. Each child was learning to inquire from primary sources in his own community, to relate school studies to his life outside of school, and to make decisions appropriate to his maturational age.

Notes

1. Interviewing skills were taught by methods suggested by ABLE Model Program, Northern Illinois University, DeKalb, Illinois, Dr. Walter Wernick, Project Director.

16

We're Not All Famous But Everyone Is Important*

Agnes Byrnes

This unit is about the importance of people. It was planned for important people. Therefore, it came alive with people—people as diversified, unique and important individuals regardless of their role in life.

Each human being needs to sense his own worth. The aim of this unit is to stress individual dignity, high self-esteem and a greater feeling of importance for each and every human life.

We began with a play in which each child in my second grade assumed a role that he would play for nine weeks. Each child received a hat or some other costume and a book that told about the career role he was playing. There were small speaking parts for each child.

Each one of the children's roles corresponded to that of an adult who had agreed in advance to visit the class and/or spend some time with that child. Altogether 25 different career occupations were included in our pantheon (see box) but obviously in any community many different roles could be included. One important note of caution: The range of occupations exhibited must be wide. If only doctors, lawyers and bankers are included, the purpose of the unit is defeated. We had beauticians, firemen, bulldozer operators, garbagemen and

*Reprinted by permission from *K-Eight Instructional Management and Leadership*, North American Publishing Company, November 1972, pp. 28-31.

many other people whose occupations may seem less glamorous, but who make a vital contribution to our lives and who, therefore, are important.

It was deemed best to visit half of the adults on their jobs. The rest came to our classroom, directly from their jobs, often still wearing their uniforms. Before each visit we saw filmstrips or read books about the job of the next visitor from the community.

Each and every adult was introduced by me, using a standard introduction, similar to this. "Boys and girls, we have a very important person with us today. His name is Joseph Smith. He is married, and marriage is a very important responsibility. He is important to his wife—that's one reason he is important. But he is also a father—he has three children—and being a father is an important responsibility. He is a son; he is important to his parents. He is a brother . . ." and so on until all of his roles in life had been brought out.

Sometimes these introductions took as much as 10 minutes (as with a man who served as a garbageman, volunteer fireman, volunteer policeman, owner of a luncheonette and was also a son, brother, father, husband, uncle, grandfather and nephew). In each case, the person being introduced stood or sat in front of the class, giving the children a chance to see what he looked like and also giving him a chance to relax a little and get over any nervousness.

With this introduction concluded, we started to ask questions concerning our guest's many roles in life. The format was like a talk-show with the important visitor in the center seat and the child who was role-playing his occupation on one side and me on the other. While the questioning took place, I took pictures because most often the visitor had a demonstration of some sort. Each and every child caught the feeling of each adult visitor almost from the moment he appeared. The adults experience some great and wonderful subtle happiness at having 25 interested souls listen to whatever it is they do. Many of the adults had not been in a classroom in many years, and most actually glowed with the recognition bestowed upon them.

You may be saying, "What is it you actually did?" In brief, the doctor came to our classroom on his day off and brought his medical bag. We talked about his education and how he had to prepare for the work he does. We always asked about the number of hours the person worked and if he was a young child when he decided he wanted to be a doctor, druggist or whatever. The children just naturally fell into the questioning, especially since each adult was anxious to talk about his work.

A similar format was followed with all visitors. The musician brought many instruments for the children to touch and play; the telephone company sent out two men with a truck and lots of equipment to demonstrate. A keypunch operator punched three cards for each child with individual children's names and symbols.

We went to watch the builders who were reconstructing the first floor of our school. The beautician demonstrated on two wigs while we all talked about her work. The bulldozer operator brought his bulldozer to our school and operated it for us. We all touched it and talked again about the years of preparation or schooling needed.

The druggist wrote out a prescription for us in Latin on the board and an 86-year-old grandmother played the piano and showed us crocheting and sewing. A truckdriver brought his tractor-trailer rig to our school and took it apart for us. We even had a major league baseball player talk about sports and demonstrate some of his skills.

We went with our school librarian to the local library, and cards were issued to those children who did not have them. We visited the bakery, the firehouse, a service station, the local borough hall. We spent an afternoon walking to two different churches in town and visiting with the clergymen. We went to the state police barracks.

We all discovered that each of the adults was absolutely essential to the community. They all work many hours every day to see that the things they are responsible for get done. They all had to practice or learn to do the particular job they did.

The items left behind by our visitors were of great importance. Each adult was asked to give us one item he felt was indispensable to him in his job, or which he felt adequately reflected him and what he did. These were all displayed under the banner "Important People Use These." Then various questions accompanied articles, such as "Who uses this?" "Does more than one use this item?" "Do you know what this does and how to use it?"

Each visitor was tape-recorded while he was telling us about himself and his job. These recordings were listened to by the children throughout the remainder of the school year whenever they had free time.

A huge mural slowly came to life in the corridor outside the classroom. It was done on pieces of homasote 4 feet by 12 feet. After each visit we added to the mural. Each child added his own rendition of the place where his role is in the community. For example, a nurse was portrayed by a hospital, the mailman by the post office, the bulldozer on the streets of the town. The mural was entitled "Important People Live Here." Other children in other classrooms throughout the building took great interest in watching the mural become a town. They often stopped to see what had been added, and it became a source of delight to the entire school.

Not only did the children begin to see significance in their individual lives, but the adults again and again were delighted to give of their time. These unique, diverse and important individuals came into our lives and by telling what he or she did, demonstrated to the children their own sense of worth. Each person enjoyed telling about what he does best and each child saw that it is necessary to have high self-esteem and a feeling of importance about the accomplishments of one's self.

The culminating event became extremely important as the unit drew to a close. Each child had experienced a day all his own—had played a role complete with hat, artifact, tape recordings and their own real life adult. Now it was time to bring the unit to an end. It was quite an impressive ceremony as each child came forward to relinquish the hat he had grown to love. (They wore these hats for each and every visit.) Twenty-five different times a child was called forward and as the hat was removed from his head and a huge VIP pin put on him, I said seriously, "Baker Jones, please come forward. You are no longer Baker Jones, but you are a very important person because you are Robert Jones." It was indeed, a most auspicious occasion.

A Potpourri of Occupations

In Pennfield, N.J., Ms. Byrnes matched 25 children to 25 occupations, each engaged in by people living in that town. Pennington's 25 occupations are listed below. Your own local occupation list is bound to differ.

Doctor	Keypunch Operator	Druggist
Librarian	Builder	Nurse
Baker	Service Station Attendant	Policeman
Musician	Mailman	Teacher
Fireman	Elected Official	Grandmother
Principal	Beautician	Truckdriver
Telephone Operator	Bulldozer Operator	Marine
Newspaper Reporter	Clergyman	Baseball Player

A Student's Guide
for Meeting Important People

1. Go to office to meet the person and bring him back to classroom
2. Sit in on interview alongside person visiting
3. See that tape recorder is ready to record event

4. Have picture taken with important person

5. Sign your name along with that of visitor in book where pictures will appear

6. Make report on your role before or after visit

7. Receive item from visitor for our bulletin board and place it on bulletin board

8. Escort visitor back to office

9. Write thank you note to your Important Person expressing thanks for the entire class

THINGS to ASK

1. When did you decide on your profession?
2. How much schooling have you had?
3. How many hours do you work?
4. How do you prepare for the work you do?
5. What do you find rewarding about your work?

IMPORTANT PERSON'S BIOGRAPHY

1. Married or Single?_____
2. Parent?_____ Number of Children?_____
3. Brothers or sisters?_____
4. Hobbies?

17

Putting Plans to Work— Some Who Have: Rahway*

Thomas W. Gambino

D iane Calder's fourth graders shout when they enter her room. "Hey, when can we work with it?" They're talking about the big tool board, which sports saws, wrenches, chisels, soldering irons, jigsaws, planes, and angles; drawers full of nails, batteries, and wire; or a surprise piece of brand-new equipment. This is all part of the New Jersey State Education Department's Technology for Children Program (T4CP), in operation in Rahway's Madison Street School for exactly one year. The program gives each child a chance to assess himself and his future potential by recognizing and developing his own special abilities, needs, and interests through manipulative experiences.

Joe Weiss, Assistant Director of Career Development in Rahway, says this program is particularly helpful to the slow learner. By being able to do things and apply all of his skills, the child can't help but keep up with classmates.

T4CP children conduct demonstrations, make things, discuss findings, and keep records of their progress. One class studied food as part of a social studies unit. They planned a morning field trip, determining the cost of the trip, mode of travel, things to eat, questions to

*Reprinted from *Instructor*, copyright © February 1972, The Instructor Publications, Inc., used by permission.

ask, and pictures to take. Back in the classroom, the class constructed a miniature bakery; then each child carried out the responsibilities of a particular job.

This is only one of the activities which give Madison Street youngsters a chance to live all kinds of occupational roles, to explore the ways in which they can influence their environments, to uncover their feelings about different jobs. Through acting out experiences, a youngster learns that outcomes depend upon his own individuality; that successes indicate his potential. T4CP is helping children become career-aware. It helps them develop wholesome attitudes toward work, cultivates self-assertiveness, and motivates them to apply their best efforts to a task.

Because a child's motor abilities often determine his feeling of independence and his confidence in coping with his environment, hands-on activities are basic in T4CP. Children work with levers, bells, batteries, paint, tools, cloth, wood, plastic, computers, typewriters, videotape recorders, printing presses. They design, measure, cut, bend, piece together. They operate businesses and write their own performances. They test techniques and apply scientific and mathematical concepts.

As in other programs, Weiss finds problems in helping teachers and children alike to correlate manipulative experiences with academic work. But the response of the Rahway community reinforces the efforts of every child and provides excellent role models. Weiss says, "Workers portray a great deal of satisfaction with their work, and they're absolutely delighted that they can talk about it."

Bill Moesch, teacher of the trainable retarded class for 14- to 20-year-olds, is extremely optimistic about the experiences his students are getting from T4CP. Although they'll never be totally independent, he thinks the skills they acquire will assist them in sheltered workshops, increase their self-worth, and help them to become more self-sufficient than they might otherwise be.

18
Putting Plans to Work— Some Who Have: West Hartford*

Thomas W. Gambino

I t showed me for proof that life has its ups and downs." That's what one twelve-year-old had to say about his visit to St. Francis's Hospital as part of the World of Work (W.O.W.) program in West Hartford, Connecticut—a pilot program, now in its second year, for 250 sixth graders in four elementary schools.

Through experiences with adults at their daily tasks, students satisfy their healthy curiosities about different occupations. Betty Burns, a team leader at Whitman School, says all her pupils wanted to be teachers, stewardesses, and football players, when they first entered the program. But now some are into such fields as computer programming and oceanography. Mrs. Burns is trying to make students aware of what they like about people; to make them ask themselves, "What qualities do I admire most?" She says, "I'm also trying to help them understand the world they may be living in someday; trying to make them adaptable."

Ruth Prosser, director of W.O.W., says that a major part of the program is seeing and talking with persons in various fields of work. "We want to go beyond the school walls and tap the human and physical resources available here in West Hartford. We want children to

*Reprinted from *Instructor*, copyright © February 1972, The Instructor Publications, Inc., used by permission.

see a given person in his entirety—to see that choosing a career means choosing a life-style."

Before and after every trip, pupils toil over detailed preparations and follow-up activities. But they don't mind when they can watch, ask questions, and even try some of their worker-teacher's techniques. During a hospital visit, a group tested suturing materials and attempted some surgical knots, while another group attended a class for operating-room technicians.

Exploring the world of work also polishes communication skills. Children learn quickly that the kinds of questions they ask determine the answers they get. New perceptions are brought back to the classroom as students commit observations to paper and increase vocabularies to understand the complex terminology of specialized fields. And of course students discover what the job means to the worker— rewards, difficulties, potential, effect on family.

Arthur Woznicki, Administrative Assistant in the West Hartford system, paints a realistic picture of the W.O.W. program. There are transportation problems due to insurance coverage limitations; some parents still don't understand W.O.W. objectives; and teachers often see W.O.W. as a burdensome new program that must be squeezed into a too short day. During the first year, the program demanded that students select an area of interest, without really knowing what interested them most. But this year the program has been divided into three phases, which involve exposure to many areas, selection of an interest, and follow-up activities in this area.

The Old Guard, a group of retired West Hartford citizens, has contributed to the progress of W.O.W. Retirees accompany students to many of the different occupational settings—often places where they have worked. So W.O.W. has given senior citizens a new sense of self-worth too.

West Hartford, one of America's most affluent suburbs, has sent some 80 percent of its graduates to college each year—but usually with little or no career guidance. With W.O.W. exposure, kids will have some idea of the directions to take to enter a particular field.

19

The Need
for Math
Seemed Endless*

Joel Smith

W atching the building of an addition to their school was obviously more interesting and exciting to Mrs. Hull's sixth grade
class than the mathematics she was trying to teach. Mrs.
Hull, a career development-oriented teacher, drew upon this interest
in helping her class to choose to implement a unit on the construction
industry.

The direction was given by the teacher, the decision made by the
students. In a planning session the class decided to divide themselves
into three groups, form companies, and bid against each other to build
the teacher a lake house.

The companies thus formed were complete with president, vice-
president, secretary, purchasing agent, architect, and the rest of the
broad array of occupations involved in the construction trades industry. Hours of research in the school library and at home (using monthly
magazines) produced the general designs that the three companies
used as a basis for bid proposals.

Further research told them that they knew little about the "in-
sides" of houses. It was at this point that they felt a need for the first
resource person who would help them get on their way.

*Reprinted by permission from *American Vocational Journal*, March 1972, pp. 50-51.

Math Useful? Amazing!

Working from a *Resource Persons File* compiled by the career development specialists, the youngsters selected and contacted an architect who came into their classroom, discussed with them the role and function of the architect, his feelings about his job, the decisions that he made in preparing for that job, and the general characteristics a person should possess to pursue a career in architecture. In addition to these intangibles, he pointed out to them the structural components of a house, the need for blueprints, and how to read them.

As the youngsters subsequently read blueprints, they became aware of the very real need for mathematics in drawing and reading them. They found that blueprints are based on measurement; they use scale, ratio and proportion, fractions, and geometry. Could it be that the very mathematics which they were studying was useful—even necessary to the architect? Amazing!

The students were then able with additional research to draw their own plans using mathematics teamed with drafting tools in the same characteristic manner as would the architect and/or draftsman.

Concurrently with these design functions, the materials procurement group for each of the three "companies" requested catalogues and brochures on supplies, materials, and fixtures. The requests were written in the form of business letters of inquiry and were typed by "secretaries" of the three companies. These letters of request, along with letters of thanks to resource persons, were checked for proper form, sentence structure, spelling, punctuation, and grammar.

Language arts were necessary in these communications. Once again the need for sixth grade schooling showed up in their unit and in the construction businesses in the community.

Using authentic bid sheets which were given them by the visiting architect, the students began to compile their bids to submit to the teacher. Many telephone calls were made requesting information on materials, supplies, and labor costs (more language arts).

The costs thus obtained were then transferred to the bid sheets. At that point the "estimators" became concerned with profit margins and thus with percentages and extensions of figures. (The need for mathematics seemed endless!)

Social Studies Too!

During this time the construction crews were busy building models of their lake houses and discussing the similarity of their work roles to those in the community. Such roles as surveyor, bulldozer operator, mason, framer, plumber, electrician, roofer, carpenter, contractor, floorer, tile man, painter, and landscaper were scrutinized for duties, educational requirements, community availability, and individual self-characteristic compatibility.

The youngsters called a local prefabricated housing manufacturer and set up a field trip to the plant. In preparation for the field trip, the youngsters discussed with the teacher the work roles they would see and the kinds of tools and equipment used in the plant and developed a technique for interviewing workers on a person-to-person basis.

Upon returning from the trip, they discussed what they had seen in terms of equipment, operation, and work setting, placing particular emphasis on their feelings about their observations.

The implementation time for this unit was about seven weeks, during which time principles of traditional subject areas were realistically applied to the unit activities. For instance, properties of materials (science) and their influence on the construction industry were graphically illustrated. Geography, climate, and natural resources (all social studies) were discussed in terms of their influence on the construction industry, as well as societal grouping patterns and architectural feats as a manifestation of our society.

A labor union representative came into the classroom and discussed with the youngsters the effects of organized labor on the construction industry—living social studies!

As they participated in various phases of the unit, the youngsters were encouraged to role-play several different occupations. As a result of this experience, they could express their likes and dislikes, interests and abilities.

Obviously no one unit could be conclusive in the determination of a student's true interests and abilities, but throughout the elementary school years there will likely occur a pattern of recognition of self-characteristics upon which a youngster can base his career goals. He will then be able to take the steps necessary to achieve those goals.

Structured But Flexible

The construction unit described above is one of 50 such units currently being implemented in Cobb County, Georgia, schools. At the elementary level the units cover occupations in the 15 clusters named by the U.S. Office of Education, thus providing youngsters a wide variety of experiences and exposure and giving them many alternatives as they formulate career goals.

The Cobb County Occupational and Career Development Program utilizes activity-centered units in grades K-6. The units are directed by the same teacher who directs mathematics, science, and language arts.

Units are so devised that they offer enough structure to create a feeling of security on the part of the teachers and yet are flexible enough to permit teachers to draw upon their own creativity and the interest of the students as they implement them.

Six Elements

In the Cobb County program teachers direct one unit each nine-week grading period, with the actual time expended per day or per week left to the discretion of the teacher.

The teacher is required to incorporate into each unit six elements: (1) a hands-on activity to give concrete experience from which abstract ideas can be drawn; (2) an all-subject matter tie-in to show the relationship of math, science, language arts, etc. to the hands-on activity and comparable occupations in the community; (3) visits by resource persons to the classroom to lend credibility and support from the real world; (4) field trips into the business and industrial community to give youngsters a firsthand look at work places and an opportunity to interview workers concerning not only their job duties but also their feelings about their jobs; (5) role-playing to capitalize upon the students' natural desire for such activity while demonstrating occupational characteristics and the need for cooperative effort to reach a common goal; (6) introduction to occupations to aid the students in becoming aware of the vast occupational opportunities available.

Obviously, these elements are overlapping, clearly demonstrating their interdependence. Perhaps for the first time for many students school has meaning. They are actually involved from planning through evaluation, and they can see tangibly how their interests and abilities can be teamed with schooling to achieve goals they set for themselves.

Unquestionably, students coming to the secondary level from such a program will know more about tools, job duties, opportunities in the community, and themselves than they otherwise would have known.

What Does It Mean?

The career development approach is underway to some degree in every state in the Union, largely through the efforts of the U.S. Office of Education. It is growing in prominence in local systems and indeed has become a top priority item nationally under Commissioner Marland. What does this mean to the vocational educator?

It means that future students will make career decisions and choose educational avenues based on their experience, exposure, and *knowledge*. It means that youngsters will choose programs to fit themselves rather than trying to fit themselves into "standard" programs. It means that youngsters will be more aware of the real occupational opportunities available to them before they choose educational avenues.

It means that youngsters progressing through a career development program will demand educational offerings that are commensurate with their career goals. It means that vocational education as a part of the broader scope of career education will serve a greater number of students who are prepared to take advantage of meaningful vocational programs.

20
The Role of the Middle School in Career Development*

Kenneth B. Matheny

T he middle school—usually grades five or six through eight—
shares with other levels of public education a concern for the
career development of students. This concern should be
translated into four major functions: (1) to provide opportunities for
the development and implementation of an accurate self-concept; (2)
to teach decision-making skills; (3) to provide vocational information
and exploratory experiences; and (4) to help students choose and locate appropriate curricula or jobs.

To identify the unique role of the middle school in career development, certain questions must be answered: What self and work experiences have students already encountered? What attitudes toward
self and work have resulted from their reactions to these experiences?
What is the student's stage of readiness for vocational planning? And
how skillful are middle-school students in making decisions?

Theoretical Base

Vocational development theories would seem to be promising
sources for answering such questions. Stages and norms derived from
these theories should help the educator plan experiences appropriate
to the readiness level of students at different ages. Such theoretical

*Reprinted by permission from *American Vocational Journal*.

information, however, is often difficult to translate into guidance practice and is sometimes misused.

Stages and norms are sometimes improperly viewed as imperatives rather than as descriptions. To make imperatives out of norms is to say, "What is, should be."

Developmental stages are not immutable. Gribbons, Shimberg, and Katz have demonstrated that the ordering of stages can be affected by a guidance program. (8,23)[**]

Moreover, individuals are not groups. Thus, group averages cannot be treated as representative of any given individual. Career guidance must be individualized in the same way that instruction must be individualized. Flanagan (6) is currently devising an approach to individualized guidance as part of a broader approach to individualized instruction. Despite dangers of misuse, stages and other normative data should prove helpful in establishing career guidance goals. Unfortunately, career development theory is still so embryonic that it is more important to research than to practice. Nevertheless, it is important to review such contributions as Super's stages of career development, Havighurst's stages of vocational development, O'Hara's stages of vocational learning, and Katz's outline of a guidance-oriented curriculum. (24, 11, 20, 15)

According to Super, middle-school students are in the exploratory stage of vocational development. At this stage, the student is exploring self-attributes and dimensions of the world of work which will later prove useful in preparing for, entering, and adjusting to an occupation. He first makes a tentative selection of a field and level of work, later specifies a vocational preference in a transition substage, and finally, in a trial substage, converts his specified vocational preferences into reality by commitment to employment or specialized training.

While college-bound youth continue this upward progress during their college years, high school terminal students and early-school-learners must accomplish this growth in much shorter time; otherwise they will not be ready for employment by the time they leave school. A planned work-exposure program at the middle-school level can be especially valuable in helping these noncollege-bound youngsters through the exploratory years.

Question of Maturity

Super and Overstreet in their Career Pattern Study, and Flanagan in Project Talent, found the vocational interests of ninth graders

[**]Numbers refer to references.

too unstable to recommend specific vocational choices at that age. (25,7)

Super later found, however, that the amount of vocational information possessed by ninth graders was positively related to their career behavior at a later age. (26) Super implies that the career development goals of the middle school should be confined to teaching students to achieve a planning orientation and to take responsibility for personal decisions.

It would seem untimely, then, to urge middle-school youth to make vocational decisions, but desirable to furnish them with opportunities to explore work both as observers and participants. By exploring broad occupational areas, students increase their understanding of the nature of work, the characteristics of workers and the differences in work settings. They also become aware of their own preferences and distastes.

In summary, while the middle school has special responsibility for teaching basic habits of industry, it shares with elementary and senior high schools the responsibility for teaching decision-making skills. The middle grades should be a time for self- and occupational exploration, for becoming planning-oriented, acquiring decision-making skills, and learning the habits of industry. Except for a few early-school-leavers, the selection of a specific occupation should be discouraged.

Recommended Practice

Concern for career development should be consistent throughout the entire middle-school curriculum. If the relationship between all courses of study and the world of work is emphasized, student interest in even unpopular subjects (like math and languages) will be aroused. Unfortunately, lack of teacher interest and scarcity of materials that fuse vocational and academic learning defeat this aim in most schools.

The guidance worker can play an important role in highlighting the need for "vocademic" education by locating promising materials and encouraging teacher interest.

Other life concerns (such as the proper use of leisure time and the establishment of sound interpersonal relations) should also be stressed throughout the curriculum. As such concerns are creatively interwoven within the curriculum, the entire educational experience becomes more meaningful even to potential dropouts.

Community as Laboratory

The career guidance programs should more fully utilize community resources, a point recently supported by the Secretary of Health, Education and Welfare when he stressed the importance of providing inner-city youth with lifelike educational experiences within the community.

The "schools without walls" concept has been amply demonstrated by Philadelphia's Parkway Project, which makes extensive use of the community as an educational laboratory. (27) The Project depends exclusively upon nearby offices, stores, laboratories, museums, factories, and jet airports to provide the "nuts and bolts" of its educational program. While the merit of such exclusive use of community resources may be questionable, it is apparent that the community has much to offer.

Attempts to use the community as a laboratory will, of course, strain the educator's inventiveness and organizational ability and demand considerably more preparation than do normal classroom activities. However, the additional teaching effort is worth it if increased student interest is achieved.

Realism Is Catalyst

Real and simulated work experiences provide a catalyst for self- and vocational exploration. Experiential learning—with the smells, sounds, and sights of work—is definitely more stimulating to the student than stilted, boring, and often outdated textbooks.

Work experience systematically arranged to expose students to broad occupational areas should be provided to give them a realistic base for comparing the psychological satisfactions offered by various types of work. The goal in planning these experiences should be to develop understanding rather than to teach job skills. Students should be guided through carefully planned observation schedules and have their attention drawn to key job operations as well as conditions under which the work is performed.

Although it will be impossible for middle-school students to actively participate in many types of work, they can profit from seeing it done under actual conditions and performing some of the tasks in a simulated setting.

An increasing number of games and problem-solving exercises are available to simulate important aspects of certain occupations. These games not only provide an interesting means of presenting occupational information but also subtly teach the decision-making process.

Among them are self-administered career kits which introduce students to the importance of an occupation, present representative on-the-job problems, and furnish information required to solve these problems. Although constructed with high school students in mind, these kits can easily be adapted to the middle-school student. It is interesting to note that students from lower socio-economic schools consistently give more favorable reactions to the use of these kits than do students from middle-class schools. (16)

Varenhorst has made use of the Life Career Game, in which students plan the life of a fictitious student within simulated environments and receive feedback on the possible consequences of their decisions. (30)

Boocock and Schild describe a variety of promising social simulation games designed to interest students, increase their information-seeking behavior, and present accurate information regarding occupations. (1)

Katz has written a work-text oriented toward decision-making, which was found to be instrumental in increasing the functional knowledge of work and problem-solving ability of seventh- and eighth-grade students. (14, 23) And the Palo Alto schools in California have introduced a program on decision-making for ninth graders.

Sharing Experiences

Exploratory experiences should be coupled with group guidance to personalize the learning which occurs. Every time a student experiences a new work role, he should be encouraged to share his reactions in a small group. He should be led to discuss his observations of job performances and job conditions, how he felt about himself while performing or observing the work, what personal needs he feels would be met or thwarted by such work, what aptitude he feels he might have for such work, and how he thinks one goes about preparing for such work.

This group approach can result in a spiral of ever-increasing understanding of work and of self in relationship to work. Guidance functions should include the prescription of extending experiences of various kinds, insuring their availability, and helping students to derive personal meaning from them.

Many of the above-mentioned dimensions are already incorporated in a career development program now being conducted in 20 Georgia schools. (2) Called the Program of Education and Career Exploration (PECE), it offers students in the upper middle grades a set of systematically arranged real and simulated work experiences in six occupational areas based on Roe's occupational classification. (21)

After each work experience, students in small guidance groups collectively use the information and experience gained to evaluate self-characteristics, explore potential satisfactions of the work role, identify the educational avenues necessary for gaining entry into the occupation, and practice decision-making.

Because it was assumed that all students could benefit from the program, the 20 participating schools have attempted to recruit cross-sectionally from the student body. In addition, there was some evidence to suggest that work experience programs may have certain negative results if offered exclusively or even heavily to delinquent students or potential dropouts. (31)

Learning to Make Decisions

Career development programs should provide students with practice in decision-making. The occupational world is changing so rapidly that students must possess the internal equipment to cope with the changes. Adequate decision-making skills will help students face the many choices they will be forced to make in later life. Good decision-making skills will result in wiser, more personally satisfying choices, and a growing confidence in self-direction.

A feeling of self-direction leads to confidence in one's ability to make an impact on his environment. According to Coleman's study, this self-attitude is more closely related to achievement in school than all other school factors put together. (4)

Decision-making skill involves learning (1) how to identify alternatives and where to obtain information regarding them, (2) how to predict one's success in each alternative, (3) how to estimate the depth to which each alternative will accord with one's values, interests, and abilities, and (4) how to construct a plan of action. Some of the simulation games mentioned earlier provide highly interesting vehicles for practice in decision-making.

Motivational Factors

Career development can be accelerated by motivating students to seek self- and occupational information. A number of studies have demonstrated the effectiveness of operant conditioning and/or social modeling in producing information-seeking behavior. (17, 28, 22)

According to other reports, career decision-making will soon be aided by the development of computer-based information-dispensing systems. The computer talks with the student about steps that are important to the making of occupation decisions; processes information regarding his values, interests, and aptitudes; and offers matching data on job opportunities, satisfactions, and requirements. (29, 3, 12, 19)

Most of these systems are in the early stages of development, but their ability to store, process, and retrieve thousands of bit of information and to make them immediately available to inquiring students promises to significantly revise the role of the guidance worker.

Inner-City Needs

Inner-city youth often need special assistance in career development. Havighurst suggests that a student's identification with a productive worker is the foundation upon which all other vocational-developmental tasks rest. (11) Without this identification, other tasks such as acquiring basic habits of industry, acquiring an identity as a worker, and becoming a productive person cannot be properly handled.

Many inner-city youth need to have their occupational aspiration-levels heightened. In the past, Negroes and other minority groups have been limited mostly to unskilled, semiskilled and service occupations. Their aspirations commonly reflect these limitations.

Although new opportunities are being made available as a result of the efforts of Equal Employment Opportunity, JOBS, the Urban League, and other organized efforts, the aspiration of minority-group students, in many cases, lags behind growing opportunity.

The Developmental Career Guidance Project in Detroit has attempted to raise the educational-occupational aspiration level of inner-city youth through a program of counseling, information dissemination to both students and parents, and exposure to work. Among other positive results, students in the experimental schools have demonstrated significantly higher levels of aspiration than control groups. (18)

Evaluating Results

The evaluation task is more difficult for middle schools than for senior high schools, since there is a lack of terminal criteria such as employment or enrollment in post-secondary institutions. For the most part, evaluation in the middle school will be concerned with measuring the increased vocational maturity of students.

Four commendable instruments are now available for maturity measurement. The Case Development Questionnaire is a group-administered, paper-and-pencil instrument for observing the student's information-seeking behavior in a simulated situation. (10)

Two other instruments are based on a definition of vocational maturity as stated by Super and Overstreet, and Gribbons and Lohnes have developed an interview schedule called Readiness for Vocational Planning. (25, 9)

The Vocational Development Inventory constructed by Crites is designed to measure involvement in the process of vocational choice; orientation toward the problem of vocational choice; dependence in decision-making; preferences for factors in vocational choice; and conceptions of vocational choice. (5)

In addition to using these measures, the alert guidance worker can construct standard situations for checking students' ability to identify needed information, locate such information and use it once it is found.

Career development goals are ambitious ones. A serious attempt to judge the value of efforts directed toward their accomplishment is in the best interests of students, educators, employers, and taxpayers.

References

1. Boocock, Sarane S., and Schild, E. O., eds. *Simulation Games in Learning*, Beverly Hills, Calif.: Sage, 1968.
2. Bottoms, Gene, and Matheny, Kenneth B. "Occupational Guidance, Counseling, and Job Placement for Junior High and Secondary School Youth." Paper presented at National Conference on Exemplary Programs and Projects in Vocational Education, March 1969, Atlanta, Ga.
3. Cogswell, John F., and Estevan, D. P. *Explorations in Computer-Assisted Counseling*. Document TM-2582/000/11. Santa Monica, Calif.: System Development Corporation, 1965.
4. Coleman, James C. *Equality of Educational Opportunity*. Washington: Government Printing Office, 1967.
5. Crites, John O. "Measurement of Vocational Maturity in Adolescence. I: Attitude Test of the Vocational Development Inventory." *Psychology Monogram*, no. 595 (1965).
6. Flanagan, John C. "Project PLAN: A Program of Individualized Planning and Individualized Instruction." Paper presented at Project ARISTOTLE Symposium, Washington, D.C. Palo Alto, Calif.: American Institutes for Research, December 1967.
7. Flanagan, John C. "Stability of Career Plans." In John C. Flanagan and William W. Cooley, *Project Talent One-Year Follow-Up Studies*. Cooperative Research Project No. 2333. Pittsburgh: University of Pittsburgh, Press, 1966.
8. Gribbons, Warren D. "Evaluation of an Eighth-Grade Group Guidance Program." *Personnel and Guidance Journal* 38 (1960): 740.45.
9. Gribbons, Warren D., and Lohnes, Paul R. "Predicting Five Years of Development in Adolescents from Readiness for Vocational

Planning Scale." *Journal of Educational Psychology* 56 (1965): 244-53.

10. Halpern, Gerald. "Assessment of Decision Processes." *Proceedings of the 75th Annual Convention, American Psychological Association.* Washington, D.C., 1967.

11. Havighurst, Robert. "Youth in Exploration and Man Emergent." In *Man in a World at Work,* edited by Henry Borow. Boston: Houghton Mifflin Co., 1964.

12. Impelliteri, Joseph T. *The Development and Evaluation of a Pilot Computer-Assisted Occupational Guidance Program.* Pennsylvania Department of Public Instruction. Final Report, Project No. 18033. University Park: Vocational Educational Department, Pennsylvania State University, July 1968.

13. Johnson, Lyndon B. *Manpower Report of the President.* Washington: Government Printing Office, March 1967.

14. Katz, Martin. *You: Today and Tomorrow.* Princeton, N.J.: Cooperative Test Division, Educational Testing Service, 1957.

15. Katz, Martin. *The Name and Nature of Vocational Guidance.* Educational Testing Service Research Memorandum 68-1. Princeton, N.J., 1968.

16. Krumboltz, John D., and Bergland, Bruce. "Experiencing Work Almost Like It Is." *Educational Technology* 9 (March 1969): 47-49.

17. Krumboltz, John D., and Schroeder, W. W. "Promoting Career Exploration Through Reinforcement." *Personnel and Guidance Journal* 44 (1965): 19-26.

18. Leonard, George E. "Vocational Planning and Career Behavior: A Report on the Developmental Career Guidance Project." *Educational Technology,* March 1969.

19. Minor, Frank, J. "An Experimental Computer-Based Educational and Occupational Orientation System for Counseling." Paper presented to 16th International Congress of International Association, August 1968, at Amsterdam, The Netherlands. Yorktown Heights, N.Y.: IBM Advanced Systems Development Division (Xerox).

20. O'Hara, Robert P. "The Theoretical Foundations for the Use of Occupational Information in Guidance." *Personnel and Guidance Journal* 46 (1968): 636-40.

21. Roe, Anne. *The Psychology of Occupations.* New York: John Wiley and Sons, 1956.

22. Ryan, T. A. "Effect of an Integrated Instructional Counseling Pro-

gram to Improve Vocational Decision-Making of Community College Youth." Cooperative Research Project No. HRD 413-65 5-0154. Corvallis: Oregon State University, February 1968.

23. Shimberg, Benjamin, and Katz, Martin. "Evaluation of a Guidance Text." *Personnel and Guidance Journal* 41 (1962): 126-32.

24. Super, Donald E. *The Psychology of Careers.* New York: Harper and Row, 1957.

25. Super, Donald E. and Overstreet, Phoebe. *The Vocational Maturity of Ninth-Grade Boys.* New York: Teachers College, Columbia University, 1960.

26. Super, Donald E. "Floundering and Trial After High School." Cooperative Research Project No. 1393. New York: Teachers College, Columbia University, 1967.

27. Thrombley, William. "No Classrooms or Teachers in High School Experiment." *Atlanta Journal,* 19 Feb. 1969, p. 3-C.

28. Thoresen, Carl E.; Krumboltz, John O.; and Varenhorst, Barbara. "Sex of Counselors and Models: Effect on Client Career Exploration." *Journal of Counseling Psychology* 14 (1967): 503-508.

29. Tideman, David, et al. *Information System for Vocational Decisions: Annual Report 1966-67.* Cambridge, Mass.: Harvard Graduate School of Education, 1968.

30. Varenhorst, Barbara. "The Life Career Game: Practice in Decision-making." *Simulation Games in Learning.* Beverly Hills, Calif.: Sage, 1968.

31. *Work Study Program, Progress Report Number Four.* Kansas City Public Schools, Kansas City, Mo., 1967.

21
Career Guidance in the Elementary School: The Classroom Corporation*

Nina Rosenthal

As part of a sixth-grade social studies unit on capitalism and free enterprise versus communism and socialism, it was decided to organize a corporation. Officers were elected, and shares of stock were sold at 10¢ each with a limit of 250 shares being issued. Approximately 200 shares were sold.

The class wanted to find ways to make money, and the children decided to hold a bake sale. Money from the shares was used to purchase the necessary ingredients. Groups were formed, and the classroom was turned into a bakery.

After the baking we discussed production costs and then set fair selling prices for each item. The children soon discovered that adding too much flour or sugar was a costly mistake, especially when forced to throw away two batters of cookies and a bowl of would-be taffy. They quickly decided to use cake mixes thereafter.

In addition, after the sale, the children realized that many prices were confusing and making correct change was difficult, so they limited their next sale to 5¢ and 10¢ items. It was found that cupcakes were easier to handle than sliced cake, and this influenced their decisions on production.

Several bake sales were held throughout the year and stock values climbed. New ideas came out, and the class switched to pop-corn sales when they discovered that more profit could be obtained. When the weather became warmer, the children sold lemonade and Kool-Aid.

Children new to the class were allowed to purchase shares at the "going" rate. This made newcomers feel a part of the group and more interested in the project.

The corporation branched out into manufacturing and selling gift items, such as paper clip necklaces, tissue paper flowers, wire animals, and mobiles. As a result of this ongoing experience:

1. Children learned about free-enterprise and capitalism.

2. Problem solving skills were developed and used in areas such as cost, mark-up, and selling price.

3. Cooperation and decision making became very important be-cause ideas were either used or eliminated. A mistake might mean a loss, and the children had to anticipate the outcomes of various deci-sions.

4. Children learned the technique of brainstorming in producing many varied ideas.

5. Children learned about investing and reinvesting their money to earn more money. Since profit was placed in a savings account, in-terest was also gained. In one class the shares climbed from 10¢ to 40¢, making a total profit of $58.64.

6. Methods for the expansion of the business were also explored.

7. Simulated experience in the world of work included: sales per-son, craft designer, stock broker, shareholder, and bookkeeper.

22

Career Education and Culture*

Charles Ellis

C areer education is having considerable impact—perhaps the greatest ever upon the direction of American education. At the state level, plans, directives, and means for implementing career education programs are being produced. The *Agenda for Illinois Education*, from the office of Michael J. Bakalis, Illinois Superintendent of Public Instruction, indicates that:

> By July, 1973, a system of financial support for career education will be developed consistent with other educational funding practices in the state.
>
> By 1975, provide occupational information for elementary school pupils and career education for all students in high schools, post secondary schools and four year institutions.

The implementation of career education programs in our nation's schools is moving education toward the goal of providing all students with the means of building successful, productive lives. Career education programs are just being introduced, however, into the area where they will meet their greatest challenge as well as their greatest potential for benefit—the inner city schools. If they are to succeed in the inner city, a reevaluation of certain social and cultural factors must be

*Reprinted by permission from *Illinois Career Educational Journal*, Spring 1970, pp. 17-20.

undertaken, particularly if school studies are to be related to the child's out-of-school activities.

The design of career education programs is at best secondary to the ability of the individual teacher. Teacher educators who will help prepare teachers for inner city schools must identify some of the cultural and social considerations that should be taken into account in planning instructional programs to be used by prospective inner city teachers.

For instance, most inner city students already view education in utilitarian terms, i.e. in terms of job or career potential.[1] Unfortunately they discover at an early age the frustrations inherent for them in the view that education automatically opens the door to occupational opportunity. There is still little assurance that upon completing his education the black or minority inner city student will in fact be allowed to pursue his chosen career. And when the bubble of verticle mobility bursts, it can lead to negative attitudes toward education as well as to a general mistrust of society. A major task of the inner city teacher is to equip the student not only with the skills to become a part of the world of work, but also with attitudes and tools to help him deal effectively with obstacles that would keep him from using his skills. A teacher who can draw upon real life experiences for content in teaching can better prepare students to cope with the realities of life situations.

It should also be emphasized that mere exposure to career information or to adult career models in no way assures that the student will be positively motivated toward accepted educational and social goals. Studies by Robert K. Merton support the contention that such activities, if mismanaged, can produce the opposite of the desired effect.[2] When certain socially valued goals (such as money, career, material effects, etc.) are internalized without the corresponding internalization of the procedures necessary to achieve those goals, the result may be anti-social or illegitimate behavior. The tendency in some schools has been to expose students to adult models of successful careerists (resource people), through special programs and field trips, in the hope that students will be motivated to emulate that success. Some teachers, on the other hand, will maximize the effect of resource people and field trips by relating them to skills and to actual instructional content, demonstrating not merely what one might become, but how to prepare and to achieve.

A career education model may well employ some aspect of adult-student interaction and utilize some variation of the interview theme. Here again a knowledge of minority cultures would be helpful to the aspiring teacher. For example, the relationship between a black child and an adult is essentially different from that between a child and an adult in the white or middle class culture.[3] Within the child's own peer group the art of discussion is practiced with some degree of skills, but that same type of discussion is discouraged in a child-adult relationship, particularly where the child assumes a role equal to that of the adult. Consequently, the difficulty some black students may have in communicating with adults is not necessarily a lack of verbal facility. More likely it indicates the surfacing of a cultural more which—unless the teacher is familiar with it—could be misinterpreted and cause the child to be branded dull or slow. A knowledge of black culture will allow interviews to be structured to take this situation into account. Role playing and other opportunities for the pupil to become comfortable in child-adult communication activities may be provided as a prelude to interaction with community resource people.

Perhaps the most crucial need of teacher-education programs is to dispel the view held by some that inner city children cannot learn effectively because of environmental, cultural or nutritional deprivation. While debilitating conditions have hampered the learning processes of all too many inner city children, the majority are bright, eager, capable learners. They are stigmatized only by the indiscriminate labeling of all inner city children as "slow learners" or "culturally deprived." This negative view only lowers the teacher's expectations for the pupil and inadvertently lowers the pupil's own achievement level and his inner development potential.

Positive reinforcement to the learner's image of himself, his family, and his community is necessary. Encouragement to inquire from those primary sources around him will increase the degree of human contact in the child's learning experience. By involving him realistically in vital, people-centered career education experiences the teacher will exert positive influence on the "child's inherent desire to become." As the child's scope of potential interests widens, the emergence of a strong self-image rooted in who he is, and what he can become will be even more evident.

While these are but a few considerations for teacher-educators to ponder, they clearly underscore the point that if career education is to be successful in the inner city, teachers must be taught to utilize instructional methods which reflect a knowledge of the culture and the particular needs of the children they propose to serve. The following recommendations provide direction for teacher-education programs and are influenced by a belief that actual experiences are the most effective teaching aids. Consequently, the major emphasis is on providing student teachers with authentic, life-centered experiences which provide natural bridges between the university classroom and the teacher's actual world of work. These recommendations are as follows:

1 Methods courses should develop techniques and skills for the incorporation of career education concepts into existing educational programs. Career education promises great benefit for inner city schools, but teachers must be able to work through existing educational programs in order to be effective. Such courses should require familiarity with the various career education designs and their strengths and weaknesses, so the teacher will be able to adapt them to the needs of the community in which they will be taught and to the needs of the individual student.

2 Inner city teachers utilizing career education in their instructional programs should be involved with the teacher-education staff in planning, supervising, and evaluating student teacher experiences. Workshops conducted by these teachers and career development programs, such as ABLE Model Program, should become an important part of the student's education. The sharing of concrete experiences by persons actually practicing career education concepts can lend practical credence to the abstract theories of career education. Such cooperation should insure that career education concepts in the inner city remain a theory of practice rather than mere classroom theory.

3 In order to get a better understanding of black and other minority cultures enrollment in minority or black studies courses should be a requirement for the prospective inner city teacher. A grasp of the concepts upon which ethnic pride are based is very instrumental in helping the teacher understand why, and perhaps how, certain values are internalized and in turn understand how that knowledge can be best related to career education.

4 Those students who profess a specific desire to teach in the inner city should be afforded the opportunity to practice teach in an inner city school (preferably with career education teachers). They should be encouraged to participate in extracurricular school activities in addition to their classroom duties. Insight concerning special interests and abilities can be gained from these experiences and interests.

5 "Field-terms" in the inner city during summer months constituting course credit should become a part of the program of the prospective inner city teacher. This independent study basis course would consist of working with urban programs such as Vista, Headstart, Upward Bound and Neighborhood Youth corps. These groups

work with inner city residents in various service capacities. In addition to the insights gained into the educational needs and career aspirations of inner city families, the field-term could be instrumental in helping students form more positive attitudes toward the realities of life in such areas.

Career education clearly has the potential of giving positive direction to education in the inner city. It is to this end that teacher education programs must insure that teachers will be able to utilize the obvious benefits of career education in the most positive ways. They must produce teachers who cannot only help the student identify his goals, but also teachers who can offer realistic ways of achieving those goals. They must produce teachers who will emphasize the positive rather than dwell on the negative aspects of the child's abilities and environment. Finally, they must produce teachers who will work to convince the child that he can and will succeed in his education, in his career, and in his life.

Notes

1. Edmund W. Gordon and Doxey A. Wilkerson, *Compensatory Education for the Disadvantaged* (New York: College Entrance Examination Board, 1966), p. 18.

2. Robert K. Merton, *Social Theory and Social Structure* (New York: Free Press; London: Collier-MacMillan Limited, 1968), p. 187.

3. Kenneth R. Johnson and Herbert D. Simons, "Black Children and Reading: What Teachers Need to Know," *Phi Delta Kappan* 53, No. 5 (January 1972): 288.

23

Occupacs for Hands-On Learning*

Marla Peterson

I f an educator had walked into the public schools of Lombard, De-
catur, Marshall, or Martinsville, Illinois, during February and
March of 1970, he would have seen some of the following sights:

First graders viewing slides of an electrician at work, listening to
tapes on the work of an electrician, and wiring up light bulbs and
switches to get the feel of what an electrician does.

Fourth graders making study models of dentures by using the
rubber molds, plaster-like materials, and other materials that dental
assistants use.

Sixth graders setting up cash register drawers, writing sales slips,
and using state sales tax guides to simulate the work of a retail sales
clerk.

He would have seen little teacher assistance taking place because
all of the children were guided by taped and printed directions in an
individualized instruction approach.

In short, he would have seen a multimedia approach to presenting
occupational information that meets needs expressed in many schools.

No Debate

The question of whether or not career information should be pre-

*Reprinted by permission from *American Vocational Journal*, January 1972, pp. 40-41.

sented in the elementary school is no longer debatable. Attitude, needs, values, and interests—vital elements in the eventual choice of a career—are influenced by the learning experiences presented during the elementary school years.

The approaches to be used for presenting K-9 information are however debatable. Certainly the printed job information format so commonly used in the high school cannot be the major career information vehicle in the elementary school. Field trips, interviews, and other often-suggested procedures for supplying career information at the high school level can be used in the elementary school too.

No matter how energetic or resourceful a classroom teacher or elementary counselor may be, he cannot be an encyclopedia of information on careers. New approaches are needed.

NEW APPROACH EMERGES

The OCCUPAC Project, with headquarters at the Center for Educational Studies at Eastern Illinois University, is developing and testing materials in an attempt to meet this need for new ways of presenting K-9 career information. The materials are based on the following needs:

New Approach Need No. 1: Materials must be developed which are not solely dependent on the teacher or counselor. Elementary school occupational information should be extended beyond the "community helpers" approach which has been so prevalent in the past. The fireman, the policeman, and the grocer have worthwhile occupations, but so have the licensed practical nurse, the office secretary, and the electrician.

New Approach Need No. 2: Materials must be developed which expose elementary school children to a variety of occupations. The narrow range of occupations which has been presented at the elementary level, coupled with the fact that many classroom teachers are oriented toward the professions, has unintentionally built in the eyes of many children a low prestige image of some occupations.

New Approach Need No. 3: Materials must be developed which build wholesome attitudes toward all useful work. Children learn by seeing, talking, listening, and doing. Seeing, talking, and listening have generally been included in traditional approaches for presenting K-9 occupational information. However, *doing*—the very thing to which career information readily lends itself—has been neglected.

New Approach Need No. 4: Materials must be developed which use a multi-media approach. Seeing, talking, listening and doing must all be included. Trying out, testing, and exploring should be made part of the career development program.

The four Illinois schools mentioned earlier served as the first field testing sites for the OCCUPAC materials. The OCCUPAC Project, which derives its name from the packages of multimedia materials being developed, is supported from funds from the Professional and Curriculum Development Unit of the Illinois State Division of Vocational and Technical Education.

The project staff is housed in the Buzzard Laboratory School of Eastern Illinois University—the school in which pilot testing of the OCCUPACS takes place.

PROGRESS TO DATE

During the first year of operation, 15 prototype OCCUPACS were developed. As illustrated earlier, tapes, slides, sounds of work, simulated work activities, and props of all kinds from the real world of work have been assembled in the packages.

Many dimensions of an occupation are presented. For example, in the package for the licensed practical nurse, children are told that LPNs sometimes have to work during evening hours and on weekends and holidays. LPN's also must expect to do some lifting and they will undoubtedly see people with injuries and broken bones.

The self has not been forgotten. After children look at and work with the various materials in the secretary package, the taped commentary asks them questions like, "Do you think you would enjoy answering the telephone? Are you a neat person or are you messy? Would you like to do what your boss asks you to do? Did you enjoy trying to write some shorthand?"

FUTURE OF OCCUPAC

Public school demand for the OCCUPACS has been so intense that 14 school systems have been selected to serve as field testing sites during the 1971-72 school year. The 14 systems were selected from among many that had applied. The number had to be limited because the OCCUPACS are not yet being made available to schools on a mass production basis.

Ways to mass produce the OCCUPACS will be explored. The supporting preservice and inservice training materials to prepare teachers for presenting all types of K-9 occupational information will also be developed.

OCCUPACS are meeting a need being expressed by public

schools—the need for occupational information and career development materials specifically geared to the cognitive and the interest levels of elementary and junior high school students.

It is through the use of materials such as the OCCUPACS that a truly developmental approach to career preparation can take place in American schools.

24

Career Guidance in the Elementary School: Take an Idea and See Where It Leads You*

Mary Stell

Take an Idea and See Where It Leads You

The real worth of an idea can be found in the words of a teacher who actually tried it with children in the nitty-gritty of everyday life in the classroom. With this in mind, I appeared at the doorway of Linda Hyyppa's classroom one day after school in early September. Linda had used the idea of a florist as an organizing center last fall.

After we introduced ourselves, I told her that I was getting ideas for a brochure on workers in a floral shop. Her eyes lit up with excitement, and she talked about how she had become involved with the idea. The whole idea came about when the class was studying living things. The children thought it would be a good idea to plant seeds and watch them grow. So June Hart, a teacher across the hall, and I decided to go along with it. They wanted to learn how to care for the plants. It was decided to visit the grower at a greenhouse. The grower was most helpful, and the children learned much that goes into producing the flowers sold at the floral shop.

Following the visit to the greenhouse, the children decided to have a greenhouse sale. They made things to sell and brought additional materials from home. In the process of setting up the green-house, the children learned that many things are needed to finance a new enterprise. They had to have a source of money. A discussion of the need for an initial investment led to the children's each contribut-ing a nickel. This, in turn, led to a discussion of borrowing money and taking out loans. Another decision that required planning was the number of hours that they would be open on the day of the sale. When the day came, they sold out in one-half hour, so a discussion was held concerning the need for the owner to predict how much to buy for re-sale and when to buy it.

The class made a total of $30. Naturally, there was much talk about how to spend it. They finally decided to use it to help stop pol-lution. An outdoor education teacher who taught in the school was in-vited to talk to the class. The money was eventually used to buy books and filmstrips for the school library.

The children felt so good about the outcome of the sale that they wanted to have another sale in the spring. They had learned much from their previous experience so the second endeavor came off more smoothly. This time they made $40 and decided to buy trees for the school yard. A resource person was invited to advise them on how to buy and care for the trees.

A teacher can take as little time or as much time as she wishes on an organizing center. Children learn to make decisions, to plan to-gether, to begin to see the relationship between what they are learn-ing and real life. They are pleased when a person comes to the class and speaks with them. One of the most rewarding things I learned was that the children thought of good ideas and made them succeed.

As I drove away from the school, I began to see that a phrase such as "Take an idea and see where it leads you" had real meaning for ca-reer development.

Part 3

Secondary and Post-Secondary Career Education

The concept of life-long learning is probably never more true than when interpreted in terms of career education. Dynamic growth and change are an earmark of our technological times. They demand that an individual continually refresh, up-grade, and/or learn new employable skills. To ignore this demand is tantamount to death. One who does not continue to learn, to keep pace with the changing times, will surely choke in the trailing dust of progress.

In keeping with this theme, James Wykle sets a proper tone for the secondary and post-secondary section of this book when he reminds us that career education extends through secondary education into the adult years.

Starting with the junior high, Thomas Gambino explains that early adolescent students have typically been assigned low status on the educational ladder. All-too-often, the throes of budding adolescence cause teachers and administrators to assume a caretaker role toward their students. Junior high school was considered a place where only the basic elements should be taught. Gambino shows how career education can be a viable element of a junior high school curriculum.

High schools, on the other hand, have long been accused of slanting their curricula to the college-bound student. With the advent of the technological age, an increasing number of studies have exposed

171

this narrow-minded view and recommend added emphasis on career education. The form and kind of career education to adopt and implement, however, is subject to conjecture. One of the more relevant and meaningful ways of providing career education experiences is by having the student gain first-hand knowledge of a given line of work. EBCE, Employer Based Career Education, as explained by Rex Hogans and John Svicarovich, is one modern-day variation of the work experience concept available to high school age students.

Opportunities for first-hand experience with given careers are currently offered in many career education programs in the form of OJT (on-the-job-training), cooperative work-study, internship, apprenticeships, and vestibule training. Of the foregoing, vestibule training is probably the least familiar and least understood. Riley Carroll does a fine job of putting it in terms the reader can easily understand.

Further opportunity for quality career education exists in the community college, a relatively new level in the American system of education that has been evolving for the last two decades. In general, the mission and goals of the community college can be summarized as providing (1) the first two years of baccalaureate education; (2) personal development through counseling and guidance; (3) continuing adult education (including the breadth of community services); and (4) career/vocational/technical education. The relative importance of career education to the community college can be measured favorably in terms of the ever-increasing enrollment in baccalaureate-oriented courses. These figures indicate there is a demand for career education at the community college level. Amo de Bernardis explores this demand in greater detail in "What Career Education Means for the Community College." "Where the Action Is" goes on to demonstrate how career education can and does occupy a significant role in the overall community college curriculum.

Sometime competitors of the community college and a growing force on the career education scene are the proprietary or private vocational schools. For years, they seemed to linger in the shadows of the healthily endowed public school systems, but with the entrance of major industrial firms (such as Bell and Howell and IBM, to name a couple) into the field, the funds and management expertise are now available to make proprietary schools a viable contributor in the educational marketplace.

It is acknowledged that their motive is profit-oriented. This, coupled with the fact that as private schools they are generally not subsidized by a political unit, means that their tuition is necessarily and significantly greater than that of public schools. Nevertheless, the proprietary school is receiving increasing enrollments because they are turning out as good or better a product within a period of time shorter than most regular academic terms. Hence, a student can begin his career much sooner. These and other attractive features of the proprietary vocational/technical schools are discussed by Stephen Crew.

More recently, colleges and universities have begun to regard career education as strictly a means of providing vocational-technical skills or trade-learning. Yet the fact is that one of the few areas in which colleges and universities show growth in recent years is in the area of continuing career education for the professions. Jean Arnold and Max Otte provide added insight into this more recent career education development.

In "Serving The Community Through Marketing and Management Seminars," Jack W. Fuller reminds us that a successful and meaningful career is more than just getting and holding a job. Continual inservice training and skill up-grading are basic ingredients of a happy and productive work force. While the curricula and delivery system will vary with the nature and purpose of the program, the mission is the same: to optimally complement the employees' overall skills and knowledge. Business managers from all levels are often afforded this opportunity through short seminars and workshops, many conveniently scheduled into their regular work week.

In final analysis, however, if career educators were ever asked to prioritize their efforts, they could probably make no better choice than to direct their immediate attention to the unemployed and the underemployed. If such persons had been exposed to effective career education programs throughout earlier stages of their lives, there would be less need for it at this late point in their development. But the fact of the matter is that career education has come into its own only recently. And because of its belated arrival, there are many who are desperately in need of guidance. John Connolly illustrates the point quite well in "New Careers: A Challenge to Adult Education." Phyllis Kopelke and Moses Koch go on to illustrate how one "New Careers" program was successfully implemented at Essex Community College.

There should be no question by now that career education is a continuing responsibility of everyone. Andrew Hendrikson examines this very real and imminent challenge in "Problems and Issues In Career Education For Adults."

25

Junior High:
The Exploratory Years*

Thomas W. Gambino

Career education in New Jersey as elsewhere across the nation is a recent thrust. The number of school districts in the state that offer their students a fairly comprehensive career education program, preschool to adult, is somewhat limited.

Although a large number of schools conduct the programs described in this article, only several operate the complete package.

It should be noted that in addition to the programs discussed here, there are others funded under the Vocational Education Amendments of 1968, such as Employment Orientation, WECEP, and programs for the disadvantaged and the handicapped, that operate as part of the career package in many school systems.

No Best Approach

It should be mentioned also that no one approach to career exploration is recommended above the others. In New Jersey we believe that a wide variety of settings and techniques for career exploration is the best approach. The programs described below illustrate that belief.

Career Clubs. The career club for Grades 7, 8, and 9 is not of the usual

*Reprinted by permission from *American Vocational Journal*, March 1972, pp. 222-224.

hobby variety. Students go on mini trips, toting cameras, audiotapes and video recorders; they role play jobs, set up and operate business, and conduct surveys; they visit with goal-oriented students in high school and community colleges, and publish their own career newsletter.

Summer Programs. Summer career exploration programs, also for Grades 7, 8, and 9, have worked well for disadvantaged children. Since the outreach and follow-up elements of this program are critical, student instructors working with the teachers are invaluable.

The activities are on the same lines as those carried on by the career clubs, but in addition to exploratory experiences in specialized vocational-technical areas, the social, cultural and recreational needs of students are significant considerations.

Plans are to expand these opportunities for disadvantaged students by basing additional summer programs in New Jersey community colleges.

Part-Time Jobs. Boys and girls in Grades 7 to 9 are eligible for numerous part-time jobs in parks, homes, farms and schools. Such job experiences with related counseling and remedial instruction are extremely helpful to students who are not enjoying a very high level of success in the regular school setting.

A chance to work with adults in a different environment, to learn how important it is to follow instructions, and how school and work are interrelated, can awaken a student to his career responsibilities.

IV Programs. Introduction to Vocations emphasizes the development of occupational awareness in students at the junior high or middle school level, typically in the eighth or ninth grade. Exploratory, manipulative, classroom, shop and laboratory experiences are offered in a wide range of occupational areas. These experiences, especially when combined with the resources of business and industry, can be very helpful to young people in planning more realistically for careers.

Students are scheduled for a minimum of five cycles (one daily period throughout the year) in such occupational areas as health, manufacturing, business, and marketing and distribution. A career guidance unit, "Know Yourself," is included in the year-long program.

Intensive Skill Training. Some salable skills can be developed by the student who plans to leave school at the end of the eighth or ninth grade. Counselors and teachers cooperatively identify such students and help them determine the areas they want to explore and follow up with training for a specific entry-level job.

The program succeeds best in communities where good school-industry relations prevail. Industry provides the skill training while the school complements it with related academic studies. Placement in a job or in more advanced training courses is critical to this program.

VIDEO RECORDER IN CAREER COUNSELING

Several schools in New Jersey are experimenting with a technique still rare in counseling procedures—the use of the video recorder as a means of expanding the student's self-identity. A student's self-image is the outgrowth of a multiplicity of experiences and interactions. Letting the young person see and hear himself can be a highly effective one.

Career Resource Centers

Pulling together school and community resources for the career education projects in New Jersey are the career resource centers. Each center has at least two key staff members: an audiovisual media coordinator and a coordinator for school-industry cooperation.

As these items respond to the needs of career exploration teachers, the career resource center essentially becomes responsible for carrying out career education to the fullest meaning of the concept.

Some of the duties of the resource center team are as follows:

1. To coordinate the efforts of the various career education programs in the school system (Introduction to Vocations, Part-Time Placement, Guidance and Counseling, Career Club, etc.).

2. To provide multimedia resources and services to teachers.

3. To expedite exchange, reduce duplication, and promote efficiency in the school program.

4. To ascertain the individual needs and interests of students, to plan experiences for them accordingly, and to maintain some measure of continuity for students in the career development process.

5. To identify a core of knowledge pertinent to inservice education of teachers.

A typical service offered by the career resource center might be to students in a career exploration club who are having difficulty participating in a group project. At the request of the club advisor, the center makes arrangements to have a group session videotaped so members can see themselves in action and perhaps gain a better understanding of group relations.

Perhaps a teacher of Introduction to Vocations wants to acquaint students with certain occupational opportunities in the business and industrial community. If the materials requested—films, slides, lists of speakers, places to visit, etc.—are not already on the shelves, the staff and teacher cooperate to produce them.

Or suppose an eighth grade science teacher wants to conduct field trips in connection with a unit on "science in your community." Directories compiled by the resource center will supply him with the information on places to visit, plus supplementary material for the students to examine ahead of time. The audiovisual team may even photograph students on trips to give them a visual record for follow-up discussion.

Surveys of part-time jobs are another of the many possible services that a career resource center can provide. Plans for 1972 are to make the VIEW program and Computer Information Services available through the career resource centers.

Assessment and Feedback

All teachers play an important part in the evaluation of career education programs, but the key role is reserved for the counselor. His position on the staff qualifies him best to coordinate the resources for determining how well the program is meeting its objectives.

In his counseling of students, he is in the best position to assess their growth in career awareness and the contribution the curriculum is making to that process. He is expected to participate in research on career development techniques, processes and programs, and to produce data from all of his activities to support needed changes in the curriculum.

Some Fundamentals

No school system can develop a 7-9 career education model that will exactly suit the students, staff and resources of another school system or needs of another community.

There are, however, some minimal steps that bear repeating: establishing a philosophy that reflects the career education plan of the school system; stating objectives; developing alternate program plans that can be studied to determine the best program for the school district; designing a system of evaluation and feedback; implementing the program; and revising the program as indicated by evaluation.

Time Is Right

Above all, the program, or programs, should be planned to capitalize on the behavioral pattern of seventh, eighth and ninth graders. Boys and girls at that age are ripe for career exploration.

At that age they want to be involved in the multitude of things that are going on around them. They like to visit new places where interesting people are doing constructive things and to meet new friends who enjoy doing the same things they do. They enjoy making things that demonstrate their talents and to compete with their peers in rewarding experiences. This curiosity for new experiences coupled with the energy of youth calls for a wide variety of activities that give them opportunities to explore new materials, equipment and techniques.

Increasingly, studies are pointing up the significance of influences during the junior high school years that will have lasting impact on the career style of the student. This is not to belittle the foundation laid during earlier school years. Opportunities for self-discovery and identification of abilities and interests are important even for young children.

But what makes career exploration even more exciting to the seventh, eighth, and ninth grader is the realization that he has the potential to manipulate certain aspects of his environment—that by choosing a certain course he can expect to gain a certain end, and that eventually the decision will be his to make. Given the opportunity to develop this potential and individuality, he finds the key to open the doors to his world.

26

An Employer Based
Career Education Model*

*Rex Hagans
and John Svicarovich*

In the way it has attempted to prepare the young for adult life, our public education system too often has posed an artificial barrier between learning and living. As James Coleman has noted, today's young people live in information-rich but experience-poor environments. This is especially true of the school environment in which reality and coping with reality have usually been "taught" through the re-education of the outside world into synthetic, symbolic form.

Yet even the most artful synthesis, for all its mass efficiency, has limited effect. The fact remains that most people learn best (and like learning best) by performing useful tasks in real situations and by getting real rewards for those tasks.

The Employer Based Career Education (EBCE) concept is based on this assumption and is fitted to this style of learning. It is intended to remove the barriers between education and living—to demonstrate that in fact they are the same thing.

EBCE, so called because learning will take place at employment settings outside the locus of the school, is one of four different pilot models being tested nationally under the aegis of the National Institute of Education. Like the other models, EBCE is a test of one alternative approach to career education, a broad and ambitious concept incorporating all the kinds of education which have existed in our minds and practice: occupational training, preparation for higher schooling, political and social awareness, self-awareness. Career education is a concept designed to treat as inseparable all the roles people must learn to assume in life: producer, consumer, learner, user of leisure time, member of the civic body.

Unlike the other three models, EBCE is geared exclusively to secondary students. EBCE test sites, under the supervision of nearby regional educational laboratories, are located in Oakland, California; Philadelphia, Pennsylvania; Charleston, West Virginia; and Tigard, Oregon. And although each reflects the unique flavor of its locale and personnel, all share these basic characteristics:

• Student learning activities take place at employment settings and other community sites entirely outside the secondary school.

• The model is guided by an advisory board consisting primarily of employers but often including union representatives, students, parents, and school personnel.

• The model's curriculum is individualized and competency based. Students, in large measure, demonstrate what they have learned by what they can do.

• The model utilizes a small staff to coordinate the learning activities of students, but the basic learning experiences are supplied by employers.

• EBCE students represent a cross section of students in the geographic area of the model site in terms of aspirations, backgrounds, and general capabilities.

• The model program will qualify the student for a high school diploma.

Favorable Feature

Those of us associated with EBCE research see in the model these favorable features:

• The total community in which the student lives is recognized as the best learning resource. The various tasks of daily community life are the foundation of the curriculum.

• Students intolerant of vicarious learning have the benefit of "experiential" learning.

• All learning experiences have to have clear relevance to career aspirations.

• Students have direct exposure to a wide variety of job opportunities available in particular career areas. For example, a student might be made aware of both the vertical and horizontal range of occupations in the transportation industry.

• By making work and community settings the sites of learning, EBCE shows both students and their adult associates that education and life responsibilities are inseparable.

• Education is not delegated to a special societal group, for example, educators; adults in the total community are responsible for the education of the young in a direct way.

• In order to help students learn, adult workers who have learning facilitator roles are forced to deepen their own knowledge, occupational competency, and communication skills.

• In adult work associates, students have a great variety of behavioral models to evaluate and, in various degrees, to adopt or to reject.

• EBCE may influence both employers and employees to see supplemental educational activities as an integral part of the learning that takes place on the job. Thus, learning opportunities for adult workers might expand at work sites. For example, one can envision students and adults together studying the relative strengths of graphics versus writing, and their interrelationships, in making reports. The fallout of such activity ranges from better technical reports to a better understanding of the uses of media.

Yet if the potential benefits of EBCE are great, so is the magnitude of the EBCE task: to develop within three to five years a body of experience and research data that would document the feasibility of an entire alternative secondary education system, harnessed to the career education ideal and drawing its curriculum from the life of the adult community.

And curriculum is the key research concern of the model, even though the comparative cost of the system, child labor laws, transportation, and accreditation are also important considerations.

Basically, EBCE assumes that the raw materials for an entire secondary curriculum exist in the work and leisure setting of the adult community. Furthermore, it assumes that those resources can be directly "refined" and utilized by students to learn the kinds of things that will allow them to live satisfying lives, occupationally and personally. Thus, it is being designed to test those assumptions.

Concerns

As the design is created, EBCE personnel are coming to grips with several concerns.

First, what should the EBCE secondary curriculum be? Answering this question is an arduous task which must draw on the experience and insight of all concerned: employers, parents, students, educators. At the Northwest Regional Educational Laboratory we have used the initial inputs of these persons to design a two-part curriculum for our Tigard site.

The first part consists of eight major goal areas within which each student will participate in the design of his individual learning program. The specific objectives and learning activities to achieve them will be based directly upon the employment and community experiences the student chooses. The second part consists of 20 basic competencies which all students must master. These basic competencies represent an attempt to define a set of performances which, at a minimum, any person must acquire to live successfully. They include such life skills as obtaining and managing credit, administering first aid, and securing a job. All 20 competencies have been identified by employers, parents, and students involved in the pilot program.

The specific means by which the student will acquire and demonstrate these competencies will draw heavily on the employment and community environment. However, both the goal areas and the competencies must be regarded as tentative starting points. The program experiences of each student, which will be documented in case study form, will ultimately shape the definition of EBCE "core" goals and competencies.

In fact, this is a second key concern of the project: to identify the ways in which various traditional "disciplines" appear in work situations. For example, writing is one of the goal areas. In 50 case studies, then, we will look for the ways in which students going through various work and community experiences had to deal with written communications. If it is found that these students encountered technical reports via letters and memos as the most common form of writing, the data would have clear implications for EBCE (and public school) curriculum design.

In addition, the discovery of patterns in which various disciplines appear in business, civic, or leisure settings would contribute to the design of truly interdisciplinary curriculum. Such a curriculum would go far beyond the integrated studies of the present school environment. In the school, such learning experiences are integrated synthetically by teachers. In a real setting, the integration has greater credibility because it exists within the tasks being performed. In addition, students themselves analyze the interrelationship of disciplines required by work.

Just as it must identify what disciplines appear in work and how they interface, EBCE research also must identify the ways in which the various disciplines are learned in conjunction with and within the work setting. Data on such learning patterns will be useful in plotting the most effective sequence of learning experiences. This implies that the curriculum design of EBCE will be primarily a process rather than the creation of content in the form of materials and simulated activities. Understanding of this process will be stressed in the training of adults to assist students in using jobs and community activities as learning experiences. This training has great potential for enriching the jobs and community involvement of adults and for stimulating their own learning interests.

And, a final concern: the EBCE project must discover ways of helping youngsters draw directly on the learning resources of the total community with a minimum of mediation by adults. From an employer viewpoint, unnecessary time spent in such mediation represents a drag in the efficiency of workers. For the student, it perpetuates dependency and insulation from the beneficial impact of direct experience.

Curriculum and the work in which it exists must be mutually reinforcing. If learning does not mesh smoothly with work and community life, employers and other adults will abandon it. This implies clearly that the EBCE project must include development of student skills in information finding, self-directed learning, and decision making. Incorporating these skills into a curriculum based in employment and community settings could be a major step toward returning to students the kind of experiential learning process the schools eliminated 50 years ago.

27

Vestibule Training Takes Hold in Wake County*

Riley O. Carroll

W ake County, North Carolina schools have discovered that not all career education need or in some cases should be geared to long-term vocational programs. Evidence that this is true can be seen in the results of our participation in a project designed by John Coster, director of the Research Coordination Unit, North Carolina State University.

Dr. Coster used the term "vestibule training" to describe the short-term intensive training which is the basis for the program in his "The Implementation of a Comprehensive Occupational Education Program in a Rural School System." As used in industry, "vestibule training" refers to short-term training given a new employee before he is assigned a job.

Short-term intensive training is not new. It has been offered in various forms in the armed services, in industry, and in education, generally for adults in courses of very limited hours.

As adopted in our program, vestibule training provides the student an opportunity to obtain entrance level skills in the field of his choice. We define "entrance level skills" as knowledge of the skills required and the tools used and awareness of the physical and mental

*Reprinted by permission from *American Vocational Journal*, March 1972, pp. 44-45.

188 / Secondary and Post-Secondary Education

demands of the job. We teach all those entrance level salable skills normally available in a two-year, 1,080-hour course family.

Our ability to reduce the period of time required is made possible by designating certain sections of the regular two-year program as priority units. For example, in the machinist field we can enable a student to master the techniques of a drill press operator, although we cannot expect him to acquire the expertness needed to convert a block of metal into a close tolerance bearing.

Employability the Aim. The important fact is that both our graduate and the graduate of a two-year program are employable, but at different levels and different rates of pay. Even these differences may be minimal, however, for many companies will not start either person at a level higher than minimum wage, preferring to develop skill habits in their employees which will meet their particular labor needs. Vestibule training has, in fact, an advantage in this regard, for by its nature it does not permit the development of habits.

In developing our courses we have obtained recommendations from personnel directors, employees, students, educators, and specialists in the careers field. The length of courses, usually from 30 to 90 hours, depends on the entrance level skills and knowledge required. The courses include classroom study, shop laboratory practice, and/or on the job practice.

Course Determination. Factors considered in determining courses offered are:

1. Availability of qualified instructors. The normal working hours of a technically qualified person often conflict with the scheduled time of classes, and, in addition, many are reluctant to become teachers. The remuneration offered is the best inducement for overcoming these obstacles.

2. Availability of space and equipment. When the school itself does not have facilities, often business and professional people have allowed use of theirs. For example, a nurse's aide course was taught at a local hospital using its facilities and personnel; a dental assistant course was taught at a dentist's office in the evening. Offers for use of a dental lab, an automotive shop, and heavy equipment have been received. Supplies have been donated by electronic companies, hospitals, and prefabrication companies.

3. The employment market. Students are attracted to programs that offer job placement, both part-time and full-time, and when they can participate in such courses, their motivation factor is high.

4. The interest of the students. Although there are other reasons

for students to be interested in particular courses, job availability provides the major stimulus.

Serves Varied Purposes. Short-term intensified training can serve a number of purposes. It offers exploration of a career field without commitment of a great deal of time, thus allowing a student, if he chooses, to investigate more than one occupation during his secondary education life.

To the college and technical school directed student, it provides a means of examining his chosen field without having to eliminate other courses needed or desired.

It prepares students for part-time or full-time employment. Both summer jobs and part-time jobs during the school year are more readily available to the trained than to the untrained.

It provides a testing-ground upon which a student can examine his attitude toward and aptitude for an occupation. A young girl sees nursing as glamorous, but will she feel the same way after she empties a bed pan? Is it not better for a person to experience the demands of an occupation at the high school level than to spend his time and money at the post-secondary level and perhaps then spend a lifetime in an occupation that he neither likes nor has the appropriate abilities for?

Finally, it can bridge the gap between working in an unskilled job and commitment to the demands of a job on the apprenticeship-journeyman ladder.

Career education must consider the needs of various people in a total vocational program at the county level. Vestibule training may be the ideal way to satisfy the needs of the student who cannot enroll in a two-year vocational course, the student who has difficulty deciding what he wants to do, the dropout, the handicapped.

Continuation of Program. Because this program has worked so well in Wake County, we plan to commit some of our regular teaching positions to it. The fact that North Carolina's vocational teacher allotment is designated by man-months permits us to do this.

The planning, scheduling, and coordinating already done by Monte B. Ross, Associate Project Director, Paul M. Maultsby, and guidance counselors Annie Reams and Emma Dorssett, in combination with Principal Edward H. Wilson, will of course need to be continued to assure the program's sustained success.

28

What Career Education Means for the Community College*

Amo De Bernardis

The amazing growth of the community college during the past
decade is proof of the great need for more education beyond
high school. Students come to the community college at all
ages, from the late teens to the early 80's, each seeking to strengthen
his education and enrich his life. Many want the opportunity to enter
one of the many current occupational fields.

Many thousands of students have failed to enter career-education
programs for which they were qualified and interested because
society generally placed low value on these programs. Many schools
fail to provide dynamic and realistic programs challenging and digni-
fied enough to attract and hold those who could profit from them.

The inevitable consequence has been that many thousands of students have graduated from high school each year with preparation for
the professions as their goal in a four-year college, although a majority
did not have the interest or skills to reach that goal—nearly 75%
failed. Today 77% of our youth will be graduated from high school; of
that number 42% will enroll in a bachelor degree program. Only 21%
of those who start can be expected to earn a bachelor's degree. Only
6% will ever reach the master's degree, and only 1% will complete the
doctorate.

*Reprinted by permission from *Community/Junior College Journal*, pp. 9-42.

What will happen to these thousands of frustrated, academically-oriented students? Somehow they must find their way into productive positions. They must be able to pay their fair share of taxes and to add their individual efforts to the progress of the nation, and, even more important, develop self respect in jobs to which they aspire.

This misdirection of human resources, occurring at the most crucial time in a youth's educational development in a country which has need for technically trained manpower, cannot and need not be tolerated. If our nation is to lead the world struggle for progress and economy, if we are to compete on equal terms for our share of world trade, the dignity of work and the pride of craftsmanship must be developed.

The community college rightfully prides itself on the principle of the "open door," offering learning opportunities to every person. All students, regardless of their previous educational performance or attainments, are offered the same access to a variety of educational programs designed to meet their needs.

The "open door" concept does not guarantee an education to anyone, but it does make it possible for all to enter the college and for all to try. Each person is encouraged to explore a variety of programs to find one best suited to his own needs, interests, and abilities.

To allow the community college "open door" to be pushed partially shut by unrealistic entrance requirements, by unnecessary course prerequisites, by arbitrary academic probation and dismissal, by the accumulation of academic rigidities of any sort, is to limit the educational opportunities that should be offered to all.

Dignity for Programs

Such restricted access permits college-level education only for those who have demonstrated academic ability; this is just as unfair as it is to demand "successful working experience" from those who have never had the opportunity to accumulate such experience. The "open door" policy must be truly an "open door" and not just a revolving door; students must be effectively guided into programs where they can achieve success. Thus, the community college "open door" requires extensive counseling and guidance inside the door.

The college must practice what it preaches. Career-education programs must reflect the same quality of facilities, of development, and of instruction as other programs. The faculty who teach career courses must be recognized for their expertise just as those who hold academic degrees. The emphasis must be on performance.

The instructor who teaches welding has the same importance to the college as does one who teaches liberal arts. Each is instructing students; each is helping students achieve career goals; each should have dignity and respect in the college. The administrative and organizational structure of the community college must place the same emphasis on career education as any other educational program. Any program in the college must have complete support if it is to achieve dignity in the eyes of the students and the community.

Balance in Programs

Career-education programs are a necessity in every community, increasingly so as our society moves from an economy of developing natural resources to an economy based on developing human resources. A study by the Department of Labor shows a complete turnaround since World War II; by 1960, goods-producing industries accounted for only 37.6% of all jobs, while service occupations accounted for 62.4%. Projected to 1975, the study shows that service industries will provide 67.7% of the jobs, and employment opportunities in manufacturing and industries only 32.3%. The message for education is clear.

Career-education programs must be provided with varying length, levels, and types to meet the realistic needs of people: short-term, one-year, and two-year programs should be offered.

Labor, business, and industry must be closely involved in planning and developing course offerings. There should be a feed-back of information and evaluation to make sure that learning opportunities in the programs are kept up to date, are effective and realistic.

Realistic Programs

The community college must keep its career-education programs relevant and closely geared to needs of business and industry. Courses must be carefully designed with realistic objectives clearly stated in performance terms. Course descriptions and performance objectives should make clear to the student and the employer what the instructor will teach and what the student will learn and be able to do as the result of the course and the total program.

The time required for completion should be realistic and not determined by the semester or length of the college year.

Programs should allow students to enter and leave at any time. Feedback information and performance evaluation should be supplied continuously through close cooperative involvement of the college and its business and industrial advisory committees.

Counseling and Advising

Most students who enter the community college need counseling whether they recognize the need or not. Many want and appreciate these services, knowing the value and impact such assistance can have on their programs. All staff members must be involved in the process of helping students find suitable programs. Each student must know and feel that the human component of the college is there to help him.

The community college must provide realistic counseling and career guidance for all students. The college must create an environment which will encourage people of the community to avail themselves of these services. Informed and comprehensive counseling in the occupational fields through continuous feedback of information and evaluation from business and industry can be immediately applied to guide students in their program choice and occupational planning and to insure future program change and development.

In a technological society, careers are no longer static; change is the name of the game. Programs must be designed so that students can have realistic career ladders. No program should be considered as terminal or non-transferable. Each step in the program ladder should be developed to build on the previous step so that the students will have a place to leave the program with skills and a place to reenter when more skills are needed.

The college should take the leadership in providing a continuous program from high school through the four-year college.

All programs should be open-ended and have many options. Core programs should be developed which provide basic skills, understandings, and concepts. Many career options should be available from each core curriculum. For example, after completing the core of health courses, a student should have options in all of the health fields—dental technician, nurse's aide, doctor, dentist, etc.

High School Articulation

Skills and knowledges developed in the high school should serve as the base for building higher levels of competency in the community college, not only in the vocational field but also in the other programs.

Every effort should be made to keep movement from the high school to the community college coordinated and as easy as possible for the student; no gap should be allowed to develop in his educational experience.

High school students with advanced skills in any vocational area should be given full credit for these achievements.

Coordination of Facilities and Programs

Facilities and programs for career-education are expensive when compared with other college programs. The need for realistic learning experiences and the high costs of equipment which must be equal to that used in commercial applications add to the difficulties of supplying effective learning situations.

The community college should provide leadership for the development of career education in its region. The college is in a unique position to stimulate a coordinated program of career-education learning opportunities which may start in or below junior high school and continue to the community college. Articulation and coordination among the educational institutions and the community college are essential for an effective career education program. The college can make available to high school students advance work in career areas while they are still attending high school.

The community college, because of its unique role in post-high school education, should take the leadership in unifying the efforts of the post-high school education groups of the community for post-high school career-education programs.

It is in a position to give these programs dignity, good facilities, staffing, and the most important element—giving the student educational mobility within the institution. People from business and industry can be of great assistance in making available teaching stations.

General Education

Students in the community college deserve full opportunity to explore and learn in general education areas as well as in the vocational programs. But there needs to be greater flexibility in the general education component of most vocational programs. The usual "50% general, 50% vocational" ratio is just not realistic today.

Academic requirements must be tailored to fit the specific needs of the vocational student; there is no reason why a student must learn western civilization before he can go to work as a welder. Yet the college should encourage the welder to want to learn about western civilization.

As the student gains strength in his occupational interest, the need for related courses and for enrichment and cultural learning should be more evident to him. Where the career-education program has many general educational options and students are encouraged, they will take advantage of the options increasingly.

General education requirements should not deny the student the opportunity to develop his vocational interests, skills, and abilities. However, the college should build the concept of total education for the individual. There should be no break between the so-called vocational and academic. The educational mix should be tailored to fit the unique needs of individual students.

Perhaps the most effective way to provide the general education component for the student is through the ongoing activities of the college. The college through its staff, facilities, resource center, etc., should be a dynamic place to learn. Everything in the institution should convey to the student that the college is a pleasant place to be.

Students in career programs should be encouraged to participate in all of the learning activities of the college—art exhibits, lectures, film showings, seminars, conferences, etc. General education, if it is to be meaningful and become part of the student's behavior pattern, must be lived each day.

Placement and Follow-up

An active placement and follow-up service is an essential part of the community college program. The service must work closely with state and federal employment services to have full impact on placing graduates. To be effective, the service must have the respect of the community, of the graduates, and of other agencies. To build this respect the college must provide well motivated and qualified people to fill the positions in the community.

Not only is the placement service of great value to the student and to the employer, but is also an essential part of the evaluation process of the college. Placement and performance information is an invaluable guide to needed change and development in program and instructional activities.

Taking Education to the People

If the community college is to be a relevant institution, it must avoid the concept that education takes place only within the four walls of a school. The total community must be considered its campus. The students' campus will be wherever instruction takes place. The need for retraining and upgrading of personnel on the job is one which will continue to grow as technology becomes more complex. The need for in-plant and on-the-job training will increase. The college has the instructional expertise, the programs, and the commitment to assist each person to learn in his own way, to his own highest level.

Cooperative ways to provide this kind of career-education must be explored with business, industry, and labor. Techniques must be developed for identifying and determining which portion of each job training need can best be done on campus.

The application of new means for communication and instruction needs to be explored. Television, both closed-circuit and recorded programmed materials, computer-assisted instruction, personalized "take home" learning packets, and other methods or techniques can all make great contributions for improvement of learning.

Innovation and Demonstration

The community college concept is uniquely American and relatively new; thus it offers a great opportunity for educational innovation. Unhampered by academic traditions, the community college can seek and explore new ways to create a better environment for learning. It can put into practice what research and technologies have developed. What is needed is not spectacular, rare breakthroughs; rather, steady, stable, and professional development followed by demonstration and day-to-day application. The community college should be a leader in developing educational techniques and methods and should serve as a demonstration center for the community.

The Challenge

The community college is strategically placed to be especially effective in development of strong career-education programs, a great and growing need in education beyond the high school. Because it is a community institution, the community college can avail itself of close involvement and cooperation from business and industry, labor, and community organizations. Herein lies the seeds of community involvement in education, at all levels, not just at the community college level. Mutual understanding and support, catalyzed by a strong community college career-education program fulfilling regional needs, can extend to other parts of the educational structure.

As our society moves with increasing rapidity into the space age with a need for highly trained technicians, the community college must not fail in its commitments to provide education for all of the people. The career-education programs can be an important part in the lives of many thousands of students previously neglected.

The community college must be alert to change. Otherwise, it cannot meet the needs of a dynamic society. Society will then have to develop yet another institution to meet its needs.

Where the Action Is: College and University Business*

TRITON: Career Center of the Midwest

Triton College calls itself the Career Center of the Midwest. Its 52 different career programs help it live up to that name as does an in-plant education program of 31 courses that last year taught nearly 1,000 employees of companies in the surrounding area. But Triton is much more. It is a comprehensive community college— three schools in one: a Career School, a School of Continuing Education, and a School of University Transfer Studies. But even more it is a place, in the words of its director of community services, Jerome Long, "where the student can sample, feel himself out, get his feet on the ground without penalty."

An example of what can happen at Triton: A high school dropout who got his GED while in the Army, at his wife's insistence, took a noncredit continuing education course. Successful, he switched the following year to a certificate program in air conditioning and refrigeration. Close to completing these requirements, he anticipates continuing until he earns an associate degree. He even talks of the possibility of a four-year engineering degree.

In 1902 the first junior college in the country was established at

*Reprinted by permission from *College and University Business*, December 1971, pp. 41-49.

Joliet, Illinois. But it wasn't until 1965 with the passage of the Junior College Act that Illinois began actively financing two-year institutions of higher learning. Triton College, located in the middle of a flat, tree-filled industrial suburb of Chicago, perhaps best illustrates the progress Illinois has made in the past seven years in developing a network of comprehensive community colleges.

Triton began on a firm financial footing when its trustees saw fit to levy the full education revenue rate in 1964. This amounted to nearly $1 million in tax receipts by the time that the college opened its doors. When 1965 rolled around, Triton initiated a $34 million construction program on an 86 acre site, with the aid of state money and an initial $750,000 federal grant. That same year it opened evening classes at a local high school for 1,243 students and with a professional staff of 114. This year, with 10 of its scheduled 14 buildings in operation, 12,222 students make Triton the largest community college among the 36 in the state, while academically it has gained a reputation as one of the finest community colleges in the central section of the country.

For a community college to work it must be just that—a community college. Triton was that from the beginning. Its founding trustees were representative of the community's industrial milieu. Only four of them had degrees beyond the bachelor's. Also, one of the superintendents of the 10 high schools in the district was a trustee. Triton's career programs were developed with the industrial needs of the Chicago area and the central part of the country in mind. To make certain that the trustees had a total understanding of how career or vocational and technical education functioned in a two-year institution, since that aspect of the program was critical to the success of the school, President Herbert Zeitlin had his trustees pack their bags and hop a plane with him to visit several well established comprehensive community colleges in California, Michigan and Florida.

Today one-third of Triton's students are adults who take non-credit courses, another one-third are enrolled in career programs, and the final third pursue university transfer studies. This is the proportion that Triton will attempt to maintain as it reaches its maximum student load of 22,000 students around 1980.

The School of Continuing Education is the fastest growing sector of the college. Started in 1968 with an enrollment of 125, it has grown in three years to 5,000 students. More than 250 noncredit classes are offered in evening classes on the Triton campus; on the premises of in-district industrial plants, businesses and community centers, and at extension centers in nearby high schools and elementary schools. The

School of University Transfer Studies is the academic area of Triton that comes closest to the traditional notion of "college." From accounting, anthropology and art to social sciences, Spanish, speech and zoology, a full complement of baccalaureate programs is offered. Triton has written agreements with many of the major universities within the state and has successfully transferred students to more than 120 different colleges and universities across the country.

But the School of Career Education is where Triton is breaking new ground. The Technology Building was the first structure to be erected. A year later, Triton was the first community college in the state to install numerically controlled (magnetic tape driven) milling machines. International Harvester, among other major companies in the area, uses Triton's machine shop to introduce new employees to computer-run machines. The Health Careers Building was second to go up. The U.S. Department of Labor has predicted that for the next 5 to 10 years health services will show the greatest individual occupational growth in the country. Health careers are a major adjunct to Triton's occupational program, as well as the most costly curriculums on campus. Triton has cooperative work/study agreements with 16 health care centers in its associate degree and practical nursing programs.

For a career program to work at optimum, there must be a close cooperative feeder-type relation with the secondary schools. In its early years Triton had some difficulty in developing this articulation of curriculum because the high schools (to the extent that they have technical and vocational courses) were oriented to a traditional industrial arts curriculum. "To better integrate the secondary schools with Triton," says Triton's assistant dean of career education, Gary Hinrichs, "several of the college deans and secondary school instructors have been appointed to each other's curriculum advisory committees." Mr. Hinrichs serves in this capacity at Elmwood Park High School with the result that this year curriculum in that school is undergoing significant change. Also, Elmwood Park students are taking evening vocational courses at Triton in such things as refrigeration maintenance, and Mr. Hinrichs expects more of this. The only drawback has been the expense. Under state law the high schools must pay junior colleges the per capita cost of student instruction.

Also, Triton has 11 coordinators and department chairmen whose function, among other things, is to inform students at local high schools of the career programs at Triton. This is done with periodic "Career Days" and close contact with high school counselors. Also, several of Triton's part-time instructors in its School of Continuing Education are local high school teachers who often serve as effective proselytizers when back on home ground.

MIAMI-DADE: A Confederacy of Careers

Nine years ago the treeless, sunbaked 245 acre North Campus of Miami-Dade Junior College looked more like the abandoned air base it had been than the site of Florida's most comprehensive vocational/ technical program. But its 37 military buildings, in various stages of disrepair, represented progress to administrators and faculty members who had been housed in chicken coops, cattle barns, and other buildings of the school system's former agricultural program, and to the 3,000 students of "Chicken Coop College" or Pigpen U, as it was sometimes called.

The college was obviously meeting an educational need; it soon became known as the country's fastest growing college, and today enrolls nearly 30,000 students. New buildings on the north campus include a learning resources center, containing a 100,000 volume library, audiovisual facilities, and auditorium; a hall of science and technology with classrooms and laboratories for technical/vocational studies; a creative arts center and auditorium, health center with gymnasium and athletic facilities; a student center with cafeteria, bookstore and student lounges, and an experimental center for special programs.

The college has also expanded to two additional campuses and seven off-campus centers.

Impetus for the occupational programs came in 1959 when the Florida state legislature passed a law requiring that every community college in the state institute a vocational education program, and backed the requirement with a $6 million Vocational Improvement Act. Miami-Dade, for example, used its $200,000 share to buy equipment.

From five technical programs in 1960, the occupational program has grown to 67 technical/vocational studies and business/career programs and 15 allied health studies. Sample programs include:

Mortuary Science. Consists of four 16 week terms and one 12 week spring-summer session, accredited by the American Board of Funeral Service Education. After one year of apprenticeship and passage of state board examination, the graduate is qualified to practice as a licensed embalmer in Florida.

Career Pilot. Meets industry needs and standards in two-year flight training programs, closely coordinated with area's aviation industry.

Executive Secretary Pilot. Combines flight training and secretarial science to prepare secretaries to fly executives to meetings, take notes, then fly back to the home office.

Fire Science Technology. Prepares persons with less than three years' experience for the occupation of fire fighter or for an administrative position within a fire department.

No matter how excellent occupation programs are, they cannot be considered successful unless the student can get a job after completing them. At Miami-Dade, the effort to match students and jobs begins before the first class, with testing procedures and counseling services, and continues beyond with a placement office instituted last year.

Counseling is an important aspect of eventual job placement, according to George Mehallis, director of vocational/technical studies. Vocational education at Miami-Dade means helping students choose a suitable occupation, determining what knowledge and skills are necessary for it, and finding methods to help students learn what they need to know. If students receive adequate advice before graduation as to what the opportunities are, finding a suitable job is much easier, Mr. Mehallis believes.

Because the Miami job market cannot absorb all of the vocational graduates, a placement office with national listings is essential. "This is one area that has to be developed—and soon," Mr. Mehallis says, "but it takes a great deal of money." Although expanding the range of employment opportunities is important for the students, it can create local friction. A few years ago, for example, a New Jersey firm interviewed all of the electronics graduates—and hired all of them. Such occurrences cause legislators and taxpayers to ask: "Why are we spending all that money, only to lose the students immediately upon graduation?"

Helping legislators understand the differences between occupational education and traditional academic programs is one of the biggest problems faced by vocational educators. For example, Mr. Mehallis points out, lower average student-faculty ratios are vitally necessary because of the nature of the instruction. "You can't very well have 40 or 50 students in a classroom with limited, complicated and expensive equipment." The college's oscilloscope, for example, can easily become uncalibrated, and it costs $125 each time it is sent out for repair. An electronics maintenance man on the staff could drastically reduce repair costs, but the request has been repeatedly denied.

What appears to speak loudest to legislators is accountability—

output. Data on how many students have graduated, and, more important, how many have contributed to industry in the state mean more than how many students are interested in particular programs. "The questions posed to us by the legislature are sometimes unfair," Mr. Mehallis says. "Many students fail to complete a program, not because they have lost interest but because they feel they have learned enough to meet their goal of employment. This is not to say that these same people don't come back to school eventually."

Perhaps part of the answer is within industry. All states are concerned with attracting industry, states Mr. Mehallis, "and they can't do it without education." To date, Miami-Dade has experienced excellent cooperation with local and state industries; in fact, input from industry takes the form of various advisory boards, appointed at the departmental level, which meet at least once a semester. These boards advise on curriculum, standards and admissions, and are excellent contacts for employment.

The biggest challenge in vocational education for Mr. Mehallis is changing attitudes. "We have to convince people that their son or daughter doesn't have to be a brain surgeon."

RIT: Pursuing a Private Goal

When Paul A. Miller, president of Rochester Institute of Technology, looks out of his office window, to the right he sees the University of Rochester two miles away, to the left is a thriving community college, and surrounding him are five liberal arts colleges. RIT began providing an embryonic form of career education in 1829. Now that the public universities and colleges, and particularly the community colleges, have awakened to the need for occupationally oriented education, it's Mr. Miller's job to see to it that RIT is not lost in the shuffle. Today every private technical institution president must face that problem.

"I had always been led to believe before I came into private education that the justification for private colleges is their ability to move faster than public colleges, to have more guts," Mr. Miller says. "But many private college people I've met tend to wait for someone to solve their problems and do away with competition. I ask RIT to practice what it preaches, and if the reason for being private is to be nimble (to be able to move without red tape), then do it." RIT has to be very nimble: Annual tuition at RIT is $2,000; annual tuition for the local community college is $550.

If anything has marked an RIT student in the last 142 years, it has been an almost obsessive desire "to get on with a job" he wants to do. Mr. Miller, who served by Presidential appointment as assistant secretary of education for the U.S. Department of Health, Education and Welfare under HEW Secretary John Gardner, calls this maturity. "We probably have more general curriculum courses than many liberal arts schools, but the reason students attend RIT is that we offer them the opportunity to not only learn an employable craft or profession but also to actually work at it outside in industry while learning." Public schools literally cannot afford to do this, Mr. Miller says. He goes so far to say that there is no public school in the country which has a program that begins to compete with RIT's cooperative education program.

A student isn't about to spend $2,100 and fool the year away, especially when he is paying for his own education—and most of RIT's students are at least 65 percent self-supporting. That's also why this year half of RIT's new students were upperclass transfers. Mr. Miller foresees this percentage increasing. "I look forward to an older student body, if not in body at least in spirit, and to an increasingly married student body. But RIT will always maintain a small freshman and sophomore class, because there will always be those students who know what they want to do almost from the day they enter grammar school." To encourage this type of student to attend RIT, five-day "live-in" seminars are held for high school juniors. The program is designed to provide the high school student with a taste of "college living" through exposure to classroom and laboratory experience, residence hall living, and the opportunity to communicate with members of the RIT faculty, staff and student body.

"We are also getting, and determined to get more of, the 'second career' students," Mr. Miller says. For example, 400 of the students seeking Master's in Business Administration are in their 30s. Now that early retirement in many companies has slipped down to age 55, RIT is also getting a few energetic grandfathers as well.

Shortly after the turn of the century RIT became a pioneer in cooperative work-study education. Its program remains today the oldest such cooperative program in New York and third oldest in the country. This has not only served as an excellent source for placement of RIT's cooperative students, but company employees also have been an excellent source of students for RIT. More than 150 employees representing 36 local companies received diplomas at RIT last May. They averaged three years of study in the areas of industrial and office supervision, sales, materials handling, packaging, traffic and transportation, and motion and time economy. Begun 44 years ago with only one course offering and 10 students, this management program has expanded today to include 1,600 students and 90 course offerings.

To continue to keep on top of the job market, last year RIT created a new Associate in Applied Science degree program in health institutions management. At present, health care is the third largest industry in the country and may ultimately become the largest. The 63 semester hour program, developed in cooperation with seven area health agencies, is designed to prepare students for management positions in hospitals, nursing homes, and related health service areas. The curriculum includes courses in general education, mathematics and science, general management and business, and professional courses in health institutions management.

In 1968 RIT moved into a new $60 million academic and residence complex located on 1,300 acres five miles south of its downtown Rochester campus. The 13 new academic buildings are a fitting tribute to the international reputation RIT has gained in the fields of photography, printing and graphic arts. Altogether RIT offers 45 major concentrations giving the associate, bachelor's and master's degrees. The campus contains seven colleges: graphic arts and photography, fine and applied arts, engineering, business, science, general studies, and continuing education. It has 5,000 daytime students and 10,000 evening students.

30

Private Vocational Schools Thrive[*]

Stephen Crews

Persons seeking post-high school career training often choose between apprenticeship programs and junior and four-year colleges, overlooking a grab-bag category called the independent private school.

It is a $350-million industry in Illinois and includes the profit-making institutions gathered under the headings of business, vocational, trade, technical, art occupation, health, self-improvement, home study, and barber and cosmetology schools.

The 589 private, "occupational" schools in Illinois receive little publicity, perhaps because their profits come from tuitions rather than from the property taxpayers pocket.

Another possible reason for the industry receiving short shrift is the condescension of members of the conventional education community and the general attitude that the industry is comprised of "profit mongers."

What is known about the industry often is incorrect, perhaps because of the comparatively low esteem attached to "vocational" education in general as opposed to college preparation and the so-called professions.

An attempt to demonstrate the importance of private enterprise

*Reprinted, courtesy of the *Chicago Tribune*.

in providing career education nationwide has been spelled out in a study of the private school industry contracted by the State of Illinois Advisory Council on Vocational Education.

It will be made available on a limited basis to guidance counselors and other interested persons thru the Council's office, 524 S. Second St., Springfield, Ill.

Conducted by H. H. Katz, president emeritus of the Illinois Association of Trade and Technical Schools and acting director of Coyne American Institute in Chicago, the report reflects the biases of a private trade school officer, but makes a sincere effort to point out both the weaknesses and strengths of this overlooked, but increasingly important, business.

At the base of the report is Katz' desire to correct what he believes to be a fundamental misconception—"that technical and business education are for . . . students with low or barely average high school grades . . . [and] that college and university preparation is for citizens who are gifted with the highest mental . . . potentials."

This view ignores the importance of a person entering a field that interests him despite its reputation, Katz said. It also ignores the fact that "a high degree of intelligence can make a tradesman more successful by common standards of measurement than a less intelligent, highly educated 'professional,'" he added.

Once the field for the individual entrepreneur, the independent private school industry has become a land of giants, the report points out.

More than 85 percent of all profit-seeking schools are owned by such well-known corporations as Bell and Howell, Minneapolis-Honeywell, International Telephone and Telegraph, and Ryder Systems, Inc.

Counting both resident and correspondence courses, the schools run by these and other companies in Illinois serve more than 600,000 students annually.

For advantages of independent private schools over other forms of training, Katz referred to a 1970 report by the Republican Party Task Force on Education and Training.

Based on interviews with students, the report listed three reasons why persons are willing to pay high fees to a private school when "similar courses are available at no or low cost" at local community colleges:

• Time: "Course length in proprietary [private] schools is very short, usually falling between four months to a year. The same program in a community college would take two years and mean a loss of possible earnings."

• Course Content: "Proprietary schools' courses concentrate on teaching only the job skills necessary to specific job goals, whereas the public school philosophy requires concurrent study of nonvocational subjects."

• Placement service: "The schools, with apparent considerable success, assist their graduate in obtaining job interviews and employment since continuation of the school as a business enterprise depends upon successful placement."

The report also cited the following advantages of independent private schools:

• Because profits are involved, they are quick to respond to changes in business and industry manpower needs.

• They are quick to respond to specific needs of students—courses can be tailored to meet needs of non-English speaking or handicapped students, for example.

• Faculty members are chosen more on the basis of practical experience and, consequently, act as excellent teachers.

• Proprietary institutions tend to have more up-to-date equipment of the kind the students are likely to encounter on the job than do public institutions.

On the minus side, however, Katz cites U.S. Postal Service figures showing that in the last six years, complaints have been leveled against 385 private schools, resulting in 120 criminal indictments and 61 convictions for mail fraud.

"Some schools, because of inadequate facilities and courses, fail to control the unethical activities of representatives [or salesmen] and, because of questionable and unethical advertising and selling practices, help to cloud the entire industry," Katz said. These companies "hurt legitimate profit-making schools that try to offer honest value in the courses they sell."

Katz recommended that the industry become better organized to protect itself against this damaging minority. Government should also develop more effective controls, he said.

In the past, anyone, qualified or not, could easily open an office and call himself a private vocational teacher, Katz said. In January, 1972, nine states still allowed independent private schools to operate without any form of control. Another 21 states had enacted regulatory laws only during the last 15 years, Katz said.

"Illinois was one of the first Midwestern states to enact legislation and, thru continuing modification, is helping to establish a national standard for meaningful regulation and approval of private schools," he said.

Although Katz obviously believes that most private schools offer honest training [if for no other reason than it results in greater long-range profits], he admitted that they should complement the public school system rather than compete with it. "It is not the fundamental responsibility of the independent school to develop the whole man and citizen. This should be a public and conventional school responsibility," Katz said. In the same way, "many educational researchers conclude that specialized occupational courses, except those on a highly technical and managerial level, should be left to specialized training institutions other than collegiate schools."

He predicted growth for the industry, pointing to what he believes is a growing tendency on the part of parents to recognize that "not all children are college oriented—and that trade-technical business education may be equally and, in some cases, more meaningful."

31

Continuing
Professional Education—
A Joint Partnership*

*Jean M. Arnold
and Max R. Otte*

T he concept of professionalism is linked with a pursuit of high
standards which reflect creditably upon the professional and
the profession and has been entwined in continuing education
programs for over forty years.

Colleges, both four-year and two-year, have greatly expanded
adult education activities to include programs for professional persons
aimed at increasing their level of technical competence, assuring high
standards of ethical practice, and expanding the stock of knowledge
available about their field of specialization. Even a casual glance at
catalogs, brochures, promotional material, and journals would indicate
the fervor with which both institutions of higher education and the
profession have enunciated the need for continued education for professionals.

The term, continuing professional education, was probably originally utilized broadly to refer to the "pioneering efforts at the Michigan Community Health Project in 1931. Physicians, dentists, nurses,
school superintendents and teachers, school boards, church pastors,
dairymen, and veterinarians were permitted to take short courses at
various universities and colleges."[1] The significance of the Michigan

*Reprinted by permission from *Adult Leadership*, February 1973, pp. 250-251, 267-268.

project lies in its concerted effort to improve, to progress, to increase competence, and to acquire justifiable respect for those fields and their practitioners. In particular, continuing education is defined as a "formalized learning experience or sequence designed to enlarge the knowledge or skills of practitioners who have completed preparatory sequences. These courses tend to be more specific, of short duration and may result in certificates of completion or specialization, but not in formal academic degrees."[2]

This paper focuses upon: 1. some of the underlying concepts involved in forging joint efforts between universities and junior colleges to identify continuing education needs of professions; 2. the need to develop both long and short term objectives and philosophies; and 3. on the necessity to design strategies or action steps directly related to these needs and objectives which would most effectively utilize all available and relevant resources in providing programs, courses and other educational activities for professionals.

Although continuing education is provided by other agencies such as professional organizations, employers, proprietary schools, and consultants, the professional tends to turn to a college in his quest for further learning. In the medical profession, for example, medical schools offered 35-60% of continuing education courses as compared with 9-22% by hospitals in the period September 1, 1970, through August 31, 1971.[3]

It is recognized that there are limitations on institutional resources. In order to promote even greater degrees of efficiency in the performance of the educational public service role of community colleges and universities, mutual planning and programming must take place to provide effective continuing education for the professions. In addition, it appears almost totally counter-productive to attempt to establish parallel and competitive programs from the standpoint of funds, personnel and quality of service.

Cooperation to achieve unity in planning and administration of continuing professional education programs by, at least, the public sector of higher education would result in more effective delivery of services. Coordination is viewed as an essential ingredient in the provision of appropriate community-centered programs. Hamrick recommended "that the efforts of community schools, adult education programs, and four-year colleges should be coordinated to provide comprehensive and relevant educational experiences for residents of a district."[4] However, there are at times almost insurmountable obstacles to achieving unity in programming. For example:

1. Lack of agreement on the goals of adult education.

2. Feelings of rivalry caused by competition for target audiences because of overlapping programs.

3. Perceptions of different status groupings within the field that generate feelings of inferiority, fear of domination, and other emotions that obstruct cooperation.

4. Adult educators from various groups who enter their educational roles from different backgrounds with differences in vocabularies, philosophies, and methods of approach that interfere with communication.

5. The difficulty of constructing a coordinating organizational structure because there is no clear pattern of the field to be coordinated.[5]

It is believed that powerful and positive forces exist which favor coordination and cooperation between universities and community colleges. They include:

1. The overlapping of the markets of the various adult educational activities that results in pressure from the consumers for better integrated services.

2. The marginality of the adult educational role that induces adult educators to seek mutual support.

3. Advances in the field that cause adult educators to seek beyond their knowledge for personal growth.

4. Adult educators who look to each other as natural allies in the struggle for recognition and financial support.[6]

Competition and feelings of inferiority can be mitigated by having each respective community college or university offer those programs which they are most capable of developing, staffing, supporting, and sustaining. Scheduled informal meetings involving adult educators should aid in diminishing provincialism and isolation and help to avoid overlap and duplication in course offerings. These close associations may also foster the development of common objectives. Joint planning and cooperative offerings of courses should provide a more secure foundation for the future of continuing education programs. One university faculty member proposed the formation of a Council of Continuing Education Administrators to provide scheduled meetings and systematic planning among these educators.[7]

Community colleges and universities can help each other considerably when their respective strengths and distinctive characteristics are viewed as complementary rather than competitive. The areas of uniqueness as identified in the literature include:

Community Colleges
1. Accessibility for community residents
2. Knowledge of community needs
3. Teaching orientation
4. Preparer of para-professionals
5. Community services—a major purpose and function

Universities
1. Well-structured and staffed extension divisions
2. Accessibility to theory builders
3. Subject matter competence
4. Preparer of professionals
5. Continuing education expertise

Accessibility is a key attribute of community colleges. "The community college in many areas is the only conveniently available community of scholars. Citizens of all walks of life (including professionals) look to it for such services as scholars traditionally provide."[8]

Community service administrators are expected to know the needs of the community served by their junior college. They encourage and sustain close contacts with advisory committees for the professions, agencies, and key decision makers to maintain current information on educational needs and desires. In addition, they generally survey interests of potential participants prior to initiating a course offering.

Research is a noteworthy function of the university and teaching is considered a strong point of the community college. A relevant continuing education program could benefit from a combination of both of these strengths. Teaching and research are essential ingredients of the "what's new" philosophy of continuing education.

The career programs in the two-year college are for the most part of a technical nature. Large enrollments in these programs seem to indicate that community college graduates render essential services to society by preparing practicing para-professionals. The continued advances in technology make continuing education a requisite for maintaining the technician's relevancy to his ever expanding field.

Continuing education for both para-professionals and professionals has been provided by community colleges through their divisions of community service. "Moreover, in most community colleges the number of persons served by the program of community services exceeds vastly the number served through the regular transfer and occupational programs offered for youth and adults."[9]

Universities prepare professionals through undergraduate curricula and/or graduate programs. Emphasis is placed upon introducing the professional to research, knowledge, and their application in life situations. Community college and university faculty members with their respective competencies in teaching and research, working in unison could add a great deal to the continuing development of the professional. Harlacher's description of institutional synergy "the simultaneous action of separate agencies which together have a greater total effect than the sum of their individual efforts"[10] seems to support such a joint cooperative approach to the continuing education of the professional.

The recent passage of legislation in several states requiring professionals to participate in continuing education will no doubt have a profound effect upon such programs in colleges and universities. For example, nurses in California wishing relicensure in 1975 and thereafter on an annual basis must demonstrate evidence of continuing education.[11] The Health, Education and Welfare National Center for Health Services Research and Development's *Report on Licensure and Related Health Personnel Credentialing* of June, 1971, recommends "that evidence of continuing education be a part of the recredentialing process for health professionals."[12]

In addition, several years ago the federal government had stipulated, "that over 10,000 inactive nurses must receive refresher training to enable them to return to work."[13] Since that time the mandating of attendance at refresher nursing courses has become an employment prerequisite by a large number of hospitals and nursing homes.

Mandatory and oftentimes reciprocal requirements for continuing education for nurses and related health professionals in various states poses an ever increasing demand upon colleges and universities in terms of both quality and quantity in programming. Cooperation and coordination between educational institutions on a regional basis appears as a desirable alternative to overlapping, divergent, and all too often duplicative activities.

As example, the New England Consortium in Higher Education financed by the W. K. Kellogg Foundation was organized to foster cooperation, coordinated planning, and joint programming among higher educational institutions. A result has been the development of the New England Center for Continuing Education, established to prompt adult education agencies to efficiently serve the educational needs of broad geographical areas and diverse clienteles.

Further illustrations include the formation of regional colleges—at times the literal linking of a two and four-year institution; regional learning centers such as the Southern Medical School Consortium housed at the University of North Carolina, Chapel Hill, serving the particular needs of medical schools, their faculties, and students in the South; and the development of regional organizations as WICHE to promote coordination and cooperation in a variety of academic and administrative areas. WCHEN, the Western Council on Higher Education for Nursing, and its subdivision, the Continuation Education Seminar, actively fosters cooperation among its members—directors of continuing education in nursing.

Consortia and other cooperative endeavors between schools have not been designed to create a new and separate education entity. Rather, they are suggested as a viable means of bringing existing and at times isolated educational components into an integrated, relevant, effective and efficient learning force.

The concept of coordination and cooperation seems to generate a host of advantages particularly when applied to the continuing education of professionals. Most important are:

1. The decline in provincialism in programs.
2. The decrease in duplication in course offerings.
3. The fostering of the development of common objectives.
4. The facilitation of a common unit of accreditation.
5. The possibility of a greater balance in curricular offerings for professionals, especially those in clinical and functional positions.

It is believed that much benefit can be gained from joint planning and programming of continuing education to meet the needs of the professional. Strong efforts are being made at various levels and in various segments of society to foster economies and efficiencies in education. The identification of needs and the establishment of programs jointly and cooperatively between universities and community colleges will result in stronger, more relevant programs benefiting the professional seeking continuing education and in turn will realize cost savings and deliver efficiencies for both types of institutions. Maximization of resources would clearly assist in furthering a closer alliance between institutions of higher learning and with their publics. "Such a scheme would serve to regularize communication, build awareness of shared purposes, promote community-wide planning, facilitate cooperation, avoid needless overlapping and overlooking, and make the most effective use of limited professional leadership."[14]

By forming partnerships with other societal institutions and agencies through joint continuing education activities, colleges can demonstrate both their ability and inclination to enter the mainstream of the community to aid in meeting its educational needs.

The future growth of continuing education for professionals seems, in great measure, dependent upon a realistic appraisal of alternative models to foster cooperation and coordination in developing effective and efficient plans and programs between institutions of higher learning.

Notes

1. Robert E. Kinisinger, "Community Education: A College Responsibility," *Community Services Forum* 2, no. 2 (March/April 1970): 5.

2. Dorothy J. Hutchison, "Interprofessional Education," *Journal of Continuing Education in Nursing* 1, no. 5 (September/October 1970): 6.

3. Norris Parrell, "The Role of the Universities in Continuing Professional Education: Professional Education in University Symposium," *Ohio State Law Journal* 31, no. 2 (Spring 1971): 318.

4. Wallace S. Hamrick, "Community Services Dimension of the Nonurban Community College," *Community Services Forum* 2, no. 4 (July/August 1970): 3.

5. J. Daniel Hill, "Can Cooperative Education and Community Colleges Work Together?" *Journal of Extension* 8, no. 4 (Winter 1970): 28.

6. Ibid., p. 11.

7. Russell J. Kleis and Donald G. Butcher, "The Role of the Community College in Cooperative Community Education," *Community Services Forum* 1, no. 10 (October 1962): 1-2.

8. James W. Thorton, *The Community Junior College* (New York: John Wiley and Sons, 1966), p. 67.

9. Ervin L. Harlacher, *The Community Dimension of the Community College* (Englewood Cliffs, N.J.: Prentice-Hall, 1969), p. 14.

10. Ibid, p. 11.

11. American Nurses Association, *American Nurse*, March/April 1972, p. 8.

12. United States Department of Health, Education and Welfare, *Report on Licensure and Related Health Personnel Credentialing*, (Washington, D.C., Department of Health, Education and Welfare, June 1971), p. 76.

13. Elda S. Popiel, "The Many Facets of Continuing Education in Nursing," *Journal of Nursing Education* 8, no. 1 (January 1969): 13.

14. Nathan C. Shaw, *Administration of Continuing Education* (Washington, D.C.: National Association for Public School Adult Education, 1969), p. 70.

32

Serving the Community Through Marketing and Management Seminars*

Jack W. Fuller

S tudents of the community college movement are well aware that a major function of the comprehensive community college is to provide a well-rounded and quality program of continuing educational, cultural, and recreational services to the community which it serves. An obvious and often influential interest within most college communities is that of business and industry. For the most part, the cultural and recreational needs of employees have remained the prerogative of the individual. The forward-looking business or industry, however, has taken education to heart and made it an ongoing program in the development of its staff and employees. Perhaps this concern and need of business and industry for a continuing program of education was best explained by Dr. Glenn Jensen in the March, 1971, issue of *Adult Leadership* entitled, "Peter, Paul, and Mary."

In the article, Dr. Jensen referred to the Peter principle as pronounced by Dr. Lawrence J. Peter of the University of Southern California. As the reader will recall, the Peter principle holds that "every employee in a hierarchy tends to rise to his level of incompetence." Dr. Jensen then reminded the reader that in June of 1970, Dr. Paul Armer of Stanford University came forth with the Paul principle. The

*Reprinted by permission from *Journal of Business Education*, December 1972, pp. 117-119.

Paul Principle held that people reach a level of incompetence in the hierarchy because they fail to continue to learn. Dr. Armer proposed that sabbatical leaves be taken so that employees could refurbish their skills and educate themselves as to the latest developments in their given line of work.

Drawing upon the Peter and the Paul principles, Jensen offered the Mary principle, named after his wife. Essentially, the Mary principle is an extension of the Peter and Paul principles. The Mary principle holds that an employee will become obsolete and hence incompetent at his level of employment in the hierarchy in direct proportion to the extent that he fails to recognize or abandon traditional or out-of-date practices and ideas. Jensen cautions that the Mary principle might not sound as expressive as either the Peter or the Paul principles. Nevertheless, it should still have importance for adult educators because that is really what the entire business of adult education is all about. By way of illustration, Jensen offers an analogy between the Mary principle and a Madison Avenue expression, "If it's working—it's likely out of date."

In effect, the marketing and management seminars offered by Harper College are a manifestation of the Peter, Paul, and Mary principles. These seminars provide the businessmen with an opportunity to upgrade and refurbish skills (Paul principle) and/or to replace out-of-date practices with tomorrow's ideas (Mary principle). En route to manifesting the Paul and Mary principles, the workshops and seminars shed serious doubt upon the validity of the Peter principle. For if the members of any hierarchy continue to learn and professionally adjust to the changing times, they will remain competent and never reach a point in the organization that is beyond their ability. And as this occurs, the Peter principle will be relegated to nonsensical fiction.

Determining Need for Seminar

A broad interpretation of the Peter, Paul and Mary principles explains some of the reasons for serving the community with marketing and management seminars. This necessarily begs the question, however, as to how these and other specific community needs are determined. Probably one of the most popularly used and occasionally reliable means of determining community needs is by a survey or a questionnaire. The value of a survey of the community at-large or of the business interests in particular is usually over-emphasized. Probably its greatest redeeming value lies in its potential for revealing general areas of interest and need. But in spite of this redeeming value, sole dependency on the survey method for needed information is discouraged. Attention must also be given to other means of securing accurate feedback of community needs.

One of these other means is trade publications. Often, successfully proven programs can be gleaned from professional journals and publications, including literature of other community service and continuing education programs at other schools and business. While this method of information smacks of program thievery, it should be recalled that educational ethics permit skull-duggery under the guise of research.

Social trends is another indicator of the need for a given seminar(s). Who would deny that relevance, communication, ability, and accountability are current social trends that have found their way into the corporate minds and processes of educational and other social institutions during the last decade? To ignore the existence of these trends and to not consider their study (and others) through a seminar format would be an inexcusable mistake.

Polling the expectations of adult students who are currently enrolled in educational programs can serve as another accurate guide for directing programming efforts. After all, studies reveal that these people are the ones most likely to continue with the learning process. Offering seminars in keeping with their wants is not a sure-fire success; but it comes pretty close.

Limited success can also be experienced by playing professional hunches. Although it is not earmarked in the index or the table of contents of adult education textbooks, offering seminars on the impetus of whim has produced some surprisingly positive results. One must be prepared, however, to suffer the loss of time, effort and money (not to mention reputation and ego) that more often than not accompany such a tactic.

Probably the best way of all to build a responsive seminar is to involve representatives of the business community in the developmental process. By having the interested parties take an active role in planning the seminar, the program will be sure to meet the needs and expectations of a majority of the target population. By securing a broader participation in the planning process, the success of the seminar will be greatly enhanced and the need to recruit students will be lessened. Not only will the planners increase their firms' participation in the seminar but the seminar agenda will be more attractive to that given industry and/or other businessmen as a whole.

Planning the Program

Once the decision to hold a given seminar has been made, great pains should be taken to insure its success. For the outstanding success or the dismal failure of that seminar can hold untold consequences for future programs. It is a tough job to build a commendable program but it requires only minimal effort and time to earn a debilitating reputation. In order to achieve the former and to avoid the latter, it might be wise to consider some of the following suggestions:

1. *Students.* Identify the target group at which the seminar will be aimed. Enlist their support in planning the program and in disseminating information about its availability. It is conceivable that a seminar might go unattended if it is not attractive to the group for which it was designed.

2. *Subject Matter.* Adults enter a learning experience with an expectation for immediate use of the knowledge they are to acquire. Hence, the subject-matter content of the seminars should be loaded with information and examples that are familiar to the students' occupational environment. Moreover, the information in seminars should be practicable on the job in the near future and not a theoretical concoction that will expire from disuse before it is applied. If a seminar is not relevant and does not provide useful information, it will generate a wealth of negative word-of-mouth publicity that could bring discredit upon all future seminars as well as the one in question.

3. *Cost.* The cost of the program to the student should be kept as low as the budget will permit. Program developers must remember that there is a direct relationship between an adult desire to continue his education and the drain it will place on his billfold. While individual firms often pick-up the educational tab of employees, this is not always the case. In some instances, the employee is reimbursed at a later date. Where this occurs, a high tuition charge might discourage enrollment in the seminar. So by keeping the costs low, a program director can hedge against this possibility. Programmers should also remember that public institutions can often receive government and/or foundation funding to help cover program expenditures. Because of the availability of this funding, seminars can usually be offered for a lesser tuition rate than that which is charged by private firms which conduct similar programs.

4. *Learning Atmosphere.* Because the typical seminar participant is an adult, care should be taken to guarantee that the learning climate complements his particular psychophysiological make-up. This means that the furniture, lighting, acoustics and temperature of the learning environment should be as conducive as possible to adult learning. This also means that the adult should feel free to ask questions without being embarrassed or without raising his hand. He should feel free to

leave at any time during the seminar and for any reason. He should not be chastised for daydreaming or napping. All of this is not to say that the adult student should be coddled. But it is to say that his expectations as a learner should be dealt with in a mature manner. If his expectations are not being met by the seminar, then only incidental learning, if any at all, will occur.

5. *Teachers.* If a seminar leader can attract a multitude of students regardless of his topic and if an objective of the program is to attract the greatest number of students, then by all means use the "big names." A word of caution. Big names are expensive and they can play havoc with the budget. They can increase the cost of the seminar to a point where it discourages enrollment by the dollar-minded adult. Where the development of a comprehensive program of seminars is the major concern, however, teachers of varying reputation will probably have to be secured. Where this is the case, it is important that each seminar leader be reminded of the aforementioned principles of relevance and atmosphere.

6. *Registration.* The registration procedures for the seminar should be kept as simple and convenient as possible. Name, address, phone, firm, and money are really all that are needed. Pamphlets, fliers, brochures and other printed publicity can easily include a registration blank requesting these items.

7. *Evaluation.* Continued program success or failure can hinge on this very item. An ongoing system of seminar evaluation provides the feedback needed for the evaluation of seminar leaders and seminar content. A properly designed evaluation system can also provide insight for additional seminar topics.

Summary

In offering a comprehensive program of seminars and workshops to the community it should be recalled that corporate as well as individual needs are being served. A business is only as sound and competent as its employees. If they rise to a level of incompetence (Peter principle) because they have failed to upgrade their skills (Paul principle) or to change outdated practices (Mary principle) then the business in which they are employed will also reach a level of incompetence. When sales begin to lag and the competition begins to gain the upper hand, it may be that a given business has reached its level of incompetence. And in the last analysis, the preservation of enterprise might well be the real reason for serving the community through marketing and management seminars.

EVALUATION

Seminar_____Date_____

	Excellent	Very good	Good	Fair	Poor

1. How would you rate this session?

   _____

   _____

   _____

2. What is your evaluation of the leader in terms
   of his ability to communicate and to make the
   material meaningful to you?

   _____

   _____

   _____

3. How would you rate the appropriateness of the
   subject matter for this session?

   _____

   _____

   _____

4. How would you rate any benefit you received
   from this session?

   _____

   _____

   _____

5. Would you recommend others in your company attend this seminar?
   _____Yes   _____No

6. Of the ideas, concepts, and/or principles covered, which do you consider to be of the most value or significance?

_____

_____

_____

7. How do you intend to apply what you learned in this session in your work?

_____

_____

_____

8. Where did you learn about this seminar?

_____ a. Brochure mailed to me
_____ b. Harper College schedule
_____ c. Personnel sent me the information
_____ d. My boss sent me
_____ e. Newspaper ad
_____ f. Friend
_____ g. Other (specify) _____

33

New Careers:
A Challenge to
Adult Education*

John J. Connolly

The New Careers model is not a new arrival upon the scene. The title is new; the concept of the career ladder which it espouses, however, has been with us in other forms throughout history. The craftsman's apprentice, the graduate student research assistant, the soldier promoted to rank in battle were all "new careerists" of a sort. Each learned his skills from masters, began at the lowest level and worked upward, received continued "on-the-job-training," and proved his mettle under fire.

In the most pragmatic sense New Careers is a training program for the under employed, or unemployed; however, it is also much more than that. It is a training program of sorts, but one which trains for careers not jobs.

The fundamental principle underlying the New Careers model is that many jobs, even those of a professional nature, can be broken down into simple basic tasks which can be learned by most people. This does not mean to say that most people can perform professional functions in their entirety, but merely that they can perform segments of these functions.

The ultimate goal of breaking down professional tasks and training persons to perform segments of these functions is an increase of

*Reprinted by permission from *Adult Leadership*, December 1972, pp. 187-188.

services in areas of initial need. The increase in services would occur by providing more personnel (for instance, teachers aides, social work aides and physicians aides) and by freeing highly trained professionals from the more routine aspects of their jobs to perform strictly professional level functions.

The initial thrust of New Careers programs has been in the human service areas, particularly in programs serving the poor.

There are, of course, problems inherent in the New Careers model. One of the primary ones is resistance on the part of professionals. Some regard the presence of para-professionals as threatening. Others, however, recognize the potential for cross-fertilization and the opportunity for mutual exchange and learning: one individual passing on the particular knowledge and expertise gained through years of formal training and the other communicating the skills and knowledge shared by members of his social group but often totally foreign to the professional.

Another problem which frequently presents itself is a fear on the part of the New Careerists themselves that the jobs "created" for them are either temporary accommodations to present social forces or dead-end positions in which they may be forever stranded. Both fears may be well grounded in reality! There can be no doubt that New Careers is a response to a social force (or many forces) and it is only the continued faith and trust by those who are leading and supporting the movement, and those who are participating in it, which can maintain its viability. Secondly, many of the positions thus far created have been of very limited opportunity. It is no mean task to cause a social system, especially a bureaucratic system, radically to alter set patterns. Change is threatening to the bureaucracy and to many of its members, who have the potential for mounting very effective defenses against revolution, if not even evolution.

Crucial problems are those related to the training or education of any New Careers program. We are not here dealing with the kinds of students who have in the past fared well in school. In fact, the complete opposite is almost universally the case. Neither the value structure, the behavioral pattern, nor the cognitive style of the disadvantaged learner is that which our educational programs are designed to accommodate.

Because of these factors, our approaches to training the New Careerist should not be based upon traditional models. The very fact that the training is so directly job related has many advantages; yet this factor alone is not adequate compensation for the counter-pressure of many negative influences. Training should be field based (conceptual training built on concrete field experiences), programmed (step-by-step), short-term (in the pre-job stage) and should utilize a team or group mode.[1]

We have thus far spoken of the New Careers model as applicable to a generalized group labeled the "disadvantaged." However, since generalizations are seldom completely accurate it might be valuable to identify some specific groups who might benefit by the program. Two, in particular, come to mind: (1) the returning Viet Nam Veteran, who finds the opportunities awaiting him not vastly different from those he left behind before he entered the service—except that he now, most likely, has acquired a few basic skills, has incorporated the value of further education, has some financial support in the form of the G.I. Bill, is less likely to be satisfied with a menial, dead-end job and is more likely to say or do something about it; (2) the older worker who is planning upon retirement, but who still desires to contribute to society in an active and meaningful way. As Alan Gartner so cogently states: "While the boundaries between work and study are most often seen as a problem of youth, they also affect . . . in almost a mirror image of their impact upon youth the older person. For our system most often allows a person but 'one ride on the carousel,' but one opportunity for protracted study and preparation for work. The system is a linear three-step process—preparation for work, the work itself and then retirement and/or death. Having made a commitment to a particular course of preparation and work, an individual rarely has the opportunity to enter into a new line of work".[2]

A third, more recent group of New Careerists, might include the unemployed unskilled and semi-skilled workers who are suffering the brunt of the current economic situation. Perhaps the New Careers model would even be applicable to the many highly skilled unemployed who find the demand for their skills lacking.

Mr. Gartner also points out another problem which brings us to the role of the adult educator and the adult education agency in the New Careers movement. He further states: "The opportunity for new preparation is rarely available under conditions necessary for adults."[3] The conditions necessary are not merely classes scheduled during the evening hours. They include a sensitized faculty, a restructured learning experience, relevant education concurrent with meaningful jobs which provide career ladder opportunities financial support, and, most of all, the commitment of a large number of individuals and agencies.

The commitment from adult educators should be made in terms of training opportunities, employment opportunities, and proselytization. We are in a unique position to lend establishment support to a new and struggling concept, bits and pieces of which exist, but which demands a national effort of unification and planning. Sumner M. Rosen, in a presentation at the University of Wisconsin in the Summer of 1968, literally threw the gauntlet to his audience of adult educators. In his concluding remarks he stated: "If you make your fight and identify yourselves as agents for this kind of change in education, you will have the support of those forces in the ghetto who now look upon you, and upon all people who have made it, as the enemy. They will begin to see the connection between what you do and what they must do, and you will begin to become relevant again to the lives of the immigrants who once before and once again will make this nation or break it. I think it is a challenge that you can understand. I hope it is one that you can accept."[4]

Forward-looking adult educators must accept Mr. Rosen's challenge and join the national coalition of professional and para-professionals which Riessman and Popper[5] declare necessary for the development and fruition of the New Careers movement. Adult educators on all levels—high school and post-high school, in church affiliated and social service agencies—should explore the ways in which they can actively support and serve the New Careers movement, and will, hopefully, adopt and maintain a firm commitment to this new and promising model for adult education.

Notes

1. Frank Reissman, *New Careers* (New York: A. Philip Randolph Educational Fund, n.d.), p. 24.

2. Alan Gartner, "The Older American. New Work, New Training, New Careers," mimeographed. Paper prepared for the 13th Annual Southern Conference on Gerontology, Institute on Gerontology, University of Florida, Gainesville, Fla. January 1969).

3. Ibid.

4. Sumner M. Rosen, "An Introduction to New Careers." (Paper based on a speech to the Adult Education Summer Conference, University of Wisconsin, Madison, Wis., July 1, 1968).

5. Frank Reissman and Hermone L. Popper, *Up From Poverty* (New York: Harper and Row, 1968), p. 9.

34

A Community College Perspective on New Careers*

Phyllis B. Kopelke
and Moses S. Koch

This is a subjective account of a subjective experience, a learning experience for two teachers, the teachers being the director of Early Childhood Programs and the president of the college. The students who provided the learning in this case were inner-city residents. They were enrolled in a Head Start Supplementary Training Program at Essex Community College, one of three early childhood programs operated by the college.[1]

In getting to know the students in the Head Start Program, it was clear that teaching in Head Start required much learning on the part of the instructors and the college. The students were not oriented to the academic games we play and tended to be "themselves." The jargon we take for granted as universal is not always understood, and an instructor must be aware of his language and be ready to clarify it.

Two years of operation has amply proven that inner-city residents can be helped to function in positions of educational responsibility for children in these critical early childhood years. It is also clear that traditional college philosophy is often not adequate to meet the needs of these adults. The challenge has not yet been met. We know for certain that these adults are a great untapped human resource, one which we have been unable to utilize thus far.

*Reprinted by permission from *Community/Junior College Journal*, pp. 14-16.

Now, after two years of involvement, the college as an institution, is committed to new careers as an integral part of its total program. Not that all faculty, administrators, or board members are equally enthused. In fact, this article is an effort to present candidly the intentions and the realizations, as well as the disappointments, of the "new careers" experience thus far.

Differing Attitudes Toward New Careers

Institutional commitment in the final analysis resolves itself to people—some of whom are deeply involved and earnestly trying to learn and understand new ways of teaching and living; others who are unsure, but try not to interfere; and many who just plainly wish life could continue without new careers, like the good old days. Essex is no different, except perhaps in one very important respect—the administration is sensitive and deeply concerned that the college be part of the changing times; not just observers, but catalysts and reactors. As an example, in the summer of 1969 the president taught a sociology course for Head Start students in a ghetto area of Baltimore.

One of the new career programs is the Early Childhood Education Program. Begun in 1968 in response to the overwhelming demand for well-trained pre-professional personnel in child care, it is a broad program that prepares persons in a variety of settings as assistants to teachers, psychologists, and other professionals in schools, institutions, agencies, and organizations concerned with small children, both normal and exceptional.

It began operating with the belief that this program would not be run any differently than any other career program on the campus. In retrospect, this was a decided error in judgment in that most of the students working in Head Start are from backgrounds and experiences very different from the other Essex students. Interpreting these differences became a delicate process, for on the one hand there was the view that all students have problems—learning and otherwise—and to set any group of students apart was unfair and unrealistic. But there was no denying that previous practices of the college were just not adequate for the Head Start students. Assumptions that were made about learning processes, textbooks, registration, courses, etc., were not applicable nor working successfully with the Head Start Program.

For example: During the first semester one course was offered and this was held on campus. Physically, this was a most unsatisfactory arrangement since most of the students came from long distances, and Essex Community College is not located near any public transportation. The students rightfully complained. The college listened. The result was that two off-campus locations were located. Classes for these students are now conducted in an inner city location and in another part of Baltimore County, as well as on campus.

Another example: The initial course in the program was Human Growth and Development. The textbook that had been used and approved for this psychology course became a source of problems to the Head Start students, and during the semester the instructor advised them to use it only as a reference. He replaced it with a more appropriate one and with short articles and relevant paperback books. The problem was one of differing language patterns and erroneous assumptions by the college concerning prerequisite information which these students lacked.

All of the Head Start students were employed as teachers or aides and working with young children daily. Most of the students are married, with families. They were aware of what they needed to know about human development and they were most anxious to deal with the questions on their minds. At times the teacher had to choose between turning off their questions and thus staying with the prescribed curriculum, or as the teachers more frequently began to do, namely incorporate the needs of the students into the basic structure of the course. As an outcome teachers are now increasingly aware of modifying course content and methods to the students' level of need and readiness. Students do help determine the content and process of learning. This practice previously preached is less and less a cliché and more widely implemented, both within the Head Start Program and in other college courses as well.

Some of the students do not have high school diplomas or high school equivalencies. Essex has an open door policy that admits any persons interested in continuing their education, but they must complete their high school equivalency before graduation from the college. Essex uses form letters to remind students who don't have the equivalency that they must get it as soon as possible. In addition, the college made it a practice to withhold grades until the test was completed. Though there was some legitimacy to the content of these letters, they have proved to be discouraging and generally misunderstood by the recipients. In examining the tone of these form letters, it became apparent that a change was necessary. The outcome was that the college redesigned the letter to insure that the students understood these conditions prior to admission into any program. In addition, every form letter has been carefully reviewed to minimize possible misunderstandings, on the part of Head Start students and all other students.

The Instructor and His Attitude

According to many studies, the key to successful educational endeavor is the attitude of the instructor. A positive, success-oriented instructor, dealing with material relevant to the needs of the population, creates the climate in which effective learning takes place. His ability to be flexible, to change in response to the student needs, to confront and deal with situations unique to a particular group of students, and his ability to start where the student is, are critical requisites to the success of the group of people who, prior to the advent of the community college concept, had little or no hope of coping with the increasing educational demands of our society. Experience with this new careers program has made this college graphically aware of the institutional difficulties in reaching some of the people we have always talked about serving.

Teachers need an orientation program that familiarizes them with individualized teaching techniques. This may mean helping a student see the need to come to class on time or helping the instructor see that it is impossible for this individual to be in class on time and working out a satisfactory arrangement for both. It might be suggesting a meaningful way to read a textbook. It will mean humanizing and individualizing education and often abandoning the textbook approach.

Concurrently while working with students in the classroom, the college has tried to work with the community action agencies and the board of education to encourage and ensure creation of new job categories and better pay for students taking courses and working. As was pointed out in the February 28 issue of the New York *Times,* programs such as the ones at Essex can lead to poorly paid, dead-end jobs, unless institutions deal with all aspects of career development—including salaries and the job market itself. The institution must become a moving force in the establishment of salary schedules commensurate with the scope of responsibility. An aide in one school in Maryland with a high school diploma earns the same salary as an aide with an A.A. degree in another school. Thus, an unfulfilled need is that of providing the financial reward to the people who have, in truth, become preprofessionals.

Career Ladder Mobility

Another need high on the priority list is the establishment of a career ladder that has both horizontal and vertical mobility. At this point, employing agencies see the aide simplistically—one salary and one job category—which remain constant until she becomes a teacher.

A final, and perhaps most important factor, is the need to award degrees based on factors other than the simple accumulation of credit hours. For example, if a person is planning to teach children, the experience she may have already had working with children should earn her credits; living experiences and work experiences must be recognized. Institutions of learning can no longer restrict themselves to credit earned only within the walls of the institution.

Certainly one of the major outcomes of the new careers programs at Essex has been its spillover effect into the college generally. It cannot be denied, for example, that this program has influenced Essex as an institution and forced many teachers to look at themselves critically, asking questions about the extent to which they have stereotyped their instructional practices. How can education be made more exciting, they ask. Many of the requests the Head Start students are making, and many of the changes in programming, scheduling, and the teaching techniques could and should apply equally well to the more traditional programs in other classes. Humanizing the education process and the classroom does not mean watering down the curriculum and lowering the standards. Academicians who coin these phrases, for a variety of "well-stated reasons," need not be condemned, but rather helped to understand the stultifying effects traditional approaches often have, and the meaningless aristocracy they establish. Meeting the needs of society, our entire society, is the essence of the uniqueness of any institution of higher learning which wishes to call itself a community college.

Note

1. The other two are: a 12-week program for entry-level jobs in child care in a variety of settings, and an A.A. degree curriculum in early childhood education.

35

Problems and Issues
in Career Education
for Adults*

Andrew Hendrickson

I t would be well to start out by defining our terms. The dictionary
defines career as, "A profession for which one trains and which is
undertaken as a permanent calling." Ever since Harvard College
was founded in 1636 as a training institution for the clergy, institutions
of higher education have accepted that definition and have increasingly accepted the role of training qualified persons for the so-called
professions. Until recently the only change has been that of the vast
increase in the number of professions being trained for.

At this point one could raise the questions, *"How does 'career' as
newly defined differ from professional and vocational training as we
have known them in the past?"* Does this emphasis derive solely from
the need for the undereducated to see that schooling can open up for
them career possibilities and thus economic security and other benefits? Or is it related to the movement for accountability in education?
Or is it a combination of these and other factors?

It is curious that this new thrust toward career building should
come at a time when many of the traditional career occupations are
either very unstable or are undergoing important transformations. As
far as instability is concerned, anyone who has followed what has happened to engineers in the aircraft and aero-space industries will un-

*Reprinted by permission from *Adult Leadership*, February 1973, pp. 266-272.

derstand what I mean. The tendency toward transformation is probably best illustrated by the way the physician's role is being sliced up into specialties and subspecialties, and with many of the functions being carried on by a variety of para-professionals.

For over 250 years after the founding of Harvard College, there was relatively little change in the way a university perceived its role in preparing professionals—except for the proliferation that took place. And this proliferation has been phenomenal. It would take an occupational dictionary to list all of the professions and sub-professions that are now being prepared for. In those days a curriculum was planned at the undergraduate and/or graduate level. This curriculum sometimes carried an apprentice experience as in the case of the ministry and medicine, but more often not. At the conclusion of his "course" the graduate was assisted in his efforts at placement and then was largely forgotten; although on occasion the alumni association would follow-up a particular class to see where the members had arrived after 15 years and what kinds of salaries they were making.

In recent years some mitigation of the above picture has taken place. Course programs are less rigid. They more frequently contain practicums, and the universities are increasingly offering opportunities for renewal through such activities as workshops, seminars and bibliographical services. In addition, alumni associations keep very close tab on the progress of the graduate.

At this point I would like to discuss some more specific changes. The first has to do with what has happened to work as we have known it, not with career training as such, although there are strong implications. This is the tendency for jobs at all levels to become increasingly mechanized and narrow so that workers have become members of the bored, and it is spelled B-O-R-E-D. According to a recent AMA study, with the introduction of computers and the expanding automation of the management functions, even middle and upper management officials feel cheated out of their traditional satisfactions. They feel that they are tenders of the machine rather than part of the intellectual process by which decisions are made. Business and industrial life has become so much more orderly and routine. Systems engineers have made jobs simpler and simpler under the guise of increasing productivity; and this is happening at a time when people are getting more and more education.

The all too apparent result of this condition is shown in extreme boredom, resulting in alienated behavior, such as destruction and pilfering. It has also created the phenomenon of the mid-career switch so characteristic of the late 60's and early 70's. *What can we do to restore job significance and create job enrichment? Isn't this a job for adult education?*

This situation leads to consideration of the role of work in our society. Originally needed for mere survival, it later took on other benefits, such as aesthetic satisfaction, status designation, and social benefaction. But in today's world the Puritan ethic is wearing thin. It is no longer "Early to bed and early to rise will make you wealthy and wise." Some wag has said that this ethic has now been replaced by the three-martini lunch. This may be an exaggeration but there is no doubt that because of multiple reasons we need to revise our attitudes toward work.

There is no doubt that even in the midst of the change from a productive society to one based on service and cultural enrichment, we will for a long time to come need to look at work as a necessity. But it will not be based on a grinding need to keep body and soul together. The use of machine operations will have taken care of that. Rather it should be thought of as a means of self-expression, of social betterment and of cultural enrichment. Work should have a liberating quality. Instead of being an enforced necessity it should be undertaken voluntarily because one sees in it a means to achieve his potential—to become his best self.

With the machine having already taken over the difficult and routine jobs and with a high level of income on the part of the majority of the population we have already seen a shift away from the production of goods and toward production of services. Job surveys show a continually diminishing number of factory jobs and an ever increasing number of service ones. The occupational thrust now is toward a larger number of health services, services for personal care, travel, education, recreation, the media—and I don't mean just radio and TV. Have you noticed the recent rash of book clubs? *What is adult education's role in helping persons to adjust and keep adjusting to these kinds of changes?*

A quite different condition I wish to mention is that of overlapping jurisdictions. As long as there were only colleges and universities on the one hand and schools on the other, there was very little competition or overlap. The public and private schools traditionally through their vocational, commercial, and general programs trained office workers, and workers in trades and industry; and professional training was left to the universities. But with the recent rapid development of the junior college as an intermediate institution an opportunity for overlapping of function is present. This is not all bad. In some respects it is good, for there is enough to be done to keep all agencies busy. In the career training field an example of overlap is in the training of medical technologists and other para-professionals. My reason for mentioning it here is that by extension this lack of clarity about formal career training could carry over into the adult education aspects. This development then may be suggesting one of the tasks for this conference. *How shall we differentiate between the roles of the universities, the junior colleges, and the public schools in the education of adults for careers?*

One aspect of career building which is likely to be overlooked and which is the responsibility of all our institutions is that of new careers for older people. Oldsters' needs are varied and the options are limited. Obvious needs are those for additional income, for coping with health and family adjustment needs, and for keeping involved in the stream of life. Howard McClusky's classification of four (4) types of needs (White House Paper) are pertinent here:

Need for coping
Need for expression
Need for contributing
Need for wielding influence

Not all of these needs lead to new careers, but segments of the coping and the contributing certainly do. *What is adult education's role here?*

Well, where do these rambling remarks of mine leave us? If we agree that the major task of preparing people initially for careers belongs to the formal programs of our institutions, then maybe we can agree that the no less important supplemental and reinforcing functions are the major tasks of adult educators. It seems to me that these functions can be epitomized by a set of 3 R's—Renewal, Retraining and Readjustment. *Renewal*—helping the adult to grow and keep himself replenished in his job by thinking, by conferring with others, by use of libraries, by reading his journals and books, and in similar ways. *Retraining*—where changes are drastic leading to loss of job or need for wholly new skills, retraining—an adult education function— will be needed. *Readjustment*—training for a stance of preparedness for change; openness for new ideas, new work tasks, new personal relationships.

Some of the questions I have raised may be summarized as follows:

1. What is the significance of the new thrust toward career training?

2. What can adult education do to offset the extreme boredom experienced by workers in many of their jobs?

3. How can we help adults to adjust to the many changes that are occurring in the world of work?

4. How can we help adults develop a new work ethic which is more viable for today's world?

5. In what ways can the three (3) agencies represented here collaborate and in what ways must they work alone? To the extent that they collaborate, what mechanisms can be used?

6. How can we, working through these institutions, bring more humane qualities into career education and into the jobs they prepare for?

Part 4

Curriculum Articulation

Curriculum articulation is a many-sided coin, as illustrated in the following articles by Moss, Diminico, Whealon, Vacca, Hedrich, and Laramore. They describe how career concepts can be integrated into every level of education. They point out that it can and does take the form of speeches, addresses, brochures, articles and books on the subject. The authors show that it is science fairs, career days, trade shows, conferences, conventions, and institutes. They continue that it is recruiting enrollments, enlisting supporters, and educating the ignorant about career education. The authors also stress that enroute to these manifestations, career education necessarily becomes a congenial and mutually productive interface with other elements of the curriculum. It assumes the form of theoretical models and constructs of the career concept. It is all of this and more. But whatever form it takes, career articulation is doing whatever is necessary to make career education an integral part of the life-long process of learning.

To remain constant and unchanging is to die a slow and disappointing death. If an entity does not adjust to changing times, the world will surely pass it by. With the advent of the knowledge explosion, these words of caution are truer now than ever before. One way to avert this catastrophe is to constantly search for better ways to do what we are doing. In other words, to continually seek improvement,

Career education is no different. It, too, must look to tomorrow if it is to remain a viable force in our educational system. To this end, consider Lloyd Dull's perception of career education as a cluster concept. Robert Ristau adds a slightly different slant when he follows with still another model for career education. Winthrop Adkins offers a variation on the same theme with a model for "Life Skills Education for Adult Learners." And finally, "Career Education, Equipping Students for the World of Work" provides one more view of a model for career education.

36

Careers: Age Doesn't Limit the Interest*

Ruth Moss

K indergartners care about careers. First graders love learning about life. From the earliest grades on, career education is catching on in schools in the Chicago area.

So that students of all ages and stages can know more about the outside world, schools have brought working men and women into the classrooms, planned projects and field trips, scheduled exhibits, seminars, expos and jamborees—all geared to careers.

The following vignettes will give readers an idea of the great variety of opportunities to learn about the world of work now available for young and old.

In Maywood, pupils are proving you're never too young to learn about career education. The showcase World of Work project, directed by Diane Bernard and financed by School District 89 and the state's vocational-technical division, begins in kindergarten.

Teachers of all elementary levels are encouraged to tie in career opportunities with every learning activity. Two 1st grade teachers, Patricia Gabig and Roberta Nelson, developed a career education unit linked to the five senses.

Their young pupils in Maywood's Van Buren school tested their sense of smell, sniffing florist Fred Stebel's arrangements. Then they

*Reprinted, courtesy of the *Chicago Tribune*.

245

tried their hand in the flower business, making paper posies, pricing them for the market.

To explore careers involving the sense of touch, they interviewed sculptress Geraldine McCullough of Rosary College, tape recording her answers to their questions. Afterwards they created and painted their own sculptures using wood.

To learn about the sense of sight, they invited Dr. Fred Walker of Loyola University to tell them how their eyes worked and answer their questions about what it means to be a doctor. District band leader Russell Wagner gave them an earful about sound, before they tried to make their own sounds on the trumpet, flute, and drum he brought to class.

For tasting they went to a pizza parlor where they talked with the cook, sampled a variety of flavors, then made thumb-print cookies and planned for, shopped, and prepared breakfast for the class.

Some of the children will tell about their adventures and sell the flowers they've made as part of Expo 89 from 1 until 4 p.m. on Thursday, at the Hillsdale Holiday Inn.

At Skiles Middle School, Evanston, teacher Ron Mackert's boys are framing in windows, pitching roofs, shingling and siding, wiring and plumbing, installing plasterboard and ceiling tile, laying floors, and loving it.

Their work is part of the World of Construction project Mackert helped develop at Ohio State University. It's proving itself with the boys. Every 8th grade boy elected to enroll in the optional course.

And next fall, 40 girls also will don hard hats to pour concrete footings, place heavy beams on columns with a jenny winch boom, and walk the beams like veteran iron workers.

For Skiles students interested in the World of Manufacturing program, teacher Tony Simonaitis helps them set up assembly lines to produce CO_2-propelled cars, model rockets which they later fly, and high intensity lamps.

With students at Glenbrook High Schools, it's the real thing. For the sixth year, students are home building in the trades program conceived by John Boley, program supervisor. They've designed, planned, built, and decorated and this year, will add the final landscaping touches to this year's house.

For the last two years, male students' designs have won in competition. Next year's house, already on the drawing boards, has been designed by a girl, Dr. Florence Steiner, director of instruction and development services, reports proudly.

Meanwhile, members of Austin High School's Green Thumb Club are reassembling their award-winning "Scentuous Garden" for the 9th annual Chicago Regional Educational Exhibit Thursday thru Sunday at the Museum of Science and Industry.

Club president Larry Woods and sponsor Walter Klimek promise a show stopper—a Volkswagen turned into a sunshine mobile, with flowers and plants blooming from interior, trunk, and engine.

Altogether, students from 70 Chicago public and parochial schools will display talents in such areas as sheet metal, foundry, graphics, electronics, woodworking, and drafting. Myron Noonan, exhibit cochairman, reports.

Students will demonstrate auto emission tests, commercial art, printing, and machine tool and plastics work at the exposition, a cooperative venture of schools and business, including The Chicago Tribune, Joseph J. Dixon, an assistant superintendent of Chicago public schools, says.

Of Bloom Township's 5,000 students, 3,500 are involved in occupational education, choosing among 21 programs. The industrial education program there does double time, from 7:30 a.m. until 11 p.m., serving students and adults from Chicago Heights and five other south suburbs, vocational director Dean Wertz reports. He calls the school's welding facility "the finest in the state."

Leyden High Schools' tell-it-like-it-is seminars have attracted 3,000 students this year, Dr. Charles T. Harrington, career education director, reports.

The series of seminars, ranging from art thru veterinary medicine, was based on an Explorer Scout career survey of students, so that young persons can keep up-to-date on an increasingly complicated technological society.

Meanwhile, come-to-the-job-jamboree is the special invitation for Leyden students who want full-time employment after graduation. They'll meet personnel men and women from local companies at West Leyden in Northlake from 1 until 8 P.M. Wednesday.

At New Trier East in Winnetka, Betty G. Quick, home economics chairman, asked if an affluent, academically oriented high school in the Middle West could find happiness offering a course in career education.

Students have answered "Yes!" For four years, they've rushed to enroll in a child development course that combines classroom and practical experience at one of four nearby nursery schools.

The opportunity to put their learning to immediate use in the growing areas of behavioral science appeals to them, Mrs. Quick explains. The course is billed as the only one of its kind in Illinois for high school students.

"This great variety of programs points up what can happen when students get involved in quality career education at all ages and stages," says Richard J. Martwick, Cook County schools' superintendent.

"All schools must offer such vital programs, so that every student will have a chance to select his career goal, develop his skills, and meet men and women on the job in the industry he wants to make his own."

37

Integrating the Curriculum via Careers

Janet Whealon
and Terry Whealon

As a junior high teacher, I have always been concerned about the lack of integration of the curriculum at this level. Each teacher teaches his or her subject and has no idea as to what is happening in the other classrooms. I have often heard the science teacher comment that his students act as if they were completely unfamiliar with graph construction when it comes up in science class and he was sure that they have studied graphs in mathematics class. Students were obviously getting caught in the departmental organization of our school. Each class in their schedule was a separate entity which had no relationship to any other class.

In the hope of changing this situation, I began a career education project which I hoped would eventually involve teachers of all the subject areas. I began by casually mentioning my idea for a project involving the clothing business and the people who work with cloth in the lounge one day at lunch. The math teacher asked, "What in the world does that have to do with language arts?" I explained that through looking at people and what they do I could teach many written and oral skills. For example, we were going to interview a clothing store manager. In order to prepare for this, we were going to write sample questions, learn to listen, record his responses, and roleplay the situation. We had already written a letter inviting him to our class and we will write thank-you letters to him after the interview. At this point several of the other teachers in the lounge became interested. We began discussing all the possibilities which a study such as this might have. They asked to make the activity a group project so we could work together as a team.

The next day discussion dealt with the type of activities in which we wanted the children to become involved, people that we might contact, and the skills which we felt would be important to include. We were particularly concerned about the students seeing a relationship between academic skills we were attempting to teach and the use they would find for them in a real life situation. Each teacher listed skills she or he wanted to teach and the person or persons connected with the clothing business who would use that skill in their work.

Each time one teacher mentioned someone they wanted the children to interview, another teacher thought of how that particular interview would be beneficial in their own subject area. We began to see relationships between subject areas that we had never thought about before.

For example, when the home economics teacher mentioned that she would like to have the kids interview a seamstress the math teacher thought this would be a great opportunity to teach measurement skills. The science teacher thought that it would also help him out in that the seamstress could go into the chemistry involved in cleaning various fabrics. The geography teacher asked if we couldn't also talk about the countries from which various fabrics were obtained. The business teacher became excited about this interview because he felt it offered him the opportunity to discuss self-employment versus employment with a firm.

Another person we decided to interview was the store manager! His job involved many skills dealing with various subject areas. For language arts, we would deal with advertising and other types of oral and written communication such as letters, memos, etc. In the mathematics class, the students could study the financial aspects of his job, such as credit, overhead, profit, and bookkeeping. He would also deal with mathematics when he makes up work schedules for his employees. The art teacher would use him as a resource person for interior decorating and the planning which is involved in making a clothing store attractive as well as functional. Other aspects of store management were also going to be explored such as employee-employer relations and customer relations.

After having decided upon the resource people we wanted to use, we discussed the feasibility of making a visit to a store and having the children actually spend a day working at various jobs dealing with the clothing business. I volunteered to call a local clothing store. Frankly, I was amazed by the cooperation I received. Not only was the owner willing to cooperate but he offered to buy lunch for the teachers and the kids.

We made our visit to the store the following week. Each student spent the day working with different employees of the store. The experience was rewarding for everyone.

After our trip and the interviews with a seamstress, buyer, manager, and clerk, we felt we were ready to operate our own store! Every department cooperated in the effort. The industrial arts students made furnishings, the clothing students designed and constructed clothes to be sold, the art pupils made posters and other interior decorations. The cost of constructing the merchandise was figured and then prices were set. The students organized the store and put it into operation. Students actually purchased the merchandise. All sales were final.

For the first time, we were a community—not just departments housed in the same building. Teachers were cooperating with teachers as well as with students. Everyone was enthusiastic. Students, teachers, administrators, business people in the community, and parents were involved and became active participants in the learning process.

38

How Much Career
Education in Science?*

THE San Diego program planning committee included a major
session to discuss the role of science teachers in career education. W. Earl Sams, consultant in secondary education, State of
California Department of Education, as chairman of the session, prepared the tentative definition of career education included here. Other
program participants were Paul Van Eikeren, Harvey Mudd College,
Claremont, California; Phyllis Dietz, Fountain Valley High School,
Huntington Beach, California; Ruth Bolton, Covina Valley Unified District, California; Nestor T. Wyatt, Birmingham High School, Van Nuys,
California; Rex Fortune, State Department of Education, California;
and Lynne English, State Department of Education, California, who
provided a statement on work styles for the panel discussion.

Following is a composite of the ideas presented and the discussion
at the San Diego session.

The career education concept, in contrast to traditional vocational education, presents a real challenge to all teachers at a time
when public education is under serious indictment for failure to establish and maintain a viable and purposeful level of interest for students
of all types. It is essential that we understand that career education is
not an edict to return to the old "applied science or cookbook course."

*Reprinted by permission from *The Science Teacher*, April 1973, pp. 28-30.

Many science teachers have long been aware that probing the career interests of their students can produce results stimulating for students and teachers alike. Also, most parents need help with their children's educational plans. Consequently a prime factor in educational planning is the goal, life style, standard of living, or tentative career objective of the children and youth.

Career education can be thought of as an instructional goal which is appropriate for all subject-matter areas. Basic career education goals include career awareness, self-awareness, attitude development, educational awareness, economic awareness, consumer competencies, career planning and decision making, skill development, career orientation, career exploration, and career preparation. Each unit of instruction in biology, chemistry, physics, and other subjects should include learning activities that direct youngsters toward one or more of these basic goals. Obviously, some goals are more appropriate for science instruction than are others. For example, science teachers can promote career awareness, career exploration, career orientation, and career preparation in scientific fields. In addition, there may be special science projects designed to help youngsters become aware of their own interests and capabilities in science activities. Such projects could also be designed to develop positive attitudes toward occupations in the various fields of science. While the major purpose of science instruction is to help students discover knowledge and learn the processes by which knowledge can be discovered, an additional purpose would be to understand how scientists use these capabilities in the world of work. The use of field excursions, exploratory and work experiences, classroom visitations by accomplished scientists, printed materials and other media can help students to achieve the goals of career education.

A successful program of instruction that includes career education will also require greater cooperation among the business, labor, and industrial communities to facilitate the provision of meaningful field exercises, work experience, and job placement in the fields of science. Some examples of this kind of cooperation exist now in scattered communities. Some school districts in California, for example, have implemented environmental study programs in connection with landscaping improvement projects of the local and municipal government. Other districts have developed health cooperation programs that involve work experience (and potential employment) in local hospitals. Other possibilities may include cooperation among school districts, universities, laboratories, and other private or public science-related facilities.

Career education is partly, then, a problem of relating a conceptual science to the working conditions of a career. It must provide a set of experiences that allows the student to transfer the knowledge and methodology of a conceptual science to a set of real problems of the kind found in a typical work experience. For example,

• We must be supportive of the student's academic interest and his attempts to find a career.

• Courses must be developed that include out-of-school experiences, in such places as clinic labs or hospitals.

• Efforts should be made to obtain summer employment for students in the areas of their career interest.

• Career programs involving speakers from industry, business, and professions, as well as films, slides, written materials, etc., should be a regular part of the career education program.

We can solicit real problems from local industry or public service and establish interdisciplinary groups of faculty and students to attempt solutions. Most of the decision-making responsibility can be placed on the students, with the faculty acting as advisers. Costs could be shared by the school and industry or public service.

Some direct career experience in science may be limited by legal restrictions, such as the Federal Hazardous Occupation Laws which apply to all industry involved in interstate commerce and which prohibit any minor under 18 from working in or around areas where chemicals are manufactured and used. However, our best chance of helping a student meet entry-level requirements lies in giving him a course with a maximum of varied laboratory experiences—weighing, titrating, filtering—including stress on accurate record keeping and necessary calculations. We can also help students achieve the general mental abilities that employers seek. One such list, compiled by Jack Davison of Ceres High School, includes the ability to

• Reason
• Recognize a problem
• Organize information
• Formulate a plan of action
• Proceed in a process of study
• Make decisions

In our haste to include career education in the school systems' curricular programs, let us not forget the importance of the avocation among the satisfactions of living, particularly as the leisure orientation of our society increases. What student isn't aware of this issue, indirectly, every time vacation rolls around?

In designing avocational interests into our total career education program, we may save some future adults from the sad dichotomy so prevalent today—the drudgery of *work* so that one can *live* on the weekends.

Career counselors can make use of the individual extracurricular interests of students as well as their subject area "majors" in directing them vocationally. Furthermore, by securing the participation of nonprofessionals they can orient students toward a concern for their "whole" life and not just 40 hours out of each week. For many of our developing adults, a career can come to mean doing something they would do anyway, with or without pay. What sounds idealistic today may be a technological reality tomorrow.

While the cluster concept suggested by the U.S. Office of Education[1] is a valuable direction in our new career education programs and is also a compromise between the goal-directedness and open-endedness that co-exist in the typical student, there is need for another key concept, namely "work-style." Like its cousin term "life-style," it focuses on the psychological aspects of its subject. In other words, it by-passes formal groupings—what we are calling clusters—for an emphasis on the actual mental, emotional, and physical atmosphere in which a particular job exists.

As a part of the total information-gathering process now being initiated throughout the schools, the "work-style" of each profession and occupation could be charted in relationship to its cluster. Thus, for the Marine Science cluster we might have:

CLUSTER	WORK-STYLE				
	Authoritative	Democratic	Independent	Managerial	Creative
Marine Science	Laboratory technician	Research group member	Diver	Project manager	Free-lance writer

Inherent in this more personal approach to career education is the assistance of the school's counseling staff. Through testing and individual sessions with counselors, participants can be aided in the designation of one or more work-styles with which they might be comfortable. The challenge lies in developing work-style categories and in considering the individual's reactions in experiences with a variety of occupational styles.

Ideally this type of chart might be an excellent counseling aid, if carefully developed. One might also prepare a series of correlational charts, each balancing a different type of work-style (mental, political, physical, emotional, etc.) with job clusters.

In planning work-experience programs, we should not underestimate the *educability* (as contrasted with the *trainability*) of a student—or over-estimate the technical difficulties of most entry-level occupations—when selecting those elements to be incorporated into the school system's program.

We should favor those experiential offerings that are more expansive and generalized, so that a student may be exposed to many different facets of a chosen career cluster or clusters. The assistance of the relevant employers is invaluable here, and a program design centered around their recommendations will be more certain to explore the range of possibilities in their occupational fields.

All participating students should be given the opportunity to explore different levels of difficulty in the clusters for which they have indicated an interest. We cannot afford to be dogmatic about the level of a student's educational motivation. Perhaps an introductory office position with a research council in the community might expose the participant to keypunching, and hence to computer programming, data processing, techniques of research design, and so on. Haven't many of today's workers chosen their present occupation through such a chance set of circumstances? A brief exposure during high school, even purely observational, to a position requiring a graduate degree may be reflected in a student's behavior years after he or she has graduated and entered the world of careers.

If we remain open-minded about the potential and direction of the students we are serving (even when they themselves might have already made up their minds, or think they have), and if we use to best advantage the diversity of resources of our communities, systems of higher education, government, and so on, we will be creating a superior career education program in our schools.

Note

1. See "Office of Education Plans for a Marketable Skill for Every Student." *The Science Teacher* 39 (December 1972): 23-24.

39
An Instructional
System for Children
in Elementary School*

Gerald DiMinico

In efforts to develop a program of career exploration for elementary school children, the Ellensburg (Washington) public schools are testing an instructional system designed to present occupational information to children in Grades 4 through 6. Its major purpose is to provide children at this early age with accurate information about the world of work that will help them in the future when they are required to make tentative educational and vocational decisions.

It is fully agreed that children at this age are not ready to make a definite vocational choice. The instructional system described here is based on the premise that young children should however be provided with some orientation to the meaning of work and its importance to them and to society.

The elementary years should be an exploratory period in which the world of work is presented to children in a manner that is realistic and appropriate to their stage of development. Specifically, objectives at this level should be to let children know about the multitude of occupational opportunities, help them develop a realistic view of the world of work and their own abilities and limitations, provide them with basic information about the major occupational fields, and point

*Reprinted by permission from *American Vocational Journal*, December 1969, pp. 22-23.

out that there is dignity in work and that every worker performs a useful function.

An instructional system is a sequence of individualized learning experiences. Essentially, it is programed instruction which uses a multimedia approach to present content based on precisely defined performance criteria.

Because the system allows each pupil to work at his own pace, the components are typically self-instructional devices and individual teaching techniques. Tutorial sessions, discussions, single-concept films, and programed materials are examples of the components.

Job Families

The instructional content of the system being tried at Ellensburg is divided into five major categories or job families, namely: White Collar, Manual, Service, Farm, and Armed Forces. The descriptive term *job families* is used for purposes of appeal and clarity. Because of the variety and complexity of tasks in two of the major job families, they are broken down into sub-units. The content of the entire instructional system is shown in Figure 39.1.

Figure 39.1: Content of Instructional System

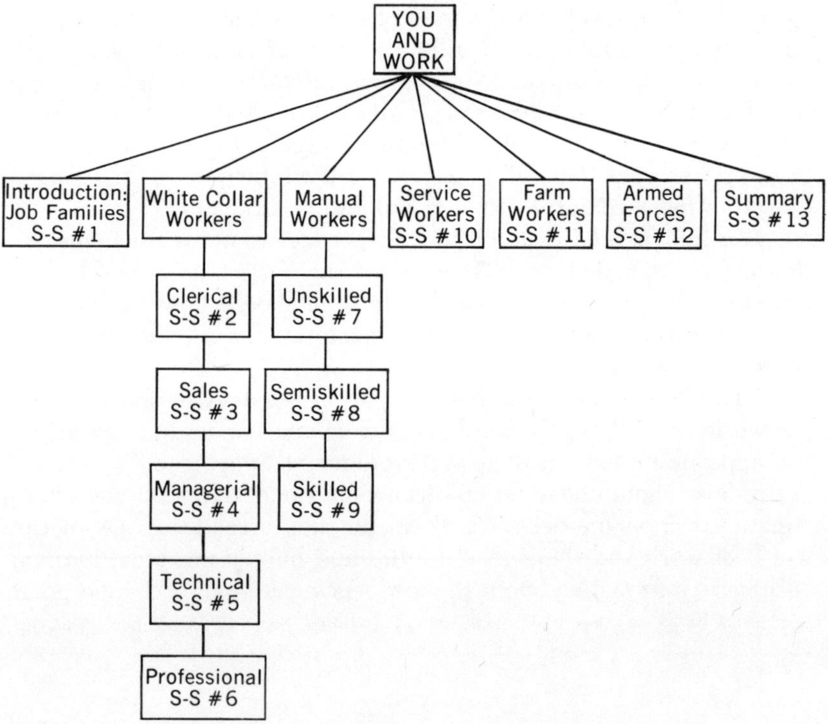

The instructional content was derived primarily from two basic sources: *The Encyclopedia of Careers* and *Occupational Guides.* The information on each occupation covers such aspects as the nature of the work, conditions of work, qualifications and education required, employment outlook, possible earnings, and chance for advancement.

Each of the 13 subsystems is a sound-slide presentation designed as a self-instructional device. The pupil works at his own pace and is individually responsible for learning at each stage of the system.

How Presented

A carousel-type slide projector, synchronized audio tapes, and a small screen are used as equipment. The basic modes of presentation are 35-mm slide sequences, synchronized sound, printed visuals and drawings, and self-testing and feedback devices.

The audiotaped presentations are designed to support information presented visually on the screen. The tapes describe the actual work being done and transmit information on such topics as the importance of the occupation to society, equipment or establishments used or serviced by the workers, beginning salary and possible range of earnings, working conditions, duties, training or education required for entrance, advancement opportunities, personal qualities needed for success in the occupation, and employment outlook.

The colored slides, all cartoon characterizations, depict the worker in his environment. Each slide focuses on the worker performing typical tasks of his occupation. Thus a skilled manual worker is shown repairing an airplane. A clerical worker may be shown typing a letter or operating a calculator.

Six hundred cartoon drawings were developed for the 13 subsystems.

Feedback Device

Self-testing and feedback devices are used frequently throughout the system. Three or four opportunities for pupils to respond are built into each subsystem. At these intervals, the pupil stops the tape recorder and answers several multiple-choice questions on an answer sheet. After he has put his answers down, he pushes the start button on the tape recorder and receives the correct answer. Thus he is given immediate feedback and additional information.

Upon completion of the subsystem, the learner is given a self-check sheet. The teacher analyzes his answers to determine if he should continue to the next subsystem. The limits prescribed for each subsystem are that the learner will score 90 percent on the performances stated in the behavioral objectives.

The effectiveness of the total instructional system is measured by parallel pre-test and post-test forms taken by each student. These tests are constructed to measure student performance described by the behavioral objectives for the total system. Evaluation of the system is based on whether or not observed responses of the learners meet the criteria established in the original objectives.

Behavioral Objectives

A major step in the design of an instructional system is to select and state behavioral objectives. Objectives are stated in terms of the behavior which the learner will acquire. Unless the objectives can be so defined, there will be no system.

Some of the behavioral objectives for the section dealing with manual workers in the experimental instructional system are stated as follows: Upon completion of this section, the student will be able to—

1. Define the term *manual work* as work done with the hands.
2. Define the term *skill* as knowledge and ability.
3. Classify the various degrees of skill required for unskilled, semiskilled, and skilled manual work.
4. Identify the operations performed by unskilled, semiskilled, and skilled manual workers.
5. State that learning a special vocational skill in secondary school can lead to a better job as a manual worker.
6. Classify each type of manual worker's employment outlook, i.e., unskilled (decrease in jobs); semi-skilled (slow increase in jobs); and skilled (great increase in jobs).
7. Order the earnings for each manual classification.

As they progress through the section, students begin to see fine distinctions among the three classifications of manual workers. At no time, however, is the role of any worker presented in a derogatory manner. Even the child who identifies with an unskilled manual worker can perceive this worker as serving a useful purpose in society. After all, not every child can aspire to becoming a brain surgeon.

Off-Focus

Vocational educators have long maintained that the overemphasis on college preparatory curricula in the public schools is unrealistic. Their contention is substantiated by statistics showing that only 20 percent of American youth complete a college degree. Moreover, of the 74 million people employed in the United States, only 23 percent are professional, technical, and kindred workers. The rest are blue collar workers, clerical and sales personnel, service personnel, and farm workers.

Thus, although 77 percent of the jobs are other than professional, technical and managerial, our public school system has focused on encouraging young people to aspire to professional and kindred positions. The ultimate result is that two out of three young persons who terminate their education early face a long period of job hunting and job jumping. It should be obvious by now that it has become mandatory for the public schools to provide students with a systematic series of experiences in which vocational and academic education complement each other.

The instructional system described here can be regarded as one technique in a grade-by-grade, developmental program which will acquaint children with the work aspect of life and increase their understanding of their own abilities and limitations.

Added Purpose

Later sequences in the program might take the form of curricular activities that relate career information to academic subjects. Course content in music, art, mathematics, English, social studies, science, etc., might include information about job opportunities at different levels in the employment fields related to these academic studies.

Non-college bound students could thus be made to see that their school subjects serve a useful purpose, that they teach important skills which might be employed in the future. If shown a meaningful purpose for their academic studies, more students would be encouraged to remain in school.

If we accept the premise that occupational information should be (and easily could be) integrated into the curriculum, the question then becomes, when should it be introduced? In my opinion, it should be done at the earliest possible opportunity. It should begin in the first grade.

40

Reading Development Through Career Education*

Richard T. Vacca

areer education and reading are strange bedfellows. Reading instruction is solidly entrenched in traditional educational thinking. Yet, some say reading is out-dated, a cool medium in modern and future curriculum approaches. On the other hand, the present is ripe for career education; its future, bright. There is a noticeable swelling of political and educational sentiment in our midst which points to the dynamic role of career education in marshalling educational reform. It is evident that present curriculum strategies generally have not succeeded in preparing young people for rewarding and productive lives.

Signs for change in our educational structure are everywhere. Clearly, career education can provide the impetus for the development of more appropriate curriculums to serve the needs and desires of students. Its essential mission is an embracing one: "The main thrust of career education is to prepare all students for a successful life of work by increasing their options for occupational choice, by eliminating barriers—real and imagined—to obtaining job skills and by enhancing learning achievements in all subjects and at all levels of education (*Career Education*, 1971, p. 2)." Reading instruction doubtlessly will play an integral part in realizing these goals.

*Reprinted by permission from the author.

Reading's role in career education, however, must be mainly functional once children have acquired basic reading skills for learning. As career education specialists attempt to develop competent practitioners and independent learners of various careers, they must assume the responsibility for guiding students not only in *what* to learn, but also in *how* to learn it successfully. To the extent that reading serves as an essential tool in this process, career education programs can provide natural contexts for students to develop reading skills as needed—functionally—in the pursuit of occupational choices.

Direct vs. Functional Reading Instruction

Teachers and administrators, especially in secondary school settings, probably have turned a corner in their perceptions of reading as a "subject" fit only for the elementary grades. There is a growing realization that students not only learn and refine skills *directly,* but need also be shown how to apply reading skills demanded by various content subjects. Visualize, if you will, a cone-shaped spiral representative of direct instruction in basic reading skills. Early (1964) suggested that at the base of this cone in the elementary grades, "the spiral is tight, to represent heavy emphasis (p. 25)." As direct reading instruction continues through the grades, it gradually tapers off as it spirals upward into high school and post secondary levels. Complete this mental picture by overlaying the cone-shaped spiral with another one, "one that begins narrowly in the primary grades and becomes broader as it reaches the upper grades (Early, 1964, p. 25)." This spiral represents the functional aspects of reading instruction where emphasis is on the application and adaptation of basic skills needed to learn content from a variety of sources and reading situations.

Operationally, then, direct instruction centers around a set of basic reading skills, arranged in a logical sequence and taught in a prescribed manner. Reading material is selected for its value in teaching the skills and providing practice once they are taught. The *New Rochester Occupational Reading Series: The Job Ahead* (SRA, 1963) is an example of a program that proposes to develop basic skills directly through career-centered reading materials.

A functional reading approach, on the other hand, allows a classroom teacher to guide those reading skills required to learn his subject matter. A functional emphasis, therefore, shows students how to apply basic reading skills that are actually needed to read a particular subject-oriented selection. Skills are not taught for the sake of teaching skills; nor are reading skills practiced in isolated drill. Instead, a teacher begins to equip students to become independent learners of his subject by combining the teaching of content with guidance in the skill processes needed to learn that content.

The Teacher's Responsibility

If reading instruction is to be incorporated into career education programs, a conscious effort must be made to develop its direct and functional components as students progress from stages of career awareness (grades K-7) into various facets of career exploration (middle school grades and beyond). During the career awareness years of a child's educational experience, direct reading instruction should be stressed as it is currently under present curriculum strategies. This means a systematic approach to the development of word recognition skills, basic comprehension, locational skills and flexibility in reading where rate is adjusted to student purposes for reading. Whenever appropriate, reading materials should reflect the career interests and aspirations of children. Career education programs have the potential to infuse real-life situations into the direct reading instructional program. Children have the opportunity to develop reading power on materials that make sense; that unlock the world of work and create awareness and interest in the occupational possibilities that lie ahead.

As pupils move out of the awareness stage and into career exploration, a teacher's responsibilities should shift accordingly. He should be prepared to "sneak" reading instruction into regular occupational settings and situations. If reading skills become an integral aspect of job success in certain career areas, a teacher must be trained to show students how to apply basic skills to job-related materials. Functional reading training, however, need not be solely task-oriented. Students preparing for professional careers must be shown how to read a variety of content-specific material in an efficient and effective manner. Classroom teachers can enhance learning by fusing the teaching of content with the teaching of skills related to learning that content. Where reading skills are not particularly needed to function successfully in a career, a teacher probably would not incorporate reading skill training into his regular instructional routines.

In conclusion, it is suggested that the reading development of young people will be facilitated through career education programs. Reading growth can be attained through direct and functional reading strategies. During early educational experiences, direct reading instruction should go hand-in-hand with career awareness activities. By teaching reading skills directly in a career-oriented atmosphere, educators will have the opportunity to capitalize on children's real-life interests and aspirations.

Moreover, a functional emphasis on reading instruction in the upper grade levels will extend the reading development of students who view reading as a necessary tool for occupational success. Such an emphasis makes reading instruction a valuable process-centered activity to students who view reading as useful—a means to an end, not an end in itself.

When appropriate, students in the secondary and post-secondary levels of education will find it necessary to refine reading skills in direct instructional settings, i.e. rate of reading training. But they will do so knowing that such instruction will lead to greater satisfaction and productivity—both personally and professionally. Career education, after all, is a life-long process, as is growth in reading. Strange bedfellows indeed!

Bibliography

Career Education, U.S. Department of Health, Education and Welfare, DHEW Publication #(OE) 73-00501, 1971.

Early, M. J. "The Meaning of Reading Instruction in Secondary Schools," *Journal of Reading*, October, 1964, 25-30.

41

Seattle's Concentration on Careers*

Vivian Hedrich

"But, *my* son is going to college!"

T he attractive young mother of a Seattle second-grader
showed more than a trace of irritation as she watched her son
Jimmy deftly handling a pipe wrench during a project demonstration at a school open house. She appeared even less impressed
when told that all children in the class, girls included, would be encouraged to try many of the common tools of the construction trades
as part of an occupational education pilot project. To her, the experience was just "not relevant" for her college-bound child.

"Parents often find it difficult to break away from the career
stereotypes they grew up with," says Tom Hodgson, intense young director of Seattle's Occupational Task Force. "And they are not the
only offenders. From the very beginning our American educational
system has regarded the child who doesn't go on to college—although
he is in the majority—as having to take second best. Just the slightest
inflection in a teacher's voice can clearly tell a child, 'You wouldn't
want to do *that* for a living.' Many teachers will have to be reeducated
out of their professional prejudices so that the children they deal with
can freely explore and find what is right for them. If Jimmy goes on to
college a decade from now—as he very likely will—he will be all the
better prepared for having this experience."

*Reprinted by permission from *American Education*, July 1971, pp. 12-15.

The Seattle Public Schools system has developed a prototype career education program that offers occupational information to students at all grade levels, from kindergarten through high school, and integrates career materials into every subject of the curriculum.

In 1965, when this approach was launched, 100 students were enrolled in assembly mechanics training classes. Since that time the number of career course offerings has grown rapidly. So has the enrollment. Of the students graduating this year, at least 40 percent will have experienced a program in career education.

"While most educators recognize that offering specialized training courses only at the senior high level is doing only half the job at best," Hodgson says, "trying to extend the scope of career education has been a long uphill battle. Now at last, however, we are beginning to understand that children cannot make intelligent career choices unless they have a chance to sift through occupations and try them out long before they reach high school. Without this opportunity they simply miss the boat."

The pilot program classes in the early grades are designed to acquaint the younger children with various kinds of workers and the roles they play in the life of the community. Classes at the elementary level promote this awareness and prepare the pupil for the higher manual skills expected of him at the junior high school level. By the time the student reaches senior high school he is ready for more specific occupational preparation in industrial arts, business education, and other areas.

Hodgson describes the task force effort as building a lattice (rather than a ladder) of career choices. The concept is to assure that no student will be so narrowly prepared for a single specialized task that he is locked into it. Instead, he should be capable—with a little further training—of branching into a number of related fields. Certainly for the 60 percent who do not continue their formal education beyond high school, aptitude in a cluster of occupational areas is essential. Too often traditional jobs are here today and gone tomorrow.

The Seattle educator defines a good career education program as one that develops and expands student concepts of work and allows them to analyze fully their individual interests and aptitudes. It is equally important, he feels, that a student's skills be continually maintained and reenforced as he progresses through school toward eventual employment, so that he is not allowed to lose ground through careless hit-or-miss scheduling.

"At one time not long ago, despite surveys showing that more than 70 percent of all high school students wanted vocational education classes, large numbers of students were forced to choose academic subjects instead because of the limited number of elective hours available," Hodgson says. "We sidestep this problem by including much of the occupational information in established subjects, rather than tacking it on to an already crowded curriculum."

This approach makes sense to students. For many it is the first time they can see practical application for their day-to-day classwork. Girls begin to consider the retailing possibilities for the items they make in sewing classes. Boys begin to understand that a good deal of mathematics is required to sell cars or houses. And the realization comes at a time when their interests are fluid and can be tested in various trades or occupations without the students being brainwashed by their elders or being obliged to make a final commitment to a career choice.

Returning to our second-grade "carpenter," we find he has the good fortune to be enrolled in Ethel Chisholm's classroom at E. C. Hughes Elementary School, one of the pilot schools in the program. The room—an old portable structure—is not much to look at from the outside, but the interior presents an attractive picture and buzzes with activity.

This morning a group of children is involved in baking corn bread in a small oven—a project that, surprisingly, is a lesson in mathematics. The pupils have just concluded the exacting task of measuring ingredients. On the previous day the father of one of the pupils, a grain inspector for a large flour plant, had introduced the study with a report on dry corn and how it is ground into meal. That introduction plus a study of supermarket ads from a local newspaper—to determine the cost of corn bread ingredients—resulted in a lively discussion of comparative prices.

Located in various parts of the room are a number of activity centers, each keyed to learning about different tools and crafts. One is a "clock shop," where each pupil receives a box containing a second-hand clock, a screw driver, and pliers. Periodically the children enjoy taking their clocks apart and, to the teacher's surprise, several have even been able to get them back together and ticking again.

A nearby sewing center contains large department-store pattern books, dogeared from use by fashion-conscious young ladies but still helpful in promoting the study of fractions required to determine the amount of material to buy. There is also a typing center and even a "bank," established after a visit to a local savings institution, where children heard talks on various careers ranging from bank president to custodian.

"Career oriented education has its ups and downs," Mrs. Chisholm admits. "At first not all the mothers were in favor of so much time spent on the program. By degrees they have been won over by our most enthusiastic ambassadors—their own sons and daughters."

As the children move on through the elementary grades their experiences include visits from community workers, selected field trips, and opportunities to work with tools on crafts projects.

Smorgasbord of Courses

When students enter Denny Junior High School the training becomes more specific. They choose from a smorgasbord of more than 30 mini-courses offered during the first period of the day. Students may set up retail outlets to sell ballpoint pens and notebooks at cost, making out their own sales records and orders. Girls collect unusual recipes and produce an attractive cookbook for sale at a school carnival. Music ensembles find themselves "booked" for paid performances at local gatherings. Through such projects the students learn the importance of teamwork and the ability to deal with the general public. Problems of student motivation familiar to every teacher at this level are countered by programs that stress the adult values of receiving pay for services rendered.

"By the time a young person reaches junior high school he has begun to refine his interests," Hodgson says. "Certain areas begin to seem more attractive than others, and job aptitudes appear closer to the surface where they can be more easily measured and evaluated—thus opening the door to occupational counseling."

At the senior high school level, the program staff maintains a close working relationship with local business, industry, and labor. New courses of study are developed only at the request of these groups and with their help, thus assuring that the training offered fits local needs and paves the way to entry-level jobs.

A recent example is a new course entitled "Marine Engine Maintenance and Repair," offered at two Seattle high schools. The idea for the course emerged from a survey of more than 300 boat dealers in the area which revealed a critical shortage of trained repair personnel. Funds were provided by a non-profit organization, Northwest Marine Industries, to send two teachers to a special summer training program. The association also purchased 12 outboard engines of sizes varying from three to 100 horsepower and loaned them to the schools for student practice. Last spring several local dealers agreed to cooperate in an on-the-job training program in which students received both pay and official school credit for the experience. A job referral service is being operated this summer.

Another successful new project involves the world's largest industry—construction. About 35 students are busy building two modular design summer homes from the ground up, with the guidance of volunteer craftsmen from the construction industry. On completion, the homes will be sold at auction, with proceeds going into a fund to expand opportunities of this kind for more students next year.

At Rainier Beach High School, instructor Roger Hubbard looks back on an adventurous year with his young crew—a year in which both teacher and students admit they learned a lot.

"We started out last fall maintaining strict teacher-student roles," he recalls. "However, I soon realized how much more effective the employer-employee relationship would be—making each student clearly responsible for putting in 'an hour's work for an hour's pay.' My observations suggested that, while students may know very well what to do in a given situation, most lack an essential understanding of how to go about it. The boys had to learn how to work by working. During the early weeks especially, I often had to move in and take over a paint roller or hammer for a while to show them exactly what was expected. I have sweated on this job and so have they."

The year has been far from "all work and no play," however. Plenty of lighter moments have sped the homebuilding along. Before they were far into the project, Hubbard inaugurated the Royal Feather Award for "outstanding achievement on the job." The prize, a colorful tail-feather acquired in a pheasant hunting expedition, is attached with a piece of masking tape to the worker's hardhat in solemn ceremony. The winner proudly wears the conspicuous decoration throughout the day's two-hour work period.

Working as a Team

Most often the boy who merits the Royal Feather is one who demonstrates planning ability and who works out a successful approach to a problem on his own. This spring, the award was given to a relatively slow learner who took the lead in organizing a timesaving project.

Not all of the students who began the year were still on hand at its successful conclusion. Some attrition has been due to class scheduling conflicts. In a few cases boys have been removed because of lack of ability to work with others.

"A sense of teamwork is absolutely essential in this kind of program," Hubbard says. "I had one very able boy who just could not reconcile himself to doing the menial but necessary jobs that were assigned. He didn't see any reason why he should become a reliable sweeper before he was given greater responsibility. But others are quick to spot someone who doesn't carry his fair share of the load, and resulting bad feeling can quickly jeopardize an entire project."

All the young workers reflect genuine satisfaction in watching "their house" develop day by day. Frequently they bring parents by for a look after school, and on one occasion, when the teacher made a weekend security check of tools and equipment, he found a student busily hammering away on the roof.

"The boy explained there had not been time to finish the job during the regular period on Friday and he wanted to get it done," Hubbard says. "That's what I call relevant occupational education."

To make sure that the training offered remains attuned to the rapidly changing job market, the Seattle Public Schools is currently establishing an information access system designed to provide computerized data that will tell students at all grade levels about new fields that are opening up and about the shifting currents in established jobs. The new system will utilize the services of the district's modern computer to feed information directly to terminal hookups in school buildings.

One area in which employment opportunities are consistently high is that of food preparation and service. The number of new careers in the food industry has expanded steadily during the last decade, and openings for trained personnel in traditional food service occupations far exceed the number of graduates qualified to fill them.

Seattle, along with a number of other school districts, is helping to prepare students for these jobs through sponsorship of FEAST (Foods Education And Service Training) programs in six of its 12 high schools. The programs' instructors, all experienced in the jobs for which they are training students, expertly relate regular school subject matter in mathematics, English, science, and art to the family of food service skills.

A recent English assignment at Seattle's Roosevelt High School required students to "prepare a menu for a restaurant that you would like to manage, making it colorful, attractive, appropriate to the establishment, and the prices right." Several of the most successful efforts were displayed in a front hall showcase of the school.

Student-made FEAST uniforms—bright gold Nehru-style jackets for the boys and attractive matching dresses for the girls—contributed to an esprit de corps. Each student in the program had one opportunity during the year to serve as catering manager for a school function, with grades based on how smoothly the job was planned and carried out. Recently, FEAST students prepared and served a dinner for 178 guests at a PTA Founders' Day observance.

Graduates of the program are encouraged to continue their education at a junior college or university specializing in food service courses. Those who show promise in advanced training may choose from many highly paid management positions.

At a recent presentation of certificates for completion of the two-year course, an attending parent of one of the graduates observed: "We are living in a changing world. I heard that here at Roosevelt, almost a third of the senior students do not graduate. They just drop out. My daughter Judy has been so involved in the FEAST program that she has not only finished but plans to go on to college. She's the first of our five children to go this far."

An on-the-fence parent offered this appraisal: "I may not be the best person to comment, because I'm still undecided about the idea of taking kids away from their books when there is so much to learn. But I will say this—I have a happy boy at home. He doesn't miss a day at school. If this opportunity did nothing but give him time to mature and keep him from losing his identity in a school of several thousand students, it will have been well worthwhile. Now he has something to build on for the future."

42

Career Education
Concept Filters Down*

Darryl Laramore

F ew declarations have had as much national impact as Commissioner Marland's speeches to the educational community on career education. The repercussions are beginning to be felt at local levels.

Although the concept that career awareness is possible at an early age has been around for some time, Commissioner Marland's pronouncements have given it new currency. State departments of education were quick to pick up the U.S. Office of Education's stress on changing the goals of general education, and in many states, this ready acceptance at the top filtered down to county offices and eventually to school district levels.

In California, the Sonoma County Office of Education early in 1971 embarked on an effort to incorporate career education concepts into the county's educational programs. Since Alameda County was considering similar steps, school officials in the two counties decided to run a combined project.

The goal of the first phase of the project was to train a cadre of teachers in six schools—an elementary, junior high, and secondary school in each county. The training would utilize existing staff and

*Reprinted by permission from *American Vocational Journal*, September 1972, pp. 45-47 & 48.

community resources to develop curriculum experiences in career education and incorporate these activities into all subject matter at each level.

An innovative aspect was the employment of paraprofessionals as career education specialists. Their job would be to help teams of teachers at each level generate ideas on methods of implementing career education concepts.

To train its teachers, the project planned a series of Inservice Days (a total of seven were conducted during the 1971-72 school year). On these occasions, teachers in a school get together as a team to develop career education experiences for their classrooms. The school's administrator and counselor must be part of the team as well as the career education specialist. Team members learn to draw on one another's creativity in developing their own curriculum packages.

(Figure 1 shows an example of the form used in planning the activity or package.)

Figure 42.1. Career Experience Evaluation Form

Teacher's Name . . . . ·
School . . . . ·
Grade Level and/or Subject Matter Area . . . . ·

1. Preparation required (Steps and/or discussions leading into experience)
2. Objectives to be met
3. Describe the experience
4. Resource people utilized
5. What curriculum areas were incorporated into the experience, and how
6. Evaluation in terms of students' enthusiasm, success, or failure (What percent of students met objectives)
7. What concept or concepts were incorporated into the experience

Activities at the elementary level must integrate with several curriculum areas. At the junior and senior high levels, they must be incorporated into the specific subject matter the teacher is teaching.

Thirteen Concepts

Each activity must include one of the 13 concepts developed by a career guidance task force in the California State Department of Education Pupil Services Division.

After the activity has been demonstrated in the classroom, the career education specialist writes up the experience on a form similar to the one used in planning the activity. This form, which includes pre-activities, terminal objectives, evaluation, and follow-up, has been found most useful to the teachers in their planning.

During the classroom demonstration, the career education specialist takes photos for a series of slides and later duplicates the slides. The slides and the written materials are made available to teachers in other schools.

Each school, however, develops its own program. The underlying philosophy is that involvement of teachers in the development of innovative practices assures implementation of these practices in the classroom. Thus the packages are not made available for classroom use, but as stimuli for other teachers in creating their own packages.

The teachers involved in the project during the 1971-72 school year are expected to be used as consultants in other schools in the county this year. The overall plan is to escalate the training each year until all interested teachers in the county have been oriented to methods of implementing career education concepts in the curriculum.

The project stresses the use of leisure time activities as part of career awareness. The reasoning behind this input is, first, that it is unrealistic to suppose that everyone in the future will have rewarding jobs and, secondly, that leisure time pursuits can compensate for careers that are not a source of lifetime satisfaction. Thus leisure time activities are included as career education concepts in the classroom at all levels.

The first step in the implementation of the project goals was to select the paraprofessionals who would serve as career education specialists in each of the six schools in the two counties. They were chosen on the basis of their potential ability to contribute ideas on ways in which career education concepts can be incorporated into subject matter at different grade levels, to help teachers locate resource people in their communities, to take small teams of students to locations offering relevant information, to use cameras and tape recorders and to train students to use these tools, and to explain various aspects of career education to community groups.

Enthusiasm Important

Those who were chosen had had junior college training in most cases. They were bright, articulate, and had had a variety of job experiences. They all were in the process of making career decisions themselves.

Most importantly, they were enthusiastic about the program, they were quick to understand career education concepts, and were easily trained by the director two days prior to their job placement. On-the-job training continued throughout the year.

The following are some examples of the career awareness activities that resulted from the teamwork of teachers and career education specialists working with resource persons in the community.

At one elementary school where the fourth grade class showed an unmistakable interest in pets, the teacher and career education specialist planned a series of activities around that class characteristic. Each student was given a slide camera and asked to take four pictures of his pet (another's pet could be substituted). The slides were developed and viewed in the classroom.

Exploring a Pet Store

Building on this activity, the teacher and career education specialist planned related experiences. On one day the specialist took an investigative team of five students to a pet store where they interviewed employees, took pictures of the different tasks being performed, and recorded this information on slides and tape. Back in the classroom, the team tape-recorded another session in which they discussed what they had learned in the pet store. All of this material was presented to the entire class, and during the rest of the week, spelling, reading, math, and social studies were related to the pet shop experience.

This process was repeated for a second team that toured a pet food factory and a third that visited a veterinarian's office, where the children saw surgery performed on an animal. During the fourth week a horse trainer came into the classroom to describe his job, after which an investigative team visited his ranch. A fifth team made a fact-finding trip to the Society for Prevention of Cruelty to Animals.

After the fifth trip, the career aspects of the investigations were brought into focus as the class discussed the kinds of people employed in animal care, the interrelationships between the different occupations, and the kinds of satisfaction that employees in these occupations might experience.

Interest was high and the children seemed to approach their subject matter with greater enthusiasm as a result of their excursions into the animal care world. As a logical sequel, the next series of experiences planned for this fourth grade class dealt with the care of people.

A Lesson in Banking

At the junior high level, a math teacher and an English teacher collaborated with the career education specialist to design a program which began with a discussion of occupations in the banking industry.

Activities included a visit from a local bank manager and a trip to his bank to take pictures and interview employees. For two weeks, the class studied the kinds of math problems prevalent in the banking industry.

As an experience related to banking, the class decided to buy a car, utilizing a loan received through the bank. A car dealer was invited to the classroom to explain his job and the kinds of problems involved in the car sale business.

An investigative team went to the car lot, looked over the cars and wrote out a contract for a loan. A second team of students who had not yet visited the bank were dispatched to seek the loan. Math problems in the classroom centered on these two activities.

Finally a car was purchased and a contract written, giving students some understanding of the kinds of problems involved in buying a car (bluebook cost, interest rate, monthly payments, etc.).

In their English class, the students wrote a play based on what they had learned about the banking and auto sales industries. They used sound effects and music, made costumes, organized a film crew and sound crew, and took photos of these activities for a series of slides.

The tape-recorded interviews at the bank, the slides depicting both the bank visit and play writing experience, and the script of the play were presented for the benefit of both students and their parents.

As a result of their exposure to these school activities, two of the parents who were in the process of buying a car decided to let their children take the initiative in finding the best buy and determining what kind of loan to apply for.

In one of the senior high schools, the career education specialist and teachers of six classes—social studies, math, business education, special education, and two English classes—organized a commuter experience. Two students from each class, equipped with cameras and tape recorders, boarded a Santa Rosa commuter bus for San Francisco. Along the way they interviewed commuters, asking questions about their lifestyles in relation to their jobs in San Francisco, and upon entering the city, simulated a day's work by touring the financial district and Bank of America world headquarters.

At five o'clock they got on the return bus and continued their interviews. Each team took its audiovisual record back to the classroom and the teacher in each class made assignments relating to the team's presentation.

These are examples of the more than 300 career education activities planned and recorded in the project schools and made available to teachers in other schools. The project has given evidence that its influence is widespread. The model developed has been utilized throughout California and part of Washington State and is reported to be very workable.

When schools ask for the recorded materials, the county offices make it a point to stress that the packages are not to be used in the classroom but as stimulators for other teachers to plan experiences relevant to their own students.

The project in Sonoma and Alameda Counties is one example of how county offices can work with local schools to implement career education concepts formulated by a state task force. It also indicates how the U.S. Office of Education has influenced states, counties and local districts to implement realistic career education experiences in the school curriculum at all grade levels.

43

Careers from A to Zoo*

Dorothy Madlee

In the past couple of years Florida's Orange County has been the destination of hundreds of thousands of visitors bent on tearing themselves out of the real world—if only temporarily—to explore the marvelous and assorted fantasies of Disney World. In odd contrast, Orange County is also the place where school children have an especially good opportunity to rid themselves of whatever fantasies they may have about the real world and to prepare for work in it. The point: There is no Mickey Mouse in the Orange County Career Development Program.

County educators are justly proud of their career program which is not only doing what they hoped it would do but has helped restore the ego to one of the county's fine old schools, now called the Wymore Vocational and Technical Center. When Robert S. Megow was appointed principal of Wymore in 1967, he took over a high school drooping from low student and teacher morale, falling enrollment, and a high dropout rate.

It had not always been so. The school in the all-black city of Eatonville, a few miles northwest of Orlando, had been known as Hungerford Academy, a black-owned private institution founded with the help of a gift from Booker T. Washington and maintained by en-

*Reprinted by permission from *American Education*, May 1973, pp. 15-21.

dowments from blacks and whites. Its academic rating was high. It had given generations of black students their starts toward college and distinguished careers in medicine, law, education, and science.

The academy, then including nearby Hungerford Elementary School, survived the Depression, but in 1950 finances dwindled and the school was taken over by the Orange County school board, which renamed it and changed its curriculum from academic to vocational. The blow to Eatonville pride soon was reflected in school apathy.

Although the general population increased, enrollment at Wymore had shrunk from 800 to 250. Many students admitted they were merely waiting for dropout age—the 16th birthday that would free them from school.

"I knew something had to be done to revive the interest of teachers and students," recalls Megow, who is now director of the Orange County Career Development Program. Megow, a squarely built, ruddy faced man, wasn't quite sure what to do, but fortunately he was gifted with tireless energy and a determination to match. In the fall of 1970 with two of his teachers he visited the huge Beggs Educational Center in Pensacola, which he had heard was solving a problem similar to Wymore's by fusing academic and vocational subjects. This was in line with his own conviction that every student— white or black, well-heeled or poor—should be equipped to make a living. But this training, he felt, should be in connection with academic learning, not a choice excluding it.

Megow's next trip was to Tallahassee where he talked with Carl Proehl, head of the Vocational, Technical, and Adult Education Division of the Florida Department of Education. Proehl suggested that Megow write a proposal for Wymore, since U.S. Office of Education funds had become available for developing career-oriented programs and testing methods.

Drawing upon his staff and a group of enthusiastic elementary school teachers, Megow wrote and rewrote a plan that included kindergarten through 12th-grade. His reward: a $245,000 Federal-State grant, renewable for a total of three years.

The Orange County school board approved the plan in May 1971, and by July, 54 teachers who would be involved directly were getting the details at a workshop. There was to be one program teacher at each grade level in nine schools chosen for their pupil flow into Wymore: three junior high schools (Union Park, Winter Park, and Apopka) and their feeder elementary schools (Bonneville, Columbia, Hungerford, Killarney, Wheatley, and Lovell). The program would be headquartered at Wymore.

At first some principals and teachers were hard to convince, fearing the program might weaken their schools' academic standing. Many teachers hesitated to accept new treatment of their traditional subject matter. They feared also that parents—many already hostile over court-ordered desegregation—might be still more upset if the classic subjects were taught with an emphasis on how they apply to to-day's occupational world.

"People naturally resist change unless you can point to a record of results and say, 'Gentlemen, this is what we have done,'" Megow says. He credits success to those teachers who believed in the idea and wrote their own curriculums during the workshop. These believers went into the schools as development supervisors, promising reluctant teachers a flow of day-to-day lesson plans, materials, and arrangements for field trips and outside speakers.

Once the program achieved a foothold things became easier. "Many of the things we were doing spread to other classrooms because of pupil pressure," Megow says. "Teachers began to consider the program seriously after a number of pupils who had observed what our classes were doing would ask, 'Why can't we do interesting things like that other class does?'"

During the 1971-72 school year, enrollment at Wymore increased from 250 to 450 and the racial mixture balanced from 90 percent black to a 47 percent black-53 percent white ratio. The additional Caucasians were voluntary transfers from other schools, boys and girls from varied economic backgrounds who were more interested in doing than in abstract learning.

"We never discourage a student's plan for college," says John Horn, project consultant. "What we do combat is the old concept that the boy or girl who doesn't go to college is necessarily a failure."

Of 51 Wymore seniors graduated last year, 12 are now in colleges or universities, two are in technological schools, 30 are employed, three are seeking jobs. The whereabouts of the remaining four are not known.

Meanwhile the Orange County program has grown to where it needs 125 teachers; the county administration expects to install extensions in 19 additional schools this coming fall; and similar career program models have been introduced in Pinellas, Brevard, and Leon counties. Many other school systems, in Florida and elsewhere, are studying Megow's plan of flexible curriculums integrating academic subjects with the working ways of the adult world.

There are 15 occupational clusters, each taking in the varied jobs within a general field—mechanics, building trades, sewing trades, food service, child care, health occupations and horticulture are among them. One cluster is made up entirely of jobs within the humanities and arts. "Historians, sculptors, musicians, and anthropologists work too," Megow smiles.

Each cluster begins with the simple "what people do" approach of the kindergarten and is carried through the early elementary level through the increasing sophistication of junior high school learning experiences to the technical job training offered at Wymore.

"I feel strongly about this program," says James C. Peery, principal of Lovell Elementary School, where the 1,060 kindergarten through sixth-grade pupils are predominantly white and from lower middle economic backgrounds. "Before this started, you'd ask a youngster what his daddy did for a living, and the answer would be, 'He works.' Most of them didn't know, or if they could name the father's trade, they had no idea what it meant.

"It's part of our way of life, I suppose, to play down certain vocations—plumbers, electricians, clerks. We don't give these people much reason for pride. Fathers and mothers go off to work and come home tired and grumpy—in no mood to talk about anything interesting or challenging that may have happened that day. The children grow up with the impression that the grownup world must be pretty dreary. What's the hurry, they think, to learn and grow up just so you can join the snail race?"

Laurel Grundish, one of Megow's original nucleus of enthusiastic teachers, entered Lovell as career development specialist, fresh from the first summer workshop and its concentrated flurry of curriculum creation. She emphasizes the flexibility built into the format, allowing teachers and the specialist to take advantage of current situations and events of interest.

One class in the project had 28 boys, chosen because they were chronic absentees. To arouse their interest they were launched in a unit on jobs connected with the zoo. In this unit they took field trips to a zoo, were visited by an animal expert who talked to them of animal lore, and were encouraged to do their own research on wild animals. Zoo history was admixed with human history: The boys learned of the animals portrayed in drawings from old Egyptian tombs and in the animal collections of the early kings of Nineveh and of ancient Greeks and Romans; they studied zoos as civic institutions in medieval Florence.

Vocabularies and reading skills increased along with the boys' zest for discussing modern zoos and playing the roles of people they employ: grounds maintenance men, compound keepers, dieticians, veterinarians, operators of vehicles and concession stands, animal handlers, and caretakers. They took note of how zoos are planned for natural settings to afford comfort for animals and spectators, and how animals should be cared for and protected.

No matter what subject or skill the boys worked at, animals were the key. In art they drew animals in their native environment; in language arts they discussed animals they found particularly appealing and wrote stories about them; in arithmetic they computed such things as construction measurements for zoo compounds, expenses entailed in feeding animals, and concession profits.

Completing the zoo unit, the class switched to airports and the jobs they offer. But by this time absences had dropped sharply; over one period of 15 days the boys established a record of perfect attendance. Throughout the year, only real illness could keep them away from school.

At the end of each unit, the teacher fills in an evaluation form on the activity. Typical questions are: Was student interest maintained throughout the unit? Was the activity at too high (or too low) a level for most students? and What improvement could be made in the unit?

Of equal concern is the question: Are the students learning anything? "Tests at the end of the school year showed that many children in the program had gained a year plus six months," Peery says. "And not one had failed to advance by at least a year."

Months before the tests were made on their children, most parents—even those who at first had disapproved of the new way of teaching—were heartily in accord with the program, although it had not always been easy to get a fair trial for it. "When they complained, we invited them to come to school and watch," Megow says. "If they couldn't come, we went to see them. We asked them to be patient with us for a few weeks, just to let us show them what we were trying to do. Before long we were getting calls from pleased mothers, telling us about children who were doing homework for the first time, because if they didn't they would not be eligible for the next day's project or field trip."

A sixth-grade class at Lovell, classified previously as low achievers, recently finished a unit on hotel-motel management.

They built a four-foot-high cardboard model of a motel right to its balconies, swimming pool, grounds, and surrounding palms. Then they were taken to one of the motels in the area where they talked with managers, maintenance men, and maids. They played roles of guests, hosts, and workers. They telephoned for reservations which were filled by role-playing desk clerks. They figured rates per day, salaries, and labor costs.

At a school assembly student committee chairmen of the project gave a comprehensive report on what they had learned. Weeks later they were happy to repeat their performance for classroom visitors. "Those particular children never would have stood up and talked before. It was a change that came from them getting involved with the careers program," Peery says.

At Wheatley School a unit on land transportation written by Eleanor Jennings for the second through sixth grades covers shipping by truck and freight car. Children learn language arts by reporting on products that are shipped, where they originate, and their use. The youngsters also study vocabulary charts with such special terms as bill of lading, tractor-trailer, switch engine, and so forth. And they learn the various responsibilities of all the people involved by role playing as truck drivers, railroad workers, shipping clerks, warehousemen, and dispatchers.

When they study math, they compute mileage and distance, fuel costs, load weights, wages and hours. In social studies they learn to read maps, and get some idea of the safety requirements, legal restrictions, and pollution problems that are all part of moving goods over land. And what better way for youngsters to study science in a meaningful context? They learn about converting the energy of steam or gasoline and air into motion. They study rock strata and road composition and the effects of heat and cold on road surfaces. They see the need for refrigeration and learn the principles involved in it.

Art too adds its own special dimension to the subject. The class draws murals of people in shipping operations. Through folk songs and records of truckers and engineers the gandy dancers come alive and Casey Jones crashes old 97 all over again.

From transportation to law enforcement is only a classroom away. A unit on police work so enthralled youngsters in the fourth, fifth, and sixth grades that 84 of them wrote the police chief in nearby Apopka that they hoped to become policemen and couldn't the recruiting age be made a little lower than 21? The surprised chief visited their classes where he talked with the youngsters. Later he arranged special orientation sessions for them at the police station. Pupils rode in squad cars, toured the jail, sat in the radio room, and had some of the administrative duties explained to them.

Each unit depends in large part on contact with actual workers and preferably in on-the-job situations. For example, a construction boom in central Florida has housing developments mushrooming around some of the schools, while at the same time an expressway is being built within yards of school grounds. Normally, these distractions are considered noisy but probably necessary evils. At Lovell

School, however, Mrs. Grundish took advantage of the house building and road construction to lead her unit out to observe what was going on. Workmen and foremen were delighted to answer questions; they showed the youngsters how to use tools and machines, and explained the sequence of steps required to put up a house or lay down a road-bed. They even furnished builders' scraps for the children to make models.

On the junior high school level, prevocational education becomes more complex. Specialists visit the schools, field trips continue, books and reference material become more sophisticated, and career clubs flourish. Ninth-grade students at Union Park used election year news as a springboard for studying current politics and researching political history. Hospital and health care careers caught the attention of eighth-grade students, while seventh-graders produced a creditable 30-minute show over closed-circuit TV at the end of a unit on broadcasting.

"Students who were bored with school are finding it has something for them," says John Daniels, career development specialist at Union Park. "Our discipline problems have just about vanished."

Back at Wymore, where the entire faculty and student body is involved in the program, real job training begins. Still it is accomplished in company with academic subjects.

"I am often asked if our students lose out in the humanities area," says Patricia Arredondo, a senior high school curriculum writer. "As a literature major, I too was bothered about that question when I joined the project. Now I can answer honestly that I don't think they lose as much as they gain. You would be amazed at the broad interest students develop from such practical courses as business law, and the taste they acquire for the study of psychology that sometimes begins with the training unit for day care aides. There's a supplemental package, too, for those especially interested in academics. Many of these students will go to college after working awhile to pay their way. I know, if I hadn't been able to type I never would have made it."

At Wymore each ninth-grade student selects a career, but any student is free to change later if he or she wants to. Meanwhile courses are open-ended, progressive from level to level, equipping the student for employment even if he should have to drop out after completing the first year of training.

After a year—or less time if one is capable and eager—a student who has chosen a career in electrical services, for instance, may receive a certificate showing that he is qualified to repair small resistive appliances such as toasters in the event he must leave school, or for summer employment. Each succeeding year he is trained for a job requiring greater skills and more knowledge. After completing four years' training, accomplished at his own pace, the student is certified for major residential, commercial, or industrial work or to enter a technological college. He is also prepared for the entrance examination required of all students enrolling in Florida's State colleges and universities.

Megow believes everyone, whether he plans to be a mechanic, a composer, or a brain surgeon, should have an immediately employable skill. But his greatest concern is for the 30 percent of American students who drop out before finishing high school and who, without a salable skill, join the cycle of poverty, hopelessness, and crime.

"The program at Wymore is not for everyone," Megow admits, and he's thinking of the person with perhaps business executive ambitions and the means to go through the Harvard Graduate School of Business Administration, for example. In the earlier school years, however, he feels it can help children of all economic backgrounds. "Our aim in the elementary and junior high schools is to make pupils aware of the interest and variety they will find in the grownup world," he says. "To give them a feeling of the dignity of work—any work."

It will take at least ten years to make a complete evaluation of the Orange County Career Development Program, for not until then will the children now in the early grades—the "awareness" phase of career development—be old enough to serve as statistical proof. For the present, the program's success can be inferred only from the enthusiasm of students, teachers, and the majority of the parents, which, incidentally, is not at all a necessarily unreliable gauge.

44

The Cluster Concept
in Career Education*

Lloyd W. Dull

C areer education is a systematic way to acquaint children with the world of work in the elementary and junior high years and to prepare them in high school and college to enter and advance in a career field carefully chosen from among many.

Career education is divided into three inseparable segments: (a) career awareness through a study of the world of work in the elementary grades (K-6); (b) career exploration and orientation in the intermediate grades (normally 7-10); and (c) career preparation conducted at the senior high level (11-12).

For students to make vocational career choices from the wide range of occupational information, the curriculum program must permeate the entire school. The subject of career education cannot be treated as an isolated subject. Rather it must be an integral part of all subjects in the curriculum and must contribute to the entire curricular motivation and enrichment of the many learning experiences of all students as they grow and develop. The program is conceptualized to involve all disciplines as they relate to student experiences and occupational information.

There are more than 23,000 active job titles in the United States today. To help teachers deal effectively with these many possible occupations, the U.S. Office of Education has broken these jobs into 15 occupational clusters:

1. Business and office occupations
2. Marketing and distribution occupations
3. Communications and media occupations
4. Construction occupations
5. Manufacturing occupations
6. Transportation occupations
7. Agri-business and natural resource occupations
8. Marine science occupations
9. Environmental control occupations
10. Public service occupations
11. Health occupations
12. Hospitality and recreation occupations
13. Personal service occupations
14. Fine arts and humanities occupations
15. Consumer and homemaking occupations.

All types of jobs are included in these 15 clusters, from basic trade skills to those requiring a doctoral degree.

The career orientation program through cluster study must present to students:

1. A more adequate knowledge of jobs and career alternatives in our technological society

2. A knowledge of the economics necessary for participating in a technological society

3. A knowledge of the kind of education or training required and work traits necessary in obtaining employment and in gaining access to jobs and careers

4. A self-appraisal regarding personal skills, abilities, and life aspirations

5. An opportunity to develop attitudes toward the world of work which enable one to fulfill his job career goal

6. An opportunity to develop the attitude that socially useful work has dignity and worth.

Many schools are using the "cluster" framework in orienting students to careers. Here students analyze the world of work through career clusters. In the analysis of a cluster, important points of emphasis are directed toward needs, varieties of occupations, and opportunities available. In grades 7 and 8, several clusters may be explored and analyzed; and in grades 9 and 10, the exploration may narrow down to a more oriented study of one, two, or three clusters. In grades 11 and 12, students may concentrate their career preparation by developing learning and skills in one cluster of vocations or, more likely, by concentrating on developing learning in one vocation within a cluster.

The theory behind the cluster is that 97 percent of the approximately 23,000 occupational titles can be grouped into a few cluster areas according to similar characteristics and purposes. For example, the communications cluster would entail the following occupations for analysis: artist, cameraman, computer programmer, film editor, offset pressman, photographer, production director, proofreader, prop man, radio-television announcer, reporter, telephone operator, typesetting machine operator, and writer. Some developmental objectives for analytical study of the communications cluster might be:

To understand the importance of communication to the well-being of society

To explore the variety of occupations available in the area of communication

To discover job opportunities within the community for individuals interested in communications careers.

Occupational cluster learning might include on-site observations, hands-on laboratory experience, role playing, and many other appropriate activities.

Some instructional activities that students may pursue in studying the communications cluster are as follows:

Students visit local newspaper printing companies.

Students write articles to be printed in a class newspaper.

Students visit local television and/or radio stations, and then role play the job of the announcer by utilizing news articles written by the entire class.

Students visit telephone offices, and then role play both the operator and the consumer.

Students make posters and develop commercials to be used as 60-second videotaped commercials.

Implications of Career Education

Many implications for successful implementation of career education seem evident. Among these are the following:

1. Career education programs should be simple, flexible, and adaptable to individual community needs. Needs and problems in communities vary in priorities. Clusters to receive curricular attention by school districts may vary somewhat because of community priorities.
2. The student program should combine work experience edu-

cation with a broad career information effort and tutoring program. The career information phase should make use of all community resource people, public and private employers, so that students can learn about jobs in many career areas.

3. The tutoring effort should also make use of workers and professionals to support classroom teachers with individualized and small group instruction.

4. Work experience education for grades 8, 9, and 10 will be largely exploratory. In grades 11 and 12 it will be more intensive in nature or allied with specific cluster vocations.

5. Teachers, counselors, and administrators must be exposed to a thorough in-service program on career education in order to develop the sophistication and commitment necessary for success in this changed curriculum.

6. The initial step for implementing career education in a school district will be informational meetings and the establishment of an *ad hoc* committee which includes broad representation of business, industrial, labor, and educational organizations. This committee will have the task of formulating plans and priorities appropriate to the local situation.

7. Career education will call for more integration of the disciplinary subject matter in high school. With the explosion of knowledge and subject matter, it seems reasonable to request that science, mathematics, English, and social studies become relevant, one discipline to the other.

8. The whole community should be used as a learning laboratory. This implies use of community people as resource speakers and use of the community for field trips and work experience.

9. Team teaching will take on increased emphasis as the collaboration of all becomes an essential requisite for the success of the program.

10. While career education is expected to be necessary for all grades K-12, there appears to be an urgency to place priority effort in the exploratory program for grades 7-10. It is in these grades that the exploratory cluster study should draw major attention.

Limitations of Career Education

Career education appears to have a promising future. However, there are many limitations that must be recognized in developing the program.

1. Care must be exercised to avoid work-study programs as a back entrance into child labor.

2. Career education must not be used to discourage the disadvantaged in seeking admission to college.

3. Educational planners must not oversell this program as a panacea.

4. The academically-oriented community must be solicited for support in order to restructure the curriculum successfully.

5. Necessary funds that might be needed to mount a vigorous restructuring of the curriculum may be difficult to secure from the electorate.

6. It is not yet known whether business and industry will cooperate in providing sufficient opportunities for work-study programs.

7. The consumption market for workers must be studied carefully by educators lest we produce too many trained people for jobs available.

8. The trend of the American economy is "anti-youth" in the sense that employers prefer to hire people in their twenties rather than in their teens. The key to successful career education—the expansion of work-study programs—runs counter to present trends. An educational campaign will need to be conducted with business and industrial leaders to overcome anti-youth employment tendencies.

9. While career education is fostered, we must continue as always to teach boys and girls how to read, write, talk, and calculate.

In summary, clustering has these educational advantages according to proponents: (a) courses can be organized around common core areas of study; (b) a student can transfer within the cluster from one job objective to another without undue loss of time; (c) once out in the world of work, an ex-student will be able to adjust more easily to related jobs; (d) schools can enter into clustering by phases (that is, start with only one or two clusters); (e) any kind of high school—large, small, urban, rural, suburban—can cluster.

If the cluster approach to learning enjoys successful growth in our schools, it will come about through the involvement of administrators, teaching staffs, counselors, and students, along with parents and community leaders from the school areas.

Counselors should redirect more of their time and energy to career guidance rather than devoting a preponderance of time on college entrance. Job placement; career information and orientation; and optional learning opportunities, such as work experience and youth volunteer activities, should become a major function of guidance counselors.

Installation and operation of the cluster approach in career education at the junior high school level provide an opportunity for these students to have a curriculum which is meaningful, realistic, and viable. If this implementation is to be a significant innovation in these schools, it will be achieved only by considerable diligence and hard work on the part of administrators and teachers working as a team with their students, parents, and community.

45

Career Exploration:
Why, When, and How*

Robert A. Ristau

The "White Shoe Syndrome." Lucy looked over at her friend, Charlie Brown, and explained, "I've made an important decision: I'm going to be a nurse when I grow up." Charlie Brown adroitly inquired, "And why have you decided to become a nurse?" "Because I like to wear white shoes," replied Lucy.

A humorous anecdote? Yes. A glimpse into a more serious problem with youth? Yes again! And so it is with career decisions: our youth make a variety of decisions throughout their lives with respect to their future careers. Unfortunately, many career decisions are based on inadequate or inappropriate information. What about this "white shoe syndrome"?

Educators have been made aware of the developmental needs and tasks of youth in the writings of career development theorists. Various people have identified occupational or career development as an integral part of those needs and tasks. Yet, the educational system has failed to respond with programs and activities that can help satisfy those needs. Too often, if anything is done at all, it can be characterized as being "too little and too late."

*Reprinted by permission of the author. First published in *The Balance Sheet*, February 1973.

Career education is a concept, and from it is an emerging educational program with dynamic federal, state, and local resources behind it. There appears to be hope for curricular reform and innovation accompanying career education. Several solutions to the problem of the "white shoe syndrome" appear to be possible. With a foundation of new educational objectives that will permit and encourage educators at all levels and in all subject areas to respond to the career development needs of youth, the structure of the school curriculum can be adjusted to provide for career exploration as part of an integrated program of career education.

Individual business and distributive education teachers, as well as the programs of business and distributive education which they teach, will play a vital part in the ultimate implementation of needed programs in career education. As new career exploration programs are unfolded, both in terms of basic and in-depth exploration opportunities, there will be new and exciting roles for teachers of business and distributive education. The "white shoe syndrome" must be looked at in terms of needs and solutions.

The Need

The young people of America are generally shielded from the realities of the world of work. Many factors, including our advanced technology, the specialization of jobs, a post-industrial society, and a variety of child labor restrictions, combine to prevent young people from gaining important insights into jobs and the work which people perform. Yet, this very knowledge is basic and vital to the career development of our youth. Too often, too many know too little about work and work roles.

The responsibility for correcting this problem lies in large measure with the educational community. The current surge of interest and commitment to career education is causing educational leaders to take a new look at the curriculum of our schools, and career orientation and exploration loom as prominent components of emerging models for career education. (See Figure 45.1)

It is evident that young people will make a variety of career decisions. Many of these decisions will have an impact on their future lives. In spite of their importance, these decisions too often are made without the necessary facts and information which ought to undergird them. The need for adolescents to "see" the big picture of the labor market, to gain a "feeling" for a broad spectrum of occupations, and to obtain in-depth knowledge of several occupational areas must be met. Business and distributive education teachers, with a firsthand knowl-

Figure 45.1

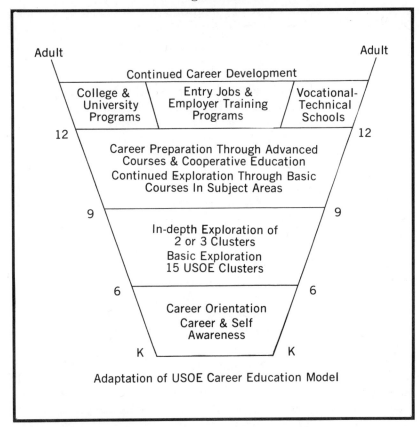

Adaptation of USOE Career Education Model

edge of the business world and a close working relationship with business and industry, can play a key role in the total picture of career orientation and exploration.

The failure of the schools to respond to what is generally recognized as a vital stage in the development tasks of youth is due to a number of factors, including the following: (1) priorities that too often leaned toward college entrance preparation rather than career preparation; (2) a lack of suitable materials which addressed the various levels of the career development process; (3) a general lack of real concern on the part of educators; and (4) a curriculum which tended to be crowded, rigid, and unable to respond to newly identified needs. The picture appears to be changing. Signs are evident which hold promise of curricular reform, and changing attitudes toward the task of public education will encourage a positive response to the needs of adolescents. Our young people must be given accurate information about work, be made aware of career opportunities, and be given an opportunity to explore a variety of occupations as an important part of their educational programs.

The Critical Years

Career orientation and exploration is a lifelong process. The young child who first begins to relate to the job of policeman, fireman, nurse, or teacher is becoming aware of careers and is developing a career orientation. In later years, youth begin to relate to other less visible occupations and learn about relationships between occupations, education, and life styles. Throughout life, as the individual works on part-time and full-time jobs and associates with a variety of persons in various work roles, the process of career orientation and exploration continues.

There appears to be a time in the developmental process of youth when curiosity about work is at a peak. These years are generally encompassed in middle schools, junior high schools, and the early stages of high school. At that time, schools should respond with an organized and realistic program of career exploration. Students must become actively involved in a process designed to enhance career exploration.

A study of several thousand sophomores and seniors conducted in Wisconsin in 1968, entitled "Vocational Education Reports," revealed that prior to their reaching the eighth grade most young people began thinking seriously about the jobs they might ultimately hold. Students in the survey overwhelmingly stated their need for more and better information about occupations. This was a random sample of several thousand sophomore and senior students enrolled in 34 high schools; the schools ranged in size from very small to very large and were located in communities with varying economic bases. The study documents a general need which exists among young people today, and it calls attention to the need for providing timely information.

Research has identified the need for youth to internalize a knowledge of occupations as a vital part of their developmental process. Students all tend to be relatively disadvantaged when one looks at their exposure to and knowledge of occupations. Whether students are in large or small communities, affluent or poor, they tend to be lacking when it comes to career exploration and knowledge of the world of work.

The following is a summary of what can generally be expected of business and distributive education teachers:

1—incorporate more career information into all of their classes and subjects;

2—give students an opportunity to explore occupations as part of their normal class work;

3—develop special courses, or units of courses, to give all students an opportunity to explore careers in the world of business before enrolling in subject-matter courses;

4—work closely with guidance counselors to provide them with information about business and distributive careers; and

5—learn about career development theory—what it is, what it means in terms of working with students, and how it can be put into practice.

It is time for the educational community to respond. What will you do?

46

Life Skills Education
for Adult Learners*

Winthrop R. Adkins

Following the passage of the Adult Education Act of 1966, there was a great expansion of Adult Education programs throughout the nation benefitting those citizens who, by virtue of economic circumstance, migration, discriminatory practice, family responsibilities and a variety of other factors, were not able to take advantage of public schooling earlier in their lives. Although program development was uneven, and the special learning problems of adults proved to be more intractable than was at first imagined, there was a great improvement in the quality and availability of Adult Education programs. Yet as Mezirow found in his national study (1970), there still are a number of problems which continue to limit the effectiveness of Adult Education programs and result in high rates of attrition and poor attendance. One major failing he identified was that students coming to Adult Education programs have not received sufficient help in clarifying their vocational and educational goals in dealing with the many difficult life problems which interfere with their training and employability. He urged a greater programmatic emphasis on helping students to develop what could be called coping skills, or life skills.

The current expansion of programs in Career Education throughout all levels of the educational enterprise is an attempt to highlight the

*Reprinted by permission from *Adult Leadership*.

fact that a major purpose of education is the preparation of students for adult work and adult living. Taken seriously, Career Education would imply a much broader range of programming alternatives for Adult Education. It has been the author's view for some time (Adkins et al., 1965) that adult programming must include more than reading and math. Such programming must not only offer vocational skills, but also must prepare the adult learner for coping more effectively with his many problems in living. Adult students have many complex and interrelated psychological, social, familial, medical and other problems which, if not dealt with effectively, will prevent them from taking full advantage of educational training and employment opportunities. Indeed, in the author's view, without some programming focused on life problems, all other components of Adult Education will be less than effective. Yet if the adult learner does get help in learning how to choose, find, get, hold and advance in a job, how to make use of the resources in his environment, how to deal more effectively with family pressures and conflict, how to improve his nutritional level and get better health care, then he will be more likely to attend his adult classes and sustain effort through the period of his training well into employment.

It is not surprising that typical adult students have a myriad of problems, considering the conditions of life with which they have had to deal. Adult Education students are a most heterogeneous group of individuals with respect to age, sex and ethnic background, but, with few exceptions, they share a common background of educational and cultural disadvantage. It is therefore not unusual to find that such students have not had the opportunity to acquire many of the subtle and necessary skills for mastering problems in the home, in school, on the job and in the community which middle class persons take for granted. At the same time, adult students frequently possess many strengths, insights and understandings, but these are not often enough taken advantage of in the design of educational and training programs.

Educational progress for disadvantaged adults is slow and it is easy for them to become discouraged. Since most students come at night, often with no stipend and after working all day at low level jobs or caring for numerous children, they must be able to manage the many life problems that occupy their time and energies if they are to persist with the program. While some are able to maintain the strong conviction that the sacrifice is worth the chance to better themselves, and are thus able to keep a positive balance between reasons for coming and reasons for dropping out, others are not. The balance is always precarious, and the burden placed upon Adult Education programs is great. Unless the student's motivations for coming are strengthened by the program with visible signs of progress toward his goals, and unless he gets help with the life problems that beset him, he may be forced to leave.

In general, most Adult Education centers have no formal programs for helping their students to cope with life problems. If help is given, it comes informally from reading and math teachers as part of the general classroom activities. In centers where some formal provision is made for helping students with their non-academic problems, two general approaches are followed:

Counseling Methods. Counseling in Adult Education programs suffers from a number of problems. First, there are too few counselors to be much help to students with multiple problems. Secondly, counselors often lack the appropriate experience, preparation and understanding of their clients (Gordon, 1964; Trueblood, 1960). Thirdly, counselors are too often burdened with administrative work, testing or crisis-solving.

Perhaps a more basic reason why counseling is not more effective is that, lacking effective tools, many counselors have relied heavily on non-structured discussion methods as the primary means for helping students to resolve difficulties and make appropriate plans. Yet there is growing recognition that traditional talk-centered individual and group counseling methods which were developed mainly with middle-class clients, have limited effectiveness with the disadvantaged. The author (Adkins, 1970) has observed the following about such counseling methods with disadvantaged persons:

—Without structure, students find it difficult to sustain focused discussion on any one topic and instead tend to flit from problem to problem with insufficient attention or effort on any one.

—Without an effective means of acquiring new knowledge, groups tend to share and perpetuate their misconceptions and ignorance.

—Without the opportunity to acquire new experience and reflect on it students find it difficult to discover new ways of handling current situations or to understand the new situations they will be confronting.

—Unless talk is related to action and an opportunity given for goal-setting and reflection, students tend to become apathetic or overenamored with discussion for its own sake.

—Without a means for practicing the application of knowledge to specific problems of living, they do not acquire skill in doing so.

Materials-Assisted Group Discussion. In addition to or in lieu of counseling, Adult Education programs employ a second approach for assisting students with life problems. This approach takes its name from its reliance on reading-discussion, film-discussion and lecture-discussion methods. Examples are programs with such titles as Urban Survival Skills, Social Living Skills and Human Relations Training. Such programs have the virtue of breaking down complex problem areas into manageable task areas and thus avoid some of the problems regarding the lack of focus and sharing of ignorance which have been noted previously as weaknesses in traditional counseling. However, few life problem programs have been developed with the systematic care and attention to detail which are required. Their major disadvantage is that they aim mainly at increasing the understanding of students. Rarely do they go beyond understanding to focus on new behavior to be learned, or provide a means for the student to translate his previous and new knowledge into action in his own behalf.

What is needed, therefore, in addition to improved programs of reading and math and vocational training, is a much greater programmatic emphasis upon helping ABE students to develop what could be called coping skills or *Life Skills*. In keeping with this objective there is the need for more powerful learning methods. Specifically, what is required is a method (1) which can be used by the average classroom teacher without massive retraining, (2) which employs a learning model based on sound pedagogical principles, and (3) which structures the learning situation with a series of well-conceived learning experiences and accompanying materials designed to culminate in new student problem-solving behaviors. The development of such a learning method is embodied in the *Adkins Life Skills Education Model*.

An Alternative Approach:
The Adkins Life Skills Education Model

Over the past nine years the author has been working to develop better methods for helping disadvantaged adolescents and adults learn the necessary behaviors for coping with their problems in living. The Life Skills program was originally conceived by the author in a small YMCA training program for Black adolescents and adults living in Bedford-Stuyvesant and an early version was originally tried out in a successor program—Training Resources for Youth (Adkins & Wynne, 1966; Adkins, Rosenberg & Sharar, 1965). That experience led to the creation of the present training model which was also adapted for use with Indians in rural Canada (Adkins & Rosenberg, 1968a; 1968b). Life Skills Education is essentially a program area and an innovative method for teaching and learning. The program area is defined by the sets of pre-vocational, motivational and social problems in living adult learners experience which interfere with their ability to profit from training and employment opportunities. Such problems are frequently those identified by counselors. They create anxiety and other forms of emotional stress and unless dealt with and resolved can lead to patterns of alienation, anger and withdrawal. Yet they are also cognitive problems. They persist because the learner lacks useful methods for defining them, knowledge, resources and techniques for using them, and basic problem solving strategies and skills which work. As previously described, such problems are not dealt with easily with global methods, e.g., counseling and materials-assisted-group-discussion. If they are to be overcome they must be attacked one by one, part by part until cumulatively, the learner begins to see himself regularly as one who is successful at solving problems and handling successfully the specific difficult choices, dilemmas and challenges he encounters in training, work and other areas of his life.

In many respects the Life Skills program employs a combination of methods regularly used by excellent teachers and counselors, but which are not often faithfully or fully carried out by "average" teachers and counselors relying solely on their own resources. A basic assumption underlying the program is that there will never be enough superior teachers and counselors for adult programs. Therefore, through Life Skills an effort is made to provide a series of pre-planned but open-ended structured learning experiences with accompanying materials which can be implemented by typical Adult Education teachers or counselors.

The Life Skills curriculum, when fully developed, has the following characteristics:

(a) It is focused on the specific vocational, educational and personal problems experienced by the majority of the trainees.

(b) It takes full advantage of the positive peer relationships of adolescents and adults by maximizing group activities on areas of common concern and yet it provides for individual needs through individual programming.

(c) It builds on the experience, knowledge and skill trainees already possess and provides a means for improving problem-solving skills while acquiring new life experiences, knowledge and new life skills.

(d) It provides trainees with alternative strategies for perceiving and resolving life problems and encourages them to make a series of conscious but informed choices about their personal values and objectives.

(e) It is sufficiently structured to permit the group to deal with one problem at a time and to experience success and cumulative progress in resolving an increasing number of related problems.

(f) It requires trainees to actively engage in exploring their environment and provides a means of reflecting on their experiences and setting and implementing new goals.

(g) It demonstrates the utility of knowledge and the value of learning by reading, study and research as well as by experience and discussion.

(h) It enables the group to apply their accumulated and newly acquired knowledge to simulated and real life problems and provides an opportunity for trial and practice.

To accomplish the above, the Life Skills program utilizes a "Problem-Centered Structured Inquiry" model. The process of curriculum development itself consists of two parts and four stages. Part one deals with *what* is programmed (the problems). Part two deals with *how* it is programmed in four sequential stages of learning experience (the structured inquiry).

Deriving the Problem-Centered Life Skills Syllabus: Part One

The first step is essentially that of identifying and collecting problems. The central notion here is that most of the inputs should come from members of the target population. The basic idea is to find out what concerns and troubles them, in essence, "where they hurt."

With the assistance of the students as curriculum development aides it is not difficult to obtain a fairly comprehensive listing of virtually all of the problems in living the students are experiencing. By checking and double-checking with several groups of students the staff obtains a sense of the importance of specific problems of the students, the frequency with which they are mentioned and the degree to which they are shared by students with similar and different characteristics.

It is also important to ask persons in close contact with members of the target population (family, friends, teachers, employers, etc.) to identify important life problems on the basis of their experience with many generations of students at their particular developmental level. The ideas from these resource persons as well as ideas from the literature can be very helpful, but the general principle remains that actual statements from members of the target population should be given priority.

Various techniques are used to record and sort trainee problems into manageable categories or clusters. It is not unusual to collect up to two hundred different problems from one group. These must be grouped into a number of manageable gross categories to provide a basic organizational framework for the syllabus. When the first rough list is completed, the students and resource persons are consulted again to insure that the categorization process has not significantly changed the problem statements and to provide further guidance to the development staff on problem details and their perceived priority. Through successive rewriting and rechecking a reliable list of problems is created. These are then analyzed into task and sub-task components, recombined and stated in behavioral terms.

Gradually, a syllabus consisting of ordered parallel and sequential tasks emerges and is refined. At this stage, the tentative instructional objectives on a general and specific level, following Mager (1962), are stated. Ideally, these objectives should describe the observable, behavioral actions which will be accepted as evidence that the student has mastered the intended outcome of the lesson—the action, not just the insight. The use of instructional objectives serves the purpose of giving trainees clear "benchmarks" in judging their progress and plays a critical role in determining the general effectiveness of the educational training program.

Table 1 shows an example of the syllabus organization created in a previous collection and categorization of problems for adolescent and adult students. The four tracks listed and their representative units demonstrate composite objectives which were derived inductively through the above process.

The Four-Stage Structured Inquiry Model and Its Development: Part Two

Once the syllabus has been created, priority units and lessons are identified and the lesson design and development process begins. Part Two of the Life Skills model involves the development of structured learning experiences following a basic four-stage model. The model was adapted from the work of Wolsch (1969) and revised with the assistance of Rosenberg (Adkins & Rosenberg, 1969) to make more explicit the processes and roles of both the educators and the learners.

The four-stage model is a sequence of learning experiences which are designed to frame the problem in an exciting, motivationally arousing way, dignify what the student already knows about the problem-task, add what he needs to know for mastery of the task and give him experience in translating his knowledge into action. Each pre-designed lesson follows this four-stage sequence. A fundamental notion employed here is that experience followed by reflection, followed by goal-setting, followed by further experience, reflection and

Table 1

MAJOR CURRICULUM TRACKS AND REPRESENTATIVE UNITS

Tracks	Representative Units
(1) Managing a Career	Identifying and developing one's interests and abilities, choosing an occupation, locating jobs, conducting interviews.
(2) Developing One's Self and Relating to Others	Caring for health needs, presenting one's self effectively, dealing with conflicts.
(3) Managing Home and Family Responsibilities	Becoming a parent, meeting needs of wives and husbands, budgeting and buying, dealing with the landlord, helping children in school.
(4) Managing Leisure Time	Planning one's time, changing mood and pace through recreation, participative vs. spectator activities.
(5) Exercising Community Rights, Opportunities and Responsibilities	Dealing with representatives of welfare, health and employment organizations, handling discrimination, finding one's way around the city.

so on in the process of implementing goals is an effective means for encouraging self-induced behavioral change.

Stage I: Stimulus Stage. Each Life Skills learning sequence begins with a provocative classroom encounter with a selected problem. The main objectives of the stimulus stage are to frame the problem, stimulate the emotional arousal of the students, focus their attention on that particular problem, and create a readiness for discussion and sharing of ideas. The task of the individual designing the stimulus is to select a controversial or emotionally charged aspect of the problem situation. The forms that the stimulus can take are as varied as the imagination of the designer; they have frequently taken the form of films, videotapes, group exercises and tape recordings or articles expressing a controversial or otherwise stimulating viewpoint. This stage in the sequence takes into consideration the important relationship between arousal and readiness to learn and, if properly designed, greatly increases the likelihood of interest, involvement and participation on the part of the trainees. As development proceeds, it is essential to try stimuli out in an exploratory fashion with members of the target population.

Stage II: Evocation Phase. Once discussion is initiated, the next objective is to evoke or call forth from each of the group members what he knows about the problem based on his own experiences. The main intent is to help the student become aware of how much he and others know about the problem and thereby dignify him as a learner. Other purposes are to facilitate problem definition, to encourage the free expression of ideas and feelings on a focused topic in a supportive, nonjudgmental atmosphere, and to familiarize them with the multiple sources of knowledge now utilized by the group. It is most important that the discussion leader be receptive and that he set a tone similar to that of brainstorming sessions by insisting that all have the opportunity to speak and that there be respect for each person's contribution.

During the discussion the Life Skills Educator also acts as a recorder of ideas by writing the ideas, words, phrases or images on the blackboard, flip chart or blank 5x8 cards in the original form in which they are expressed. He may fill boards on all sides of the room as he attempts to exhaust the knowledge of the group on the subject. He also liberally dispenses verbal rewards for effort in the manner of an art teacher attempting to get students to express themselves freely on a blank canvas. The blackboard or flip chart recording tends to give the contributions of the group a semi-permanent status instead of allowing the comments to disappear immediately after utterance. Members feel that they have been heard and their ideas have value for subsequent analysis and discussion. Moreover, having been given an opportunity to describe what they know about a topic, they can psychologically afford to admit what they do not know. The novel concept of "I have been a learner" seems to translate into "I am a learner" and leads to curiosity and further inquiry.

The curriculum development task in Evocation consists of preparing a sequential set of leads which move the group from a generalized reaction to the Stimulus to a definition of the problem, to specific experiences with the problem, to the definition of possible solutions, and finally to the identification of questions needing answers and the knowledge which must be obtained.

Stage III: Objective Inquiry Phase. Having probed the limits of their own knowledge, the major objective of this stage is to encourage and assist members of the group to explore a variety of other sources of knowledge about the problem. After identifying major questions of interest and what new knowledge is needed, the group is led to assign its members tasks for obtaining information. The LSE shifts his role from question-asker and recorder to resource person and question-answerer. He assists teams and small groups of learners to make full use of the specially prepared multi-media kits which are boxes containing pre-selected films, film-strips, pamphlets, books, pictures, tests, maps, lists of lectures, addresses of libraries, cards listing suggested field trips to places of employment or points of interest, persons to talk with, things to count, subjects to research and additional sources of information.

After the teams of learners have found information relevant to their assignment, both outside and inside the classroom, the LSE helps them use it to plan their presentations as experts on a subject before the whole group. As groups become more familiar with the process of searching out information, they become less dependent on the multimedia kits and the LSE and discover their own sources of information. In the process of completing their tasks, students learn how to operate projectors, find books in the library, plan trips, improve their reading and discussion skills, carry out simple research, take tests, talk with and interview experts in a given field, prepare presentations, analyze results and hopefully to think more clearly. The desired outcome is not only that they will obtain useful information about a specific problem, but that they will have a variety of new experiences and learn the basic skills of inquiry and resource identification.

Stage IV: Application Phase. It is not sufficient to merely obtain, discuss and present information since it is likely to be forgotten if not put to use. The main objective of this stage, therefore, is to demonstrate the utility of knowledge by providing the initial application projects, helping the group to evaluate their performance on projects and frequently assisting the students in developing and carrying out their own applications. Since many of the first application projects tend to be simulations, the notion of student-designed applications suggests even greater possibilities for participation, involvement and transfer of learning from the educational setting to the real world.

Application projects can take many varied forms. If the subject of the unit is "selecting an occupation," an appropriate project for an early lesson might be to make an inventory of one's interests and abilities based on information and categories gained in the Evocation and Objective Inquiry stages. If the subject of the unit is "making your emotions work for you," and the lesson deals with controlling one's anger, the project might be to role play techniques of reperception and delayed response learned in the Objective Inquiry stage to a simulated anger situation. In a unit aimed at the adult which explores "the role of the father in a family," the project might involve tutoring a youngster. In another unit where the subject is "presenting oneself effectively to others," the project might be to make a videotape of a job interview conducted with a cooperating employer using new knowledge about verbal and non-verbal communication.

Flexibility of the Model

When projects are completed, the four-stage model for the learning experience is recycled. If the next lesson is an extension of the lesson just completed, and motivation is quite high, it is possible for the Stimulus phase to be eliminated. If the group decides to move on to a new unit, then the new lesson would begin with the Stimulus phase as described. Cycling through all four stages may take one or several sessions.

The units selected may be designed to focus on one area in depth or they may deal in less depth with a broad range of problems. They may form the core of an entire training center curriculum or they may be used on a more limited basis to deal with pressing life problems. It is recommended that individual counseling supplement the group activities.

Life Skills and the Role of the Life Skills Educator

One can identify two broad tendencies in educational thinking about the role of the teacher. One tendency has been to romanticize the role of the teacher, to see him as a "Renaissance man" who is capable of anything. Another tendency has been to minimize the role of the teacher, basically arguing that most of what an effective teacher does can be duplicated by such technological innovations as individualized computer-assisted learning packages. The Life Skills model takes a middle position—that the classroom teacher is a necessary and important part of the educational enterprise and will always, for better or worse, be with us. Yet since it is probably quite rare for one person to be able to make all the facilitative pedagogical moves necessary for effective learning, the teacher needs support. Thus the Life Skills model can be seen as a teacher-support system that embodies a well-designed, structured learning sequence. The pre-designed learning units facilitate goodness of instruction through excellence of design.

Basically, it provides the Life Skills Educator with pre-designed learning experiences with accompanying resources which take the burden of lesson planning and resource collection or development off the teacher. It frees him for the important functions of developing effective learning relationships with students and managing the instructional process. In other words, it creates a more focused role for the teacher, a role which is more appropriate for Adult Education. From this standpoint, the learning of a new role is also apt to be less threatening and therefore less resisted than staff training programs aimed at teaching the teacher what he thinks he already knows. The Life Skills Educator can be a specially trained teacher, a counselor or a paraprofessional.

Specifically, the staff training program for the Life Skills Educator includes instruction in the teaching and counseling tasks required by the model at each stage. Typical skills include: convening a group, setting the stage for Life Skills units, asking questions which promote involvement, expressing a non-judgmental attitude, reinforcing student ideas, tailoring information and resources to the needs of students and so on. In all, the program is designed so that it can be flexibly tailored to enable both teachers and counselors to build upon their existing knowledge and skill while acquiring the new skills necessary to implement the model. The LSE training program also employs the four-stage model, thus giving the future LSE experience with its operation and a feel for what the student's needs will be as he transits the four stages.

The Life Skills Education Development Project

The author is currently Director of the Life Skills Education Development Project at Teachers College, Columbia University which is engaged in creating Life Skills units for disadvantaged adult learners. This past year the project has developed ten units focused on the problems of choosing, finding, getting, preparing for and holding a job. The ten units were selected on the basis of a thorough study of the employability needs of adult learners. Each of the units follows the four-stage sequence of learning experiences described above. This year they will be tested in adult education centers in the New York City area. In addition, a staff training program for the Life Skills Educators will be developed, tested and revised. Once the pilot testing sequence has been completed, the units will be published and disseminated within five different regions of the country. Results to date, based on observation and anecdotal reports, indicate that the units are very successful in producing the desired kinds of behaviors for which each of the units is intended. Videotape records of each of the pilot tests are being analyzed and will eventually be compiled in a documentary report of the unit test-outs. If the units developed prove to be successful in the many regions in which they will be disseminated, it is the intent of the Project to proceed to develop larger numbers of units dealing with a variety of other coping needs of adult students.

References

Adkins, W.R. "Life Skills: Structured Counseling for the Disadvantaged." *Personnel and Guidance Journal* 49, no. 2 (1970): 108-116.

Adkins, W.R., and Rosenburg, S. *Report of Research Design and Information System Task Force.* Saskatchewan, Canada: Pilots Project Branch, Government of Canada, 1968 .a

Adkins, W.R., and Rosenburg, S. *Operations of the Technical Support Center and Corporate Reactions.* Saskatchewan, Canada: Government of Canada, 1968 .b

Adkins, W.R., and Rosenburg, S. *Theory and Operations of the Life Skills Program.* Ninety-minute videotape privately produced, 1969.

Adkins, W.R.; Rosenburg, S.; and Sharar, P. *Training Resources for Youth Proposal.* New York: Training Resources for Youth, Inc., 1965.

Adkins, W.R., and Wynee, J.D. *Final Report of the YMCA Youth and Work Project.* Department of Labor Contract 24-64, New York: YMCA of Greater New York, 1966.

Gordon, J.E. "Counseling Disadvantaged Children." In *Mental Health of the Poor,* edited by F. Reisman. Glencoe, Ill.: Free Press, 1964.

Mager, Robert F. *Preparing Instructional Objectives.* Palo Alto, Calif.: Fearon Pubs., 1962.

Meizirow, J. *Analysis and Interpretation of Adult Basic Education Experience in the Inner City: Toward a Theory of Practice in the Public Schools.* OEG 0-9-422163-441 (324). Annual Report, May 1969-June 1970.

Trueblood, D.L. "The Role of the Counselor in the Guidance of Negro Students." *Harvard Education Review* 30 (1960): 252-69.

Wolsch, R. "Poetic Composition in the Elementary School: A Handbook for Teachers." Ph.D. dissertation, Teachers College, Columbia University, 1969.

47

Career Education*

Administrators of education at all levels are confronted with a major problem: How to equip their students for a world of work that bears little resemblance to what has traditionally been taught under the heading, "vocational education."

Although the problem has been growing for years—along with a haphazard proliferation of technical and vocational programs, courses, schools and institutes—most educators have only recently become keenly aware of it. Major attention is being directed to vocational programs, partly because of the increased emphasis, and money, devoted to career education by the U.S. Office of Education under the regime of Sidney P. Marland Jr. and partly because of protests from industry that education is not turning out students with employable skills.

By 1980, 101 million Americans are expected to be in the national labor force, one-sixth more than the 86 million in 1970. At present 80 percent of our youth do not graduate from college, and the unemployment rate among secondary school graduates, with or without some college, is more than three times as high as that of vocational education graduates.

This special section on what is now called career education has

*Reprinted by permission from *Nation's Schools*, December 1972, pp. 35-40.

been researched and written jointly by *Nation's Schools* and its sister publication, *College & University Business,* because the editors believe that developing effective programs for occupational education is not the responsibility of either secondary or post-secondary education alone. The responsibility must be met by education as a whole. Vocational education costs more than general education. The U.S. Office of Education figures 15 to 30 percent more. Why? Need for individual instruction is greater, equipment and facilities are more expensive, more time must be taken for counseling and job placement. The fact is, though, everybody is beginning to think it's worth it.

In the past the federal government saw little need to provide this extra money except for a smattering of students. At the federal level, it was not until the Vocational Education Act of 1963 that money was made available for students seeking *all* occupations that required less than a college degree. The 1968 Amendments to this act provided the country (for the first time) with the beginnings of a federal and state administrative structure and a funding basis to create vocational curriculum alternatives to the general education courses that 80 percent of the students in the country receive, like it or not.

The impact of the 1963 and 1968 legislation is revealed in national statistics: Enrollment in vocational education programs nearly doubled between 1964 and 1968—from 4.5 million to more than 8 million—and USOE estimates that 14 million Americans of high school age or older will be enrolled in occupational education by 1975. Dollar investment increased proportionately: USOE figures on all government levels more than doubled—from $605 million in 1965 to approximately $1.4 billion in the fiscal year ending June 1969.

In the 70s there is every reason to believe that more monies will be available for vocational education—if not from federal sources, at least from the state and local levels. (States are already spending five times more than the federal government for vocational education programs.) This optimism is primarily due to the attempt by U.S. Commissioner of Education Sidney P. Marland, Jr., to reshape college preparatory, general curriculum, and vocational training into a new, mutually beneficial whole which he calls career education.

As Marland tentatively envisions it, the reshaping of education would take the form of an inverted pyramid. Attitude building, career orientation, vocational guidance, as well as exploratory activities, would begin in the elementary grades to create a motivation for a world of work. Specific skill exploration would start in the middle grades to acquaint students with machines, instruments, tools and equipment. Simple job cluster skills would be introduced in junior high school. As the student progressed through secondary and post-secondary programs of his choice, he would have alternative choices for specific skills training, for job cluster skills training, for prevocational and pretechnical education, for advanced vocational and technical education, and for college preparatory education. Upgrading and retraining through continued education programs would also exist throughout adulthood.

Marland's emphasis on careers at early elementary levels is expected to be part of the solution to a basic criticism vocational experts have leveled at traditional secondary vocational education programs. Since most state laws allow a high school student to drop out of school at age 16, and since most children reach that age during Grades 10 and 11, it has made little sense, according to these experts, to begin vocational training as late as Grade 11, as most schools do.

If any one group is to be singled out for consistently alerting the nation's educators to the need to reshape this country's system of education, perhaps it should be the National Advisory Council on Vocational Education (NACVE). Created under the 1968 Amendments, its 21 members, who are appointed by the President, include representatives from disparate social and occupational segments of society. Since 1969, NACVE has submitted five reports that have systematically suggested strategic and tactical means for bringing vocational education into the mainstream of education. An example: The 1970 report points out that reform of American schools cannot come about if the federal government continues to invest nearly $4 in remedial manpower programs for each $1 it invests in preventive (elementary and secondary education) vocational programs.

To help lay the foundation for USOE's new emphasis on career education, Marland has directed $15 million for Fiscal 1972 to USOE's Career Education Development Task Force, under Rue D. Harris, to coordinate the development of four model career education programs: the school model, the employer model, the home-community model, and the institutional model. Development and demonstration contracts have already been let for the first three of these models.

Educators, however, are not at any loss for examples of vocational education programs, comprehensive ones that already integrate, to some extent, skills with general curriculum and college preparatory programs. The development of a network of nearly 100 community colleges in California has not only provided job-oriented education programs, but has encouraged the state's 750 public high schools to expand and develop their own vocational programs in tandem with the curriculum of the community colleges. More than one million young people received occupational education in California during 1970-71. Last year, Ohio became the first state in the nation to require that each of its public school districts gear up to offer comprehensive vocational education programs to their students by 1975. Under the Ohio law—which provides $75 million in matching funds for construction and materials—a school district has three alternatives: provide vocational courses on its own, contract for them from another district, or form a joint vocational district with other school systems. To ensure a comprehensive approach, a vocational district is defined as having no fewer than 1,500 students in Grades 9-12 and no fewer than 12 vocational programs and 20 classes.

Nationwide experience with vocational curriculum has precipitated several career cluster approaches. Rather than the old curriculum collection of narrowly defined training programs for specific jobs or skills, related courses are grouped into general occupational areas. For example Wyoming's State Department of Education has suggested that educators separate their vocational curriculum into 11 clusters: metal processing, graphic communication, electricity-electronics, health, office and family, construction, hospitality, distribution, transportation service and repair, agricultural production, community and social service. Oregon, taking the same approach, has proposed 12 clusters.

Also taking a note from technical schools and colleges, vocational educators, and those at community colleges in particular, have developed cooperative partnerships with industry. As Edwin L. Rumpf, USOE's director, Division of Vocational and Technical Education, points out, cooperative education has several obvious advantages. The student learns under actual job conditions, ensuring that his instruction is up-to-date. Often there is a built-in placement opportunity and, for the economically disadvantaged student, it can afford the opportunity to earn a training-level salary and still remain in school.

One of the better-known cooperative education programs on the secondary school level was initiated by Chrysler Corporation, following the 1967 civil disturbances in Detroit. The automobile manufacturer volunteered to "adopt" the city's predominantly black Northwestern High School. Chrysler renovated a wing of the school and established a placement office where testing and interviewing were conducted by industry personnel. It provided office and data processing equipment to update the school's office education labs and established a well-equipped auto mechanics training facility. Under a "secretary for a day" plan, girls in the program spend a day on the job at Chrysler; there are creative teaching grants of $300 to Northwestern teachers who want to develop new programs.

Recruitment of vocational counselors and vocational instructors is an area in the development of occupational education that has often been neglected. One thing is certain: There are not enough of either. On the national level, the Student Personnel Programs branch of USOE's Bureau of Adult, Vocational, and Technical Education is attempting to develop a handbook on how to organize and manage programs of vocational guidance, with hopes that this will lead to workshops in each of the 50 states. But no one is quite sure where these counselors will come from. Nor is the counseling profession making it easier to obtain them. A USOE suggestion that paraprofessionals might be of help has been criticized by many professionals because they fear it will lower the standards of counseling.

Some authorities in vocational counseling have advocated use of new technologies, such as computerized occupational information, as counseling tools. These give the individual student an opportunity to evaluate occupational and educational information against his own interests, aptitudes and goals through "career game" interaction with the machine. Harvard University's Graduate School of Education, in joint development with the New England Education Data Systems and the Newton, Mass., public schools, has developed a "computer-driven multimedia system" for this purpose. Called Information System for Vocation Decisions (ISVD), it makes use of slides, films, charts and printouts to help the student relate his personal characteristics to occupational education information.

The USOE estimates that by 1975 the country will need 345,000 occupational instructors—about 130,000 more than we have now. The government has attacked this problem by appropriating $6.9 million this year and the next, under the Educational Professions Development Act (EPDA), for development of vocational education instructor programs. Universities involved in the project include: Illinois, Georgia, North Carolina, Ohio State, Rutgers, Colorado State, Oklahoma State, California at Los Angeles, and Minnesota. Several individual schools and community colleges in the country have developed programs using paraprofessionals, experienced craftsmen, and technicians in the field. Certification requirements in most states, however, still represent the biggest barrier to recruitment of vocational education personnel.

Administrators are aware of the need to improve the vocational education programs in their schools. An extensive survey by *Nation's Schools* of public school superintendents showed that three-quarters were dissatisfied with their district's present vocational programs, considering the curriculum offerings too limited. The growth of the community college in the 1960s, at a rate of more than 50 per year, attests to the importance that post-secondary educators and the public put on vocational education.

Despite a projected rapid growth rate in the "professional" occupations, a Labor Department study of the jobs which will be available in the coming decade indicates only about one in five will require higher education preparation. The Department of Labor's Occupational Outlook Handbook projects a 13 percent increase in blue-collar jobs between now and 1980 and a 36 percent increase in white-collar positions. Service-producing industries (trade, government, health care, education, transportation, repair and maintenance, finance, insurance, real estate) are expected to grow from 44.2 million people in 1968 to 59.5 million by 1980, a 35 percent increase. The work force in goods-producing industries (agriculture, mining, construction, manufacturing) is expected to increase from 27.5 million to 30 million, a 10 percent increase.

What do these changes in the labor market portend for educators? This: That the demands on education in the next decade will be much different from those of the past decade. Not only will more students attend occupation-oriented courses at the secondary school and community college level, but the occupations of the future will require changes in curriculum. Even today, secondary and community colleges provide career instruction in such new fields as oceanography, data processing, and radiology.

If Sidney P. Marland Jr. can make his scheme to reform U.S. schools work, a grateful nation may finally remember the name of a U.S. Commissioner of Education.

Marland is the fifth man to hold the job in the past decade. Resident cynics say the post is a revolving door. But Marland is showing signs of toughness—together with a willingness to play on the Nixon team—that marks him as different from his predecessors.

One of the most important differences is the terrific push he has given to what he calls "career education." The concept is not new to him; he adapted it to the Pittsburgh school system when he was superintendent there in the early 1960s. Today he is going far out of his way to preach the career education dogma every chance he gets. He has a White House group, headed by John Ehrlichman, hopped up about it. He has brought to the Office of Education the most successful state administrator in the field, Robert M. Worthington of New Jersey, as his associate commissioner for adult, vocational and technical education.

With relatively few ($50 million, approximately) federal research and development dollars available for career education, Marland is out to change traditional voc ed patterns. Why?

"Dropouts are not created in freshman year in college," he remarked recently. "Their aimlessness is usually the product of 12 prior years of non-career-oriented education. Many of their classmates . . . drop out without attempting college." It is this aimlessness—the failure to establish goals, the failure of motivation and perhaps of pride in oneself—which Marland believes is so frustrating in U.S. schools.

He proposes "preventive medicine," in the form of occupational emphasis which the schools must start to give to children at ages eight, nine and ten. To give the medicine, however, requires "a thorough overhaul of both elementary and secondary curriculum and procedures," Marland thinks. That's what his researchers are working on, through contracts with several educational labs, which, in turn, are working with a handful of school systems.

The objective, Marland says, is "to guide youngsters to occupational awareness and desire, and to lead adults to a re-examination of opportunities missed in their earlier lives." Everyone, the commissioner believes, should "enter the world of work with readiness and pride."

He adds: "There is no longer a place for the in-betweens. We also hold that given the option to enter the world of work following high school, the young person should retain his option to enter higher education later—not unlike those under the GI Bill."

Marland stresses that vocational education is not career education: Vocational education is only a part of career education.

He sees career education as nearly a cradle-to-grave continuum, with the smallest school children starting to get a general indoctrination into the world of work—the real world, in Marland's view—even as they begin learning the Three Rs. Generalization gradually gives way to specifics as the child becomes the youth, so that somewhere midway through high school "entry-level" skills are gained, and in the last years of high school, work skills are acquired.

Marland points out that the Bureau of Labor Statistics has forecast that no more than 20 percent of all U.S. jobs in the 1970s will require as much as a bachelor's degree, and that "the remaining 80 percent will be within reach of a high school diploma . . . or non-degree post-secondary schooling."

With this in mind, he has personally pushed USOE's experiments with four career education models, the most important of which, obviously, is the one which carries children from first through twelfth grades in school.

The models have not gone untouched by criticism, however. Foremost among the critics is Hugh Calkins, former chairman of the

Figure 47.1

Federal money for occupational education: Authorizations vs. appropriations

	FISCAL 1969		FISCAL 1970		FISCAL 1971		FISCAL 1972	
	Auth.	Appro.	Auth.	Appro.	Auth.	Appro.	Auth.	Appro.
Permanent programs	$355.0	$248.2	$565.0	$320.1	$675.0	$352.7	$675.0	$397.4
Consumer/homemaking education	-0-	-0-	25.0	17.5	35.0	21.3	50.0	25.6
Cooperative vocational education	20.0	-0-	35.0	14.0	50.0	18.5	75.0	19.5
Work-study	35.0	-0-	35.0	5.0	45.0	5.5	55.0	6.0
Exemplary programs	15.0	-0-	57.5	13.0	75.0	16.0	75.0	16.0
Demonstration schools	25.0	-0-	30.0	-0-	35.0	-0-	35.0	-0-
State programs	15.0	-0-	15.0	-0-	15.0	-0-	15.0	-0-
Construction loan aid	5.0	-0-	10.0	-0-	10.0	-0-	-0-	-0-
Disadvantaged programs	40.0	-0-	40.0	20.0	50.0	20.0	60.0	20.0
Curriculum development	7.0	-0-	10.0	.9	10.0	4.0	10.0	4.0
Personnel development	25.0	-0-	35.0	5.75	40.0	6.9	45.0	6.9
Advisory council	.1	-0-	.15	.2	.15	.3	.15	.3
TOTALS	$542.1	$248.2	$857.65	$396.45	$1,040.15	$445.2	$1,095.15	$495.7

A four-year comparison of Congressional authorizations versus appropriations for various sections of the Vocational Education Act Amendments of 1968 (dollar amounts are in millions) reveals a prime problem: Appropriations have not come close to matching authorizations. Further, even when appropriations have been substantial, they are sometimes trimmed by the Bureau of the Budget via the technic of "non-release." It is significant, however, that money for the "permanent programs"—those for distribution to states on a 50 percent matching basis with state and local funds—has increased steadily. Vocational Education Act funding is designed for all levels of education: K-12, post-secondary, and adult.

National Advisory Council on Vocational Education. "Without sufficient funds, USOE is falling back on the age-old bureaucratic gambit of funding development and demonstration projects," says Calkins. "This allows maximum publicity with minimum financial output."

Calkins feels USOE would do better to pay start-up costs of research projects and let private companies or cities and states come up with operating expenses for the demonstration models.

Marland is also aware that he is open to the charge of "antiintellectualism," possibly with some justification. But he believes career education—the shoring up and rationalizing of the Protestant work ethic—will make present grade and high schools "far more realistic, with the implicit motivation for academic learning undergirding the career mode." Rather than anti-intellectualism, the more important question about Marland's career education scheme is: Will it work?

It neatly fits the Nixon Administration's larger plans, with regard to welfare and job training. It gets high marks in Congress—indeed, anything that gives even faint promise of putting welfare mothers and high school dropouts to work is hailed there.

But there is an open question in some Washington circles as to whether children can be manipulated to the extent that the career education scheme contemplates—and whether teachers will buy the program at all. For, in a sense, Marland's scheme is one more attempt to use the schools to solve social problems. Can multimedia shows and TV documentaries cure alcoholic fathers, slatternly mothers, racism and drug addiction?

The Washington cynics point to the bonepile of programs left over from the 1960s that are now frozen into the bureaucracy. Where, they ask, are the payoffs from huge expenditures on Head Start, the Job Corps, the National Alliance of Businessmen's JOBS program, the Neighborhood Youth Corps, and Title I of the Elementary-Secondary Education Act?

And those are only for openers, the cynics say. They think Marland underestimates the forces of inertia. For example, they note that a fairly simple matter like changing the high schools' chemistry curriculum took a full decade or more.

The results won't be known for years, but there is no doubt that Marland is trying.

48

Thirteen Ways
to Improve Your
Occupational Program*

Grant Venn

R adical changes in vocational education are almost upon us. In a few years, one-third of the senior high student body may be off campus—working in stores, hospitals, libraries or elementary schools. We may also see students taking jobs earlier and going to school part-time, not worrying whether it takes four or six years to complete high school. We will see many new patterns for vocational education, rather than the single pattern so eagerly sought now. But most of all, preparation for work, in the new meaning, will be part of everyone's education regardless of place of residence or station in life. Graduation may become a dead word and "academic versus vocational" a moot question.

How to prepare for the new era? Even if the district now runs a more or less traditional voc ed program, there are certain things the superintendent can do to help meet changing needs—actions which, by the way, do not cost a great deal of money. Here are 13:

1. *Exhibit strong leadership.* It gets dangerous up there, but without active, demonstrated and aggressive support, all the money, buildings and staff won't do much. In no place where there is a good vocational program was it originally opposed by the chief administrator.

*Reprinted by permission from *Nation's Schools*, December 1971, pp. 41-48.

2. *Get the support of principals.* For the past three decades, most of the direction from the central office to building principals has concerned preparation of all students for the next educational step—elementary to junior high school to high school to college. The good jobs were in the academic schools; professional advancements come through these schools. How do you get the principals to believe that career education and occupational skills do pay off and suddenly are worthwhile? It will take more than memos and statements. Most principals have little knowledge of career education, few skills, and limited experience. A plan must be implemented so they feel competent to move in new directions.

3. *Select a good director of career education.* This person must give direction to the implementation of career education at all school levels and in all areas. Career education is much more than a skill program at the high school level—it requires integrating the career concept into all phases of the education program. The appointment is crucial. If you already have a person in charge of vocational education, retraining and reassignment may be needed. It takes a different drive, style, and ambition than either the old-line vocational person or the academic administrator usually is able to exhibit.

4. *Have a job placement office.* The Parkersburg, W. Va., school system operates such an office year-round for all youths between 16 to 22. The office is open from noon till 8:00 p.m. weekdays, and all day Saturday. People who have worked as district guidance counselors man the office, with clerical, secretarial and mechanical help from students (for school credit). It has become a major student center for counseling, career planning, job entry placement, and part-time work. Entry and part-time work can be matched to student interests for learning as well as earning. Work experience programs, cooperative education, volunteer youth programs, and the Neighborhood Youth Corps program are also supervised here. It takes no new space and little equipment, and it centralizes efforts of teachers and staff.

5. *Develop work-experience and work-study programs.* Set up a continuing program for high school youths to work part-time in private businesses or public agencies, depending on need and skills. Schools generally give credit for these experiences, particularly if related to educational goals. Much of the work, however, can be unrelated and simply provide exploratory

and orientation knowledge and skills about business. It can also mold positive attitudes.

6. *Expand flexible, cooperative education plans with industry.* This is a more formal approach to work experience, tied more directly to a career choice and aimed at the development of specific job skills. Again, it requires no new facilities or equipment, but involves programs with industry under which students alternately attend school and work on a job related to their vocational studies. Cooperative programs provide income to students and can be operated any time of the day or year. Cooperative education has been traditional in the business, secretarial and distributive fields—it can also apply in any area where specific job skills can best be learned on the job through skilled supervision.

7. *Expand occupational orientation in the middle grades and junior high school.* New material aimed at these grade levels has been designed to provide information for understanding the developing career options in a technological society. Purposes of the material are: (1) to broaden options and information; (2) to act as a transition into specific preparation available in the secondary school; and (3) to give purpose and function to academic and related courses. In addition, the usual industrial arts and home economics classes for all students should provide a heavy emphasis on field trips, class visits by professionals in many areas, and visitations which give knowledge about options.

8. *Provide career information in the elementary grades.* Unless this is done, few students will ever be interested enough to choose a career curriculum, and few parents will want them to. The basic problem is a national attitude (too often that of teachers) that says vocational education is designed for somebody else's children. Attitudes, values, and life-style concepts are most often formed at a very early age. Career information through subject content and reading materials in the elementary grades provides a basis for broader career interests and expanded orientation and skill development patterns when the student reaches junior and senior high school.

9. *Establish advisory councils.* A districtwide career education advisory council is necessary. It should report to the superintendent and the board of education, and concern itself with the over-all educational program at all grade levels.

10. *Redirect counseling.* Continual criticism of counseling pro-

grams in most schools comes because there are few measurable outcomes other than college entrance. Thus, most guidance personnel find themselves spending most of their time on this single goal. Job placement, career information and orientation, and optional learning opportunities, such as work experience and youth volunteer activities, should be a major purpose of the guidance function.

11. *Develop youth volunteer experiences.* There is much to be done in every community and students are demanding to be involved. Programs such as student teacher aides, hospital and recreation volunteer work, and a host of other community needs could be met by an accredited youth volunteer program. The chance to learn ways to work with people is needed by young people.

12. *Expand time use of present facilities and equipment.* Many school districts are moving to an all-year program in the vocational education area. A new pattern of cycling courses so students may enter the labor market at different times during the year is possible.

13. *Check the budget for program integrity.* A review of the total dollar allocation in the budget against the career education goals of the district is necessary. Many times the budget is not consistent with program goals.

USOE's four models: In search of career education complete

Putting all your eggs in four baskets is a lot better than putting them in one, so the U.S. Office of Education has given its new Career Education Development Task Force $15 million for Fiscal 1972, plus some funds left over from OE's 1971 budget, for the development of four basic models to undergird Commissioner Sidney P. Marland's career education concept. The four—called the school-based model, the employer-based model, the home-based model, and the institutional model—will be designed to permit people to shift from one mode to another as their needs change. In short, they take into consideration the fact that people are not students all their lives.

The school-based model: This affects the entire grade and high school pattern. At the grade school level, the child learns about a wide range of jobs and their requirements. In junior high, he studies specific occupational clusters—"environment," "communications and media," "marine science occupations," and "personal services occupations" are among the 15 clusters for which OE has detailed schema—through work experiences and observation as well as regular classwork. By senior high, the youth is well along toward specialization and acquisition of job skills.

In mid-August, OE's National Center for Educational Research and Development awarded a one-year contract for $1,988,004 to Ohio State University's Center for Research and Leadership Development in Vocational and Technical Education to work on and, in part, support this model in six public school systems. The experimental models will be installed in Mesa, Arizona, Los Angeles, Jefferson County, Colorado, Atlanta, Pontiac, Michigan, and Hackensack, New Jersey.

The employer-based model: A consortium of public and private employers, such as unions, community groups, and public agencies, would join to provide unmotivated students, aged 13 through 18, with what OE calls "significant alternatives" to current schools. These alternatives would combine vocational training, education in academic fundamentals and work experience selected for career development possibilities. Enrollment would be open year-round and youngsters would move at their own pace.

Two educational labs, Research for Better Schools, Inc., and the Far West Regional Educational Laboratory, Berkeley, Calif., have received a total of $2 million from OE to define model characteristics. The Center for Urban Education, New York, has received $300,000 to do a "pilot study" on implementing this model.

The employer-based and the school-based models are expected to cost $5.5 million each when completed.

The home-based model: The idea here is to provide learning for young adults (18 through 25), and possibly older persons, too, who have left formal schooling. They would, presumably, increase their employability, using the home as a learning center through modern technology—TV and radio, audiovisual tape cassettes, possibly even printed materials.

OE has invested $300,000 with the Educational Development Center, Newton, Mass., to study three areas connected to this model: In-Depth Definition of Population Characteristics of Potential TV Viewers, Development of an Evaluation Plan for a National Career Education TV Series, and Conceptualization and Feasibility of Ancillary Subsystems.

The institutional model: This is sometimes called the rural-residential model. The model's purpose is to develop and implement resident career education programs for unskilled persons living in rural areas. Families would be brought to the training site so that, in the words of an OE source, "each family member can develop an appropriate career role, through employment, study, or home management, or a combination of these."

The Mountain Plains Regional Education Center has been set up at a closed Air Force base in Glasgow, Mont., and OE has sunk $4 million into the center as the start of a five-year program which will bring hundreds of families to live at the base. The project is supposed to serve as a prototype for similar projects elsewhere.

Four cases—two from big city districts, one at the state level, and one involving a community college—where innovative programs are commanding national attention

OREGON: CLUSTERING

Rarely is an educational idea two-dimensional. The Oregon State Department of Education's cluster concept for occupational training is an exception, for it is both a curriculum innovation and a facility-planning breakthrough.

The theory behind the cluster is that 97 percent of the approximately 25,000 existing occupational titles can be grouped into a few major areas according to similar characteristics and purposes. Thus a school can feasibly gather closely related occupations into a "cluster" that is at once a physical facility and a curriculum concept. For example, a health cluster might include in one location such occupations as medical assistant, nurse's aide, dental technician, and inhalation therapist.

Clustering has these educational advantages, according to its proponents: (1) courses can be organized around common core areas of study; (2) a student can transfer within the cluster from one job objective to another without undue loss of time; (3) once out in the world of work, an ex-student will be able to adjust more easily to related jobs.

In addition, the nature of the program serves to encourage individualized instruction and team teaching projects.

Oregon, which pioneered in the development of the cluster concept, expects about half of all high school students in the state to be in cluster programs by 1975. To promote this goal, the state department of education has issued a colorful brochure explaining the concept, detailing instructional guidelines, and recommending 12 clusters on the basis of present and projected employment needs in the state. They are: industrial mechanics; general clerical; marketing; agricul-

Figure 48.1. DESIGN ELEMENTS OF A CLUSTER

The design of each cluster, as envisioned by Oregon planners, would have three major zones: a resource center that contains audiovisual equipment and reference material; a laboratory for job simulation experiences with heavy machinery and tools; and a support zone that serves as an acoustical buffer between the other two zones and contains conference rooms, clean-up areas, lockers and toilets. According to Robert Mention of Mention/Hanns/Lindburg, Eugene, Ore., the architect on the planning team, the three spaces would blend together in an actual facility and could be designed in a variety of shapes and sizes.

RESOURCE CENTER

This is a flexible space designed to accommodate large groups, small group seminars and individual study areas. The center provides the various resources for the cluster or clusters which it serves. The resources include audiovisual equipment, occupational periodicals, references and textbooks. The space would be well lighted and acoustically designed to accommodate various activities in close proximity.

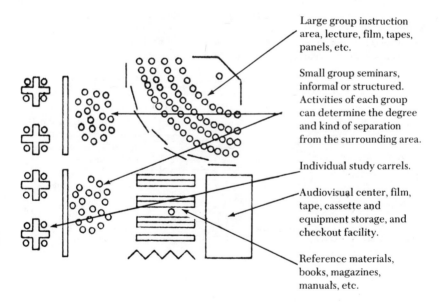

Large group instruction area, lecture, film, tapes, panels, etc.

Small group seminars, informal or structured. Activities of each group can determine the degree and kind of separation from the surrounding area.

Individual study carrels.

Audiovisual center, film, tape, cassette and equipment storage, and checkout facility.

Reference materials, books, magazines, manuals, etc.

SUPPORT AREA

This space encompasses a variety of functions which support the resource center and laboratory and thereby enables each of them to be more flexible. The area also serves as a noise buffer between the passive resource area and the active laboratory. Instructor-student conference rooms, storage facilities, toilets, locker, cleanup area and dressing rooms are some of the chief uses of this space.

Figure 48.1 continued

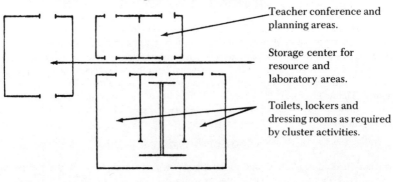

Teacher conference and planning areas.

Storage center for resource and laboratory areas.

Toilets, lockers and dressing rooms as required by cluster activities.

LABORATORY

The skill laboratory is where the hands-on skill and experience appropriate to the cluster occupations are taught. Accordingly the various tools, large scale equipment and student work stations are located in this area. Access to the outside is needed as is access to the support and resource areas. The laboratory activities should provide the student with job simulated experiences so that various activities and their relationship to each other are relevant to actual conditions. The laboratory should be as flexible as possible to accommodate program equipment and enrollment changes.

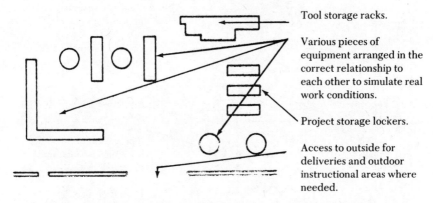

Tool storage racks.

Various pieces of equipment arranged in the correct relationship to each other to simulate real work conditions.

Project storage lockers.

Access to outside for deliveries and outdoor instructional areas where needed.

ture; food service; construction; wood products; secretarial; metal working; bookkeeping and accounting; health; and electricity-electronics.

Within the state, there are now more than 400,000 people employed in these 12 occupational groupings. Another 200,000 will be needed to fill job openings by 1975.

The cluster program in Oregon schools will involve a three-hour block of time each day during Grades 11 and 12. Each "clustered" student receives a broad introduction to the knowledge and skills appropriate to an occupational family. The program then develops competencies in a variety of jobs, encouraging the student to seek a level of knowledge and skills that is commensurate with his capabilities. Finally, the student may specialize in one occupation within the cluster. This would be supplemented by outside, on-the-job experience.

Two more advantages of the program, according to Oregon State Superintendent Dale Parnell, are that schools can enter into clustering by phases (*i.e.* start with only one or two clusters) and that any kind of high school—large, small, urban, rural, suburban—can cluster.

DALLAS: CONTRACTING

If performance contracting can work with standard academic subjects such as reading and math, why not with career education?

The Dallas (Tex.) Independent School District couldn't find any objections. And since district officials have a strong belief that performance contracting is efficient, they decided theirs would be the first district in the country to contract with outside industry for occupational training.

The result is two vocational contracts in Dallas. The first program, now in its second year, is a modest effort in traditional shop subjects for 150 students. It includes mechanical drafting for *women,* and auto mechanics and machine training for boys. Thiokol Chemical Corp., a division of LTV Industries, is the contractor, and it is being paid $385.47 from Title I funds per student.

The success of this program—industry demand for graduates is reported to be extremely high and the district says 95 percent of students reached employability—prompted a much larger performance contract for 11 of the 24 major career clusters at Dallas' new Skyline Center, a $21 million, five-building complex that is the first of five planned magnet schools for career education, traditional high school subjects, and community services. Approximately 2,500 of the Center's 3,700 students are in the career development program.

RCA is the contractor for management of the 11 clusters, and the company has guaranteed that students who finish the program (some in two years, others in three) can either get a job in their chosen fields or be able to gain admittance to college or technical school.

Cost of the contract, which includes curriculum development, is slightly in excess of $1 million, excluding the cost of teachers but including some district personnel assigned as support staff. All financing came from local funds. Because the contract with RCA also covers development of curriculum as well as a review and updating of curriculum next summer, the district has no cost-per-student figure.

Initially, Dallas had a contract with three firms—RCA, Philco-

Ford, and Thiokol—to counsel, screen and recruit potential career education students for the magnet school. More than 4,200 applications were eventually received and the three companies were paid a total of $100,000.

Following this work, which was completed early in 1970, the district decided it would be more feasible to contract for further services with only one company. The three firms then resubmitted bids; RCA was selected.

First, RCA recounseled with students and then drew profiles of certain subject "clusters" and determined what type of students would fit best into each cluster. Development of curriculum for clusters was therefore based on knowledge of student wants and their needs.

Curriculum development, completed in August of this year, consisted of writing curriculum guides, developing and assembling materials, and ascertaining equipment needs. Equipment already on hand was reevaluated.

The 11 subject clusters RCA is managing are: business management; technology; horticulture; metal technology; world of construction; electronic sciences; aeronautics; transportation services; photographic arts; television arts; world of fashion; and health, medical and dental technology.

Under the instructional phase, which began this semester and will run through June, 1972, RCA is hiring and managing teachers who work in these clusters. The teachers, however, remain under contract to the Dallas district so that if the relationship with RCA is terminated for some reason, the district is protected against stoppage of the program.

RCA has recruited many teachers directly from industry, but those without teaching experience are teamed with professional teachers within clusters. There is no certification problem with industry recruits since they may be immediately certified as vocational education teachers if they have five or more years of work experience.

The school district itself has set up industry advisory committees for each of Skyline Center's 24 career clusters. These committees meet periodically with the contractor and school officials to provide added input on curriculum. In addition, the Dallas Chamber of Commerce has assigned a full-time person to serve as liaison between the district and local industry.

Dallas has no other performance contract plans for vocational training, but hopes that its experience with Skyline Center will be beneficial when the other magnet schools are built.

TRITON COLLEGE: COOPERATING

What kind of contribution can a community college make to vocational programs at neighboring high schools? A big one if it gets the chance, say administrators at Triton College in River Grove, Ill.

Despite stumbling blocks, Triton is attempting to make a major contribution to occupational training in surrounding high schools by sharing with them its own staff, facilities and resources. To date, progress has been nothing to shout about. But the concept is significant.

For one thing, Triton's cooperative arrangement may serve as a model for other communities. For another, the idea of extending use of community college facilities—which are the fastest growing educational institutions in the country—is less costly than adding new vocational programs in secondary schools.

Specifically, Triton's effort involves a "released time" agreement that's enabled a dozen high school juniors and seniors to participate in vocational programs (and receive high school credit for them) on the Triton campus. Several of the college deans and secondary school instructors have been appointed to each other's curriculum advisory committees, with the result that high school voc ed curriculums are being updated and expanded.

In many cases, integration of staff has been even more significant, since many of Triton's part-time vocational instructors are local high school teachers. Triton has also appointed 11 "coordinators"—often department heads and deans—who inform high school students about the college's career and university transfer programs. This is done through periodic career days and close contact with high school counselors.

The college has developed close relationships with area employers as well, and last year taught nearly 1,000 employees of companies in the surrounding area. The cooperative effort has led to a number of work-study arrangements in industrial, technical and health service fields.

Triton administrators tend to see the "released time" agreements with secondary schools as most beneficial to the youngsters, who then might conceivably be graduated from high school with accredited training in any number of career fields. They expect that more and more students will want to participate.

So far, the major drawback has been the expense. Under present state law, the high school that wants a "released time" agreement must pay Triton the actual cost of instruction for each student. At $35 per credit hour, the expense is too high for most districts. State law also prevents a student, or his parents, from supplementing whatever the secondary school might be able to pay, or from paying the whole cost himself, under a released time, for-credit agreement.

Currently, Triton administrators are hoping to get a federal or state grant which would allow them to take the cost burden off the school district.

TOLEDO: COUNSELING

What school administrator doesn't fret about vocational counseling and guidance? It's a squeaky wheel in most otherwise smooth-running school districts.

Not, however, at Toledo's Jefferson Center, where officials have gone all out to gear up career counseling. A year-round vocational rehabilitation facility to be opened by next month, Jefferson places as much priority on counseling and evaluation as it does on actual skill training. A good part of the reason: The center's target population includes 15 to 20-year-old youths who have dropped out of school or who are unable to adjust to, or profit from, regular school programs.

Says R. Thomas Scherer, executive director of vocational, industrial and adult education for Toledo public schools: "Jefferson Center is an effort to work with the specific problems which are causing failure and frustration and which cannot be solved through standard and normal procedures."

To achieve an objective like that requires consistent and comprehensive counseling, he adds. And Jefferson students—45 at the beginning—will get it from specialists from Ohio's Rehabilitation Services Commission, the agency assisting the Toledo City School District in operating the center. (Indeed, the commission is footing 80 percent of the bill.)

Here's how Jefferson relies on counseling and testing to find the right career for each student:

Initially, potential trainees referred to Jefferson—by the welfare department, Ohio State Employment Service, churches, public and parochial schools, other social and employment agencies—undergo a battery of testing, one full week of psychological tests, intelligence tests, interest, aptitude, dexterity and personality tests (Wexler, Kuder, Strong, Rorschach among them) conducted by two clinical psychologists. Results of the tests are combined with previous information—provided by the referring agency and, sometimes, by parents—

on the trainee's social, psychological, medical and academic background.

If all the information shows the trainee to be suited for the center, he is assigned to a rehabilitation counselor who not only guides him in selecting a skill, but also keeps tabs on his progress during the entire 38-week program. Should he require medical attention, legal assistance, or other supportive services, he will get help in those areas, too, from his counselor. Each counselor—there will be four to start—holds a master's degree in vocational rehabilitation counseling.

The trainee then begins approximately five weeks of work evaluation and adjustment before he moves into actual skill training. This portion of the program gives him an opportunity to get acquainted with several different skills and lets counselors learn more about the trainee's interest, attitudes, abilities and drawbacks.

Can the trainee do the work? Does he accept supervision? How does he relate to his peers? Is he highly motivated? Questions such as these require answers if a wise choice of careers is to be made.

By combining results of testing and evaluation with skill preferences of the trainee, the counselor comes up with a recommended course of vocational rehabilitation in one of nine skills offered by the center—building maintenance, child care, fabric service, health care, manufacturing and construction, merchandising, office services, and warehousing.

The trainee enters a 16-week program of skill training and remedial education based on his individual needs and desires. Here training instructors (teachers) keep comprehensive records on the trainee's work and adjustment. Should his instructor and counselor find him unsuited for the field chosen, the trainee receives additional testing and counseling to find something more fitting.

At completion of the skill training period, a decision must be made by the counselor on whether the trainee seems ready for a full-time job or requires more education at the center. If it's the latter, the trainee enters a 16-week work-study program that serves as an extension of the previous phase. Or perhaps the counselor believes a student should return to a regular school program. In that case the counselor will confer with a staff member at the school to help secure the best placement for the student. Up to age 20, any individual who has completed his training at the center may return for more.

Twenty is not the cut-off age for everyone seeking the center's services, however. Starting as soon after the center is opened as feasible, Jefferson will initiate vocational rehabilitation and training for adults. Like the student program, the emphasis will be on—you guessed it—counseling and evaluation.

Part 5

Preparing
Teachers for
Career Education

This section is for anyone concerned with developing the pedagogical skills necessary for the teaching of career education. An attempt has been made to provide alternative ways to acquire these pedagogical skills.

The initial article discusses what needs to be done to meet the demand for career education teachers. It is followed by an article that provides encouragement for any teacher who is contemplating the implementation of career education in her classroom.

The preparation of teachers for career education can occur at a number of different levels. The article by Walter Wernick et al. takes a global perspective on the entire process. The article by Gene Meyer describes how pre-service career education experiences can be provided to prospective teachers as undergraduates. Terry Whealon gives an example of how school districts and the university can work together to provide in-service workshops for teachers.

The last article illustrates how one teacher set out to learn on her own about career education by attending a career education conference.

49

Meeting the Demand: Personnel Development in Career Education*

William K. Appelgate

Thomas Jefferson believed that society, in order to retain its vitality and resilience, must possess both a vision and an understanding of equality and of excellence. Equality of opportunity and recognition of excellence, contended Jefferson, exist as a rationale and cornerstone of free public education.

During the past two hundred years, some rather dramatic changes have taken place concerning the responsibilities assigned to the school. Society now possesses a growing expectation that schools not only have more responsibility to serve all individuals, but also that educational excellence means work for all; and the responsibility falls to the public schools, particularly the secondary schools and community colleges.

A review of the record indicates that public education has just not produced consistent with this expectation. Not only has the comprehensive high school and the community college failed to provide adequate amounts and variety of direct preparation for work, but they have also frequently failed to develop the individual to the point where he can intelligently make career decisions for himself.

Nearly fifty percent of the nation's youth currently make the

*Reprinted with permission from the *Illinois Journal of Education*, a publication of the Illinois Office of Education.

transition to the world of work directly from high school. Although Illinois' averages are somewhat lower, due in part to the well-developed community college system, selected urban areas are among the highest in the nation. In these districts, as many as eighty percent of those graduating from high school move directly to work without further education or training. The severity of the problem is further impressed when it is realized that the majority of students in the eighty percent figure possess no salable skills to improve their plight in an economic system which supports a small and steadily shrinking number of work roles for the unskilled.

What goals for the schools? Certainly the interpretation of multiple purposes must be a joint venture between the community, students and parents, teachers, and the State which provides support. However, the recurring concern evidenced throughout the country is that education be made more purposeful. Interpreted, education, especially in secondary schools, should either prepare the individual for work or for entry to some higher level of education.

In January 1970, a statement by Sidney P. Marland, United States Commissioner of Education, focused clearly on how schools might well begin to serve society's new expectation of education. In a presentation entitled *Career Education Now*, he provided schools with a charge to expand programming and to further detail the much needed emphasis on education for work. The rationale for this new direction of education, according to Commissioner Marland, emerged from a need for schools to perform not only more accountably to society's expectations, but also more positively in response to each student's real need for career preparation. Career education was described not as a program tract alternative for students to select, but as a conceptual alternative to the existing orientation of the total school program.

> "What I would hope for is a new orientation of education—that would expose the student to a range of career opportunities, help him narrow down choices in terms of his own aptitudes and interests and provide him with education and training appropriate to his ambition—every student leaving high school would possess the skills necessary to give him a start in making a livelihood for himself and his family. . . ."[1]

Career education has matured markedly as an educational concept in the last two years. A recognizable philosophy and a growing body of knowledge currently exist to support Commissioner Marland's early thesis. Acceptance of the career education idea is evidenced by an encouraging commitment in the level of Federal Government support to a variety of community, industry, and school-based models. State governments have assumed what can be interpreted as a major responsibility for expanding the more narrowly defined concepts of vocational and occupational education into functional educational programs of career development which begin in kindergarten and continue through college. And, most encouraging are the efforts of local school districts.

Elementary school programs of career development, designed to assist individuals in developing a realistic self-concept and improve their understanding of society's organization for work, have been articulated with experiences to provide improved career awareness. Career exploration and orientation to specific career options can now logically lead to sound decisions about direct preparation for work. Whether one chooses to prepare for work entry after high school or to continue his studies, it is important to know that the decision was made by the individual with sufficient information about himself and career options. A functional orientation toward career education places as much emphasis on vocational decision-making as on direct occupational preparation, and local school districts are beginning to make the concept work.

At the core of educational institutions and programs is the body of professional personnel who make them work—administrators, guidance personnel, and teachers. If improvements or changes in education are to occur, then educational personnel become the vehicle for that action.

If public schools are to move successfully to acceptance of career education, emphasis must be placed on developing personnel to perform. Gordon Swanson, of the University of Minnesota, clarified the importance of personnel development in career education in a recent issue of the *American Vocational Journal.*

> "There is no greater barrier to career education than the need for appropriately trained instructional and supervisory personnel.
> "Career education cannot be implemented as an educational reform by training a small cadre of specialists. Nor can it be implemented by merely returning to the deadening practice of conducting classes in each school.
> "It can become a reality by beginning a massive program of in-service training for the slightly more than two million elementary and secondary teachers in the public schools of the country. It is necessary, simultaneously, to begin a flow of adequately trained teachers from the teacher education institutions of the country."[2]

A current planning effort of the Illinois Division of Vocational and Technical Education focuses on this most critical component of the movement toward career education. The purpose of the Master Plan for Personnel Development in Career Education is to provide a series of recommendations for improving the development of personnel for career education programs in elementary schools, secondary schools, community colleges, and state institutions (e.g., correctional). Through a careful analysis of where we have been, as well as where we are going, it is hoped that adjustments can be made to fortify the complex personnel development system in Illinois.

This effort is most encouraging. For too long, too many state education agencies have failed to recognize the complex, multidimensional components of personnel development. In 1969, the Illinois Division of Vocational and Technical Education developed a special unit within its organization to support the planning and design of curricula and personnel development activities. Since that time, more than one million dollars has been invested in preservice and in-service career education personnel development and curriculum projects. Since early 1970, more than 3,000 educational personnel have participated in the in-service development workshops and programs sponsored by the unit.

Despite some encouraging signs, much remains to be accomplished. Activities of the Professional and Curriculum Development Unit of the Division have largely serviced personnel in secondary schools and community colleges. Before the career education model can be operationalized in public schools, new efforts must be initiated to focus on development of new types of educational personnel. Elementary teachers and guidance personnel require in-service activities to prepare them for roles in career education; new personnel are needed to employ the use of occupational orientation curricula in the ninth and tenth grades, and administrators at all levels need to develop an improved understanding of the public expectations for improved employability through education at all levels.

An additional factor compounds the concern for personnel development in career education. Since 1969, the amount of State and Federal support going to career education programs in Illinois has grown three times. This has simultaneously resulted in, and has been encouraged by, increases in enrollments and a wider variety of program offerings. From 1969 to 1970, the number of occupational program offerings in secondary schools in Illinois has increased by one hundred thirty percent. Community colleges are currently offering one hundred fifty-five different types of occupational programs, whereas, in 1969, the total number of different offerings was only eighty-seven. This represents an increase of seventy-eight percent.

These important systems demands for more and better personnel in a variety of types naturally motor selected changes in career education personnel development. However, the observed speed and direction of this change leaves much to be desired. Local districts, whose stake is highest, and whose interest should be greatest, often do not or cannot bring about desired changes. Problems with certification procedures or shortages of appropriate in-service programs in specialized areas are, frequently, too complex, or too far removed, for the energies of individual districts to meter and correct.

With increasing emphasis being placed on states to plan, deliver, and administer career education programs, corrective action to improve personnel development must be initiated at the state level. Efforts to bring about planned and positive changes in personnel development in career education must more fully recognize the variety of people and the importance of each group's involvement in the planning process.

What can be done? Where should the attention in personnel development be focused? Action on priority concerns expressed in the following prescriptive observations provides some alternative first steps.

Cooperative Goal Setting

The importance of improving the delivery of career development in the elementary schools, career orientation in junior high, career exploration in early high school, and direct preparation in late high school and community college is well supported by the stated intent of various statewide groups. The *Action Goals for the Seventies* report of the Office of the Superintendent of Public Instruction, the Task Force on Career Education sponsored by the Illinois Chamber of Commerce, the *State Plan for Vocational Education, Master Plan Phase III for Illinois Public Higher Education,* and the *Report of the Governor's Conference on Vocational Education* all support a renewed emphasis for improving career education and the associated processes of personnel development. However, this most desirable intent lacks focus. Failure of organizations and institutions to zero in on compatible, well-defined goals for career education restricts the potential for facilitating dollar support and dilutes energies expended toward implementation.

A major effort is needed to detail career education on a statewide basis. Such effort would not only improve the efficiency of various groups, but it would move the focus from reaction to symptoms to action on implementation. State education agencies such as the Office of the Superintendent of Public Instruction, the Division of Vocational and Technical Education, the Illinois Junior College Board, as well as the Illinois Board of Higher Education, should take the lead by establishing a committee with the charge to develop measurable goals for career education. Such action would provide an important first step in providing criteria for statewide accountability in education and associated personnel development.

Renewed Local District Action

A recent statewide evaluation of career education programs conducted by the Division of Vocational and Technical Education details the need for improved developments of personnel. Each of the fifty-two independently developed reports completed to date recommends action by local districts to upgrade personnel. These actions include: providing planned on-site development programs, improving incentives for participation in university in-service activities, and encouraging summer employment or internships in government, business, and industry. If local school districts are interested in quality and improved accountability, then such incentives and program provisions for personnel development must be initiated. Business and industry, which generally are less personnel intensive than is education, spends approximately five percent of its annual operating budget on personnel development.[3] Most local school districts spend less than one-half of one percent on such activities.

Expanded University Commitment

Currently eight public universities and one private university provide various degree-oriented preservice preparation for occupational teachers, administrators, or guidance personnel. The major emphasis is on secondary school teacher preparation in areas of business education, home economics, industrial technology, and vocational agriculture. However, despite the continuing need for such personnel and a relatively successful record of graduate placement, other critical personnel needs exist which go unmet. The glaring deficiency of in-service offerings for all types of personnel, the need for occupational teachers in developing areas of health and public service, the importance of providing career development theory and skills to elementary teachers, and the need for developing vocational guidance personnel rather than college guidance personnel—all these demand greater attention and action on the part of universities.

Institutionally, resources must be mobilized to consolidate the dispersed and often duplicated efforts of special content preparation. Statewide, resources should be focused in selected institutions to provide a critical mass of personnel and programs with the capacity to offer a full complement of in-service and preservice programs. The education personnel development are clearly more promising than continuing rivalry. The realities of limited state resources, coupled with critical personnel development needs, make it highly inefficient for a statewide system of higher education to support eight separate attempts to accomplish similar ends. Institutions willing to commit resources to comprehensive personnel development in career education should begin planning and development of programs accordingly. State educational agencies should recognize these efforts and work to provide facilitating dollar support, even if resources must be drawn from similar, less productive efforts at other institutions.

Alternative Routes to Certification

Encouraging universities to improve preservice programs by granting credit for work experience and developing new models of preparation is an important consideration for enhancing personnel development in career education. However, without accompanying changes in the certification process, real improvement is blocked. Alternative routes are needed for current state certification procedures. Provisions should be made for assessing competencies and certifying skills rather than basing certification solely on courses taken, or credit hours earned, in university professional education courses.

Rather than insuring quality, many provisions of certification requirements have worked to insure a rather questionable sameness from one program or institution to another. Opportunities for institutions or individuals to experiment, to test alternate routes to personnel preparation and development are limited by the current guidelines.

Competency-Based Development

Curriculum revisions, in terms of courses required, application of new technologies, or changes in instructional forms, frequently fail to insure lasting, improvement unless they are measured against changes in personnel performance. As long as courses which are essentially content-oriented form the basis for the curriculum, little real progress will result.

Needed is a major overhaul of the curriculum for career education personnel. Emphasis on process-oriented, competency-based programs provides a most worthwhile alternative to current program offerings. Identification and validation of skills, attitudes, and understandings required for good performance by personnel in a career education model provide the basis for competency development. Thus, information gathered from evaluating performance becomes the basis for personnel development programs.

Whether the intent of career education personnel development programs is preservice or in-service, a competency-based curriculum provides an accountable method for taking a prospective or practicing teacher, administrator, or guidance counselor from where he is to an improved level of performance. This orientation toward performance not only recognizes the public call for improved accountability by eliminating program elements, which are unnecessary, but it also has implications focusing on the value-added by a particular educational program. Seldom has any idea such as competency-based personnel development provided a format for simultaneously improving the efficiency of preservice and in-service development and insuring quality in the process.

Placing Priority on In-service Development

While needs for new types of personnel are apparent, the priority concern for personnel development must be a vigorous commitment to improved in-service programs. Introducing personnel to the career education concept and providing them with competencies to implement programs in local schools are prerequisites to realizing the career continuum. To accomplish such an objective for seventy-two thousand elementary and thirty-six thousand secondary public school teachers and one thousand two hundred administrative personnel in Illinois is a formidable task. Yet, if an honest commitment to career education is to be made, a major in-service effort must be initiated.

Previous in-service efforts in career education have generally been offered by public universities. Most have been provided in the form of workshops conducted during the summer, and nearly all have been funded by the Division of Vocational and Technical Education. Few universities have committed resources to include ongoing, in-service development as an integral component of their program offerings despite the apparent need. Part of the problem has been the statewide funding mechanism. Universities are supported essentially through credit-hour generation in degree-oriented programs. To mount a major effort of in-service career education personnel development, alternative reimbursement procedures reflected in operating budget formulas must be provided. Forcing in-service programs into credit generating workshops held during the summer when faculty are less fully employed, severely restricts the impact of the already limited in-service offerings.

The type and variety of in-service activities must also be reconsidered. In addition to summer workshops, provisions must be made for weekend seminars, correspondence instruction, local personnel training programs, and supervised internships in business, industry, and government throughout the year.

New Types of Occupational Teachers

A major component in the concept of career education is programs of direct occupational preparation. While figures from the United States Office of Education generally indicate a growing demand for occupational instructional personnel, employment needs in selected areas dictate that a shift in emphasis on the types produced may be desirable. While teachers of home economics, office occupations, and industrial technology comprised almost seventy percent of the occupational teachers graduated from Illinois' universities in 1971, virtually no instructional personnel graduated were qualified to prepare individuals for employment in health and public service occupations. Yet, critical needs currently exist in these two areas and employment projections point to a steady increase for associated employment opportunities. For example, one out of every four jobs created in 1971 in the United States was in government. In the cities this figure increases to two out of five, and most of these jobs are in service areas such as health, welfare and related services, police, fire, and education.[4]

Business, Industry, and Government Participation

The benefits of functional relationships between potential employers and occupational education has been well established. Local schools utilize advisory groups in the planning and conduct of occupational programs.

Cooperative education curricula, utilizing the concept of employer-based training, are important components of direct preparation. Nearly 20,000 high school students and community college students are currently enrolled in these programs in Illinois.

Such education-employer relationships are encouraging. However, they represent only one dimension of potential interactions beneficial in a Career Education Model. More exposure to how communities are organized for work, production, and service is a major intent of career education. In practice, implementation calls for more than additional field trips to business and industry. A two-way flow of personnel, educators, and employers is critically needed to improve the relevance of career awareness, orientation, exploration, and certainly the direct preparation of individuals with marketable skills.

Universities must seek to build improved relationships not only with business and industry, but also with government agencies which provide an increasingly high proportion of new employment opportunities. Recruiting potential teachers and administrators with experience in occupational specialties, establishing business and industry advisory groups to career education personnel development programs, utilizing the facilities and resources of industry in the process of preparation and joint design of cooperative in-service programs for technical teachers are examples of relationships which give promise of improved quality development.

Ultimately the success of career education is dependent upon the success of efforts to provide programs of career education personnel development. While quantitative concerns for new types of personnel are strikingly apparent, qualitative demands derived from emerging public expectations of education for work deserve commensurate attention. Clear thought about needs, an increased commitment to planning, and evaluation of performance rather than promise provide some necessary initial steps, if education is to deliver on the expectation.

Notes

1. Sidney P. Marland, Jr., "Career Education Now" (Speech delivered before the Convention of the National Association of Secondary School Principals. Houston, Tex., January 23, 1971).

2. Gordon I. Swanson, "Career Education: Barriers to Implementation," *American Vocational Journal* 47 (March 1972).

3. Carl J. Schaefer. "A Rationale for Comprehensive Personnel Development in a State" (Address delivered before the meeting of State Directors of Vocational Education, Columbus, Ohio, September 1971).

4. Jean Couturier, "Higher Education for Public" (Address delivered before the Illinois Assembly of Higher Education and Public Service Careers. Allerton House, Monticello, Ill., April 5, 1972).

50

Any Teacher Can: Guiding Career Exploration*

*Norman Gysbers
and Earl Moore*

A relatively new concept in education—career development, or career exploration—may provide a basis for redirecting school experiences to make them meaningful, relevant, and human. No less influential a figure than Jerome Bruner has suggested that we put vocation and intention back into the educational process.

> "... I would like to explore, in the interest of relevance, whether we might not recapture something of the old notion of vocation, of ways of life, or to use the expression of so many undergraduates today, of 'life-styles'. ... I really believe that our young have become so isolated that they do not know the roles available in the society and the variety of styles in which they are played. I would urge that we find some way of connecting the diversity of society to the phenomenon of the school, to keep the latter from becoming so isolated and the former so suspicious."[1]

Others are saying the same thing, though sometimes in different words. United States Commissioner of Education Sidney P. Marland, Jr., has called for a clear focus on career education at all levels from early childhood to adult life. Career education, in broad terms, encompasses those structured programs and activities in home, school, and community which help shape an individual's career decisions and development. Clearly, these activities have a place in the elementary school. As Matthews and Sylvester suggest, childhood is the period when the lifelong construction of one's career identity begins.

If you're a teacher who is mostly concerned with getting subject content across to your class, you probably recognize the potential of a career program for teaching traditional academic skills. But if you're truly a careerwise teacher, you not only appreciate this approach—you use it for the opportunities it affords students to develop a personal sense of self-worth, to examine the interrelationship of work and leisure in the shaping of individual life-styles, to become more aware of their abilities, and to assure them of marketable skills upon graduation.

While bringing out the unique qualities of each student, a career-centered classroom will be a democratic one. Where the content-oriented classroom often creates passive, dependent students, and fosters competition for grades, the career-oriented classroom encourages students to help one another. And this interdependence provides the security and confidence with which each student can achieve individual goals.

Since career exploration is a personal rather than a competitive goal, each student can explore at his own pace, in his own way, and still be assured of a measure of success.

Incorporate exploratory activities into every phase of your regular curriculum—math, art, social studies. Plunge into the world of work by first helping children relate the skills they acquire in school to future applications in an occupational setting. Let the local community assist you in teaching basic knowledge and skills.

Resource personnel, parents, and students themselves can bring the career world into the classroom. Use action-oriented, learning-by-doing processes. If you're studying transportation, go to the railroad station, airport, bus depot. Observe. Ask questions. Invite a bus driver, railroad engineer, pilot, stewardess, or reservationist to talk to the class. Examine all aspects of an occupational field. As a career-minded teacher, you should encourage individual planning and self-accountability too. In Santa Rosa, California, for instance, teams of students organized a worker visitation unit in their community. Using recorded interviews of workers talking about their jobs and photographs of them on different jobs, each team prepared a narrated slide presentation to share with other class members and their parents. *Who is responsible?* All members of the school community have a shared responsibility for establishing career exploration programs. But right now, very little is being done on a systematic basis. Leadership is needed to bring people together in activities which help students relate school life to life in the outside world. More is needed than a once-a-year field trip to a local industry, or a one-hour talk from the counselor about career planning. School-age children at all levels should be able to explore their interests every day in the context of career possibilities. With the following guidelines, any teacher can establish a classroom environment rich with career explorations.

• Take the responsibility to sample the career world and share your findings.

• Plan activities that parallel or simulate different work settings.

• Provide procedures and resources for students to explore careers.

• Provide media, worker role models, and appropriate support personnel.

• Plan for each student's career needs.

• Plan cooperatively with counselors, administrators, and other teachers.

• Establish and maintain self-accountability procedures for these programs.

• Encourage the establishment of advisory groups among parents and local businessmen.

Where will you get the necessary funds for a continuing program? The major source of available money is the federal government. Part D of the Vocational Education Amendments of 1968 (Public Law 90-576), authorizes the use of federal funds for career development programs in the elementary school. To secure funding under this program, prepare and submit a proposal to your state education department or the United States Office of Education.

Title III of the Elementary and Secondary Education Act of 1965 provides still another possible source for funding career programs. Under this Title, as with other funding sources, proposals must be developed and submitted. Query local school administrators or appropriate state personnel for procedures. WHAT DO YOU DO UNTIL THE FUNDS ARRIVE? First of all, keep in contact with your state department. It will alert you to funding sources as well as state program guidelines. Simultaneously, organize appropriate career activities for your class and recruit the enthusiasm of other teachers to do the same.

Your school and community may need a major reeducation program to accommodate these new attitudes and philosophies. Most teachers and administrators haven't been trained to operate their classroom and schools along the guidelines suggested by career education concepts. Therefore, teachers, counselors, and administrators must initiate training programs involving the total community.

• Along with college courses, in-service programs, speakers, and consultants, use activities to encompass the total school operation.

• Establish a K-6 committee to prepare a comprehensive school staff reeducation plan. The committee should include members from all grade levels, and from administrative, supervisory, and specialty areas, so that the plan worked out will support all disciplines. The committee will need to consider media to be used, names of possible consultants, and conference formats. Consider cooperative programs with other school districts.

• Embark on a community-involvement program. Contact businesses and industries, service institutions, parent groups, service clubs, and professional groups. Use news releases, speakers bureaus, and face-to-face discussions to inform and enlist community support. Form an advisory council which includes a wide occupational range of community members.

• Assess possible resources; then experiment with some career exploration activities. While there is a lack of educational materials and formalized texts at present, in the near future there will be a rapid increase in textbooks with a career-world base, multimedia career exploratory kits, and specialized materials representing career development approaches. Meanwhile, try creating your own materials.

• Contact personnel who can supply you with the materials, transportation, and service support to carry out community-based projects.

To take advantage of the current and future emphasis on career development as a way of making education relevant, you need to begin now. Examine your current teaching techniques and goals from a career exploration perspective. As you accomplish this, you take an important step—one that any teacher can.

Note

1. Jerome Bruner, "The Process of Education Revisited," *Phi Delta Kappan*, September 1971, pp. 18-21.

51

Career Education for Elementary School Teachers*

Walter Wernick et al.

eacher educators can see the career education movement as a strategy to make job training for specific occupations synonymous with secondary school education—or they can perceive career education as a positive force for more effective personal development of individual human beings. We've chosen the latter view. Our research and development project has attempted to refocus the work of the schools upon people[1].

Changes in Basic Human Relationships

"You've come a long way, baby!"

And you won't grow up in the same environment either. Work activities have moved outside the home and a fantastic array of information about the world has moved in—by means of television and other forms of mass media. The catalog of changes in our ways of life would make a large volume, and the index of educational needs to meet these changes would be longer than the lists of course descriptions found in curricular guides.

We intend to focus upon only a few changes in the ways children and adults can relate in our technological world, suggest ways that

*Reprinted by permission from *Journal of Teacher Education*, Summer 1973, pp. 97-102.

teachers can help learners cope with their educational needs, and then present recommendations for teacher educators to help prepare teachers to meet the needs of children.

CHILDREN NEED ADULT MODELS

Perhaps the teacher in today's world knows the importance of adult models in child development, but does he realize that many children are now virtually adult-deprived at the same time they have an affluence of sophisticated devices, an abundance of world knowledge, and an overabundance of outside stimulation? Children now need adult models more than they need information-givers.

Each prospective teacher must be prepared to serve as a model of a working adult, since he will be the only adult that many of his students will have an opportunity to observe at work for any length of time, day after day. But just as important, prospective teachers need to understand the world of work themselves; they must be able to relate to other working adults. They must know how to put their students in contact with these other adults in meaningful ways—ways that will compensate for the briefness of the exposure.

Teachers can serve as models, especially for the development of inquiry and value clarification skills, and they can serve as managers to maximize the learning opportunities available within the school, home, and community.

MODELS MUST SHOW HOW HUMANS RELATE TO CHANGE

The model of the "happy" worker is insufficient for our dynamic times. Children need to learn about the work people do and they also need to learn how human decisions are made. Children need to observe the development of plans and their consequences—a kind of learning which goes far beyond learning to accumulate and repeat facts. The tools for inquiry and for working with values have to be included directly within the curriculum. We will need a focus on skills that will relate school studies to life outside the classroom, and we will need resource people who, within themselves, represent content about human decisions and their consequences.

Teachers must replace inert subject matter with life-centered activities. Our dynamic world requires active content, content which lives within the activities of working adults. Children must learn from direct experience with adults how to participate in today's fast-moving events—and to believe their personal interventions can have a favorable effect within their own lives.

To paraphrase Mark Twain, *Everybody talks about change, but very few people are doing anything about it.* Teacher educators can!

They can plan programs which provide opportunities for college students to learn more about child-adult relationships; about the life-careers of a variety of adults; about social, political, and economic trends; and about methods of planning to involve a greater range of human resources within the mainstream of instructional activities.

Skills to Implement New Programs

"Information-givers" are prepared by filling them up with information and then helping them learn "information-giving" skills to impart what they are expected to give. Teachers who are to implement new programs by managing a wide variety of resources must be prepared through completely different means. Their skills must be nurtured within carefully selected laboratory experiences and then evaluated with reference to real people in real situations. With our information-rich and experience-poor environment, it might be safer to assume that our college students already have background of the "subjects" than to assume that they have experienced the necessary human relations and management skills with which to readily implement a career education program.

A Developmental Approach to Learning Management Skills

Do our novice teachers have the technical skills to identify children's interests and blend them into curricular programs? If not, then our college students must be helped to diagnose children's interests and refocus traditional content into a variety of experience settings. Students should be asked to demonstrate skills in relating to children, of course, but they should also have the basic management skills to plan sensory activities for small groups of children. Management skills should be as much a part of teacher (and in-service) preparation as child development; teachers have to learn to plan to utilize the internal resources of the school system in order to construct sensory and sharing opportunities to meet specific objectives.

Most school districts provide support systems for the instructional efforts of their teachers. Do teacher preparation programs show how teachers can utilize existing instructional support systems? Or do they feature a heroic model wherein a person knows his "stuff," has a good personality, and goes it alone? A good management approach would enable beginning teachers to get off to a more effective start, work with established traditions, and then create support systems of higher quality to serve more sophisticated needs.

A Focus upon Skills for Utilizing Human Resources

Most teacher educators see the need for developing competencies in the area of human relationships, but they usually translate that to mean teacher-child relationships. They may fail to see the need for examining competencies in the broad range of working relationships necessary for the planning and implementation of a life-centered program.

Can our college students relate to adults? Can they draw upon the services of accessible adults to provide direct experiences for their learners? A simplistic stereotype of the elementary school teacher is "not being able to relate to the real world of the adult." This view needs to be transformed into an image of the teacher as a mature adult working with other adults, as well as with children, to provide quality learning environments. If not, how are career education programs to utilize adults as models of human activity and for information about the world of work?

For most college students, learning to communicate with people "in the real world" for the purpose of preparing relevant instructional activities will probably require the learning of new skills. There should be many opportunities to practice these skills before as well as during student teaching situations.

SKILLS TO MAKE DECISION-MAKING VISIBLE AND CREDIBLE

A packaged approach to curriculum is doomed to failure unless it draws forth the teacher's imaginative energies. Our creative dimensions for career education are not add-ons to instructional activities; they are built-in necessities if teachers are to be tuned in to the opportunities they can gather together within their plans.

Perhaps more than any other human development program, career education demands activity in the mind of the teacher. Diagnosing children's needs, examining instructional resources, relating content from many disciplines of knowledge, and planning for individual as well as social activities require a continuous flow of decisions. The teacher who works to make reasons (as well as decisions) visible to his class is helping children learn career development skills; they will learn that being human means being capable of making decisions, living with them, and meeting their consequences.

Children need to learn from credible models how this can be done and how these human processes can be constantly improved. These processes of thought and action are put in practice by many active adults in our communities—and one need not be working for pay to use imaginative energies to plan and to perform with people. These skills are becoming increasingly significant to personal, social, and economic survival in our dynamic, thing-centered world.

Whether the best exemplary models are teachers or whether better models would be other adults in the community is unimportant to this discussion. The fact of the matter is that elementary school teachers *are* providing, whether they like it or not, one of the most readily accessible models that elementary school children have. By every action (or nonaction) they are creating images for developing minds.

Our college students are learning how to use multi-media approaches to present information. Are they learning how to use themselves as credible models for the examination of decision-making skills?

SKILLS FOR EXPLORING THE FUTURE WITH CHILDREN

It may seem strange that an institution just recently freed from its dependence upon the past for its source of content should be declared irrelevant because it now seeks to relate to the present. Yet, if education today does not become more future-oriented, our programs will become increasingly impotent. The future has become a legitimate area for study, one that has to be a focus for school studies as much as any other content area in the curriculum.

In brief, college students need to help children reach beyond present happenings to examine what they might become—and what their environments might become, too. Working with a child's imaginative energies is a different kind of involvement than working with facts, instructional media, and groups. Our novices will need preparation for involvement with the self-images of their children, especially as the children project themselves into their futures. Technical skills in this area will enable our teachers to explore a great variety of adult roles and models, to bring out the historical and affective dimensions of adult lives, and to focus upon the career opportunities that appear to meet needs, interests, abilities, and values.

Elementary school children will need help in meeting the future but not memorizations of job descriptions or early training in specific vocational skills. To help children explore the future, teachers need to plan for the following concepts: (a) people change their minds about what they like to do with their time, energies, and resources; (b) dynamic forces shape business, industrial, and governmental operations; (c) a free society requires individuals willing to assume responsibility for part of their own futures; (d) many of life's activities require cooperation with people of diverse origins, interests, and abilities as well as individual initiative.

Images Drawn from the Real World of Teaching

The following section describes a few activities planned to include opportunities for career development. The "newness" of these endeavors is not that the children participated in completely different activities from their regular program; rather, it is the mindful attention of the teacher to life-centered goals and the refocusing of instructional energies to meet these goals.

One third grade class in an inner-city Chicago school began by exploring work stations in their own community. By selecting those in black-owned businesses they were able to focus on their own identities and potentialities. For example, a small snack shop took on new significance as the children discovered—through a field trip and interview with the owner—the amount of expertise needed to operate such an enterprise. Besides inquiring about the work involved in each separate business, the class assessed and recorded the contributions that each business made to the community as a whole.

After this nearby exploration plus a week and a half spent studying and researching black businesses outside the immediate community, the children embarked upon a business venture of their own. They conducted informal polls to determine the marketability of certain products and chose popcorn as the most saleable. The problem of available capital was solved by individual donations and an emergency loan from the teacher.

An advertising campaign was launched, then jobs were created and assigned to various students. The children determined the best source of popcorn, silk-screened their own labels onto their packaging materials, and did the work of preparing and selling the merchandise. After selling their entire stock, they "balanced out" to see if they had made a profit.

Specific content skills were not neglected during the project. By refocusing arithmetic, reading, social studies, and language arts lessons upon real people's activities, the teacher was able to demonstrate that education is a relevant—and more important, a *usable*—commodity. Apparently the class learned the lesson well. With the capital from their successful business venture, the students decided to establish a bank from which other classes now borrow (with interest) in order to launch career education projects of their own.

After learning of this project, several other teachers in the school decided to attend a Career Education Conference being held at nearby Northern Illinois University. They listened to other teachers describe how they had introduced career education concepts into their instructional programs. They examined samples of students' work, asked questions, became involved, and formulated their own plans.

"People who work with foods" formed the organizing center for one first grade teacher's planning, while another first grade teacher focused on farming and related occupations. Basic interviewing skills were taught first, with the children practicing by interviewing each other and the teacher aides. After they became comfortable with the interviewing process, several resource people from the community were contacted. The manager of a local produce market visited the classes and was interviewed. A mother related her farm experiences to the group and aided the class in making butter and applesauce. During these weeks, the teachers developed social studies, arithmetic, science, and language arts lessons which drew their content from the interviews.

These teachers reported that class response was overwhelming. There was a marked improvement in attendance, and discipline problems seemed to decline as the children's energies were channeled towards active learning experiences. The children appeared to be much more self-directed. As one teacher commented: "When I can clearly identify my own instructional objectives and goals, the children know what I expect of them and seem to work more independently. The organizing center approach has helped me plan more effectively."

In an upper middle class suburb outside Chicago, three teachers in an elementary school—working within their districts' regular curriculum goals—planned life-centered activities which incorporated resource people, cooperative planning, doing activities, and discussions of the changing world of work.

In the first grade, interviews with resource talent drawn from the parents of the class produced information about people and the work they do, but the teacher also planned for vocabulary development, writing, reading, and math skills. She insisted that career education should also be good academic education. For example, the children said, understood, and spelled words such as interview, facilitator, auditorium, income, analyst, department, and manager. Communication between children and adults increased dramatically as the semester progressed. Parents noted the positive effects of the people-oriented program upon mastery of basic academic skills and endorsed the teacher's efforts without reservation.

Two second-grade teachers worked from a traditional base of academic skills but greatly expanded their range of content by following interests into areas they had previously left unexplored. As a result of an interview with a child's father who was a veterinarian, they were able to carry their science learnings far beyond grade level. Children were constructing "experiments" by using their own ideas for "hypotheses" and were able to make bulletin board displays showing the procedures they followed.

As routine practice sessions of grade-level skills were replaced by interesting and varied exchanges with active adults, more time became available for individual conferences and group sharing sessions. Personal meanings were "turned on" and focused upon the real world, enabling teachers to gather and develop insights that would have been almost inaccessible in media-centered programs.

All of the teachers found they were making more frequent decisions concerning the flow of materials, ideas, children, and activities. They declared that they learned more about the world of work than did the children. They had mixed feelings about their roles as value clarifiers but enjoyed their efforts to facilitate inquiry skills. Sometimes they felt overwhelmed by all the activities they had going on in their classrooms, but they claimed they learned how to manage themselves better and in so doing managed their classroom environment more effectively.

None of the teachers was especially prepared for his renewal as career education professionals, but all were able to build upon their existing pedagogy, learn from consultants, and develop their own procedures. It should be noted that their maturity and experience with community organizations facilitated their development. They were not new teachers just out of school; their previous participation in many varied life activities helped them manage their own roles.

The Support Systems Concept

A school, or a community, can be regarded as a structure of facilities and services. Instructional programs can draw upon this structure to go beyond texts and autoprogrammed materials. Activities can be complex or simple, depending upon the imagination of the teacher.

We believe that the creativity with which the structure is utilized can be developed. If teachers understood what support systems are available and how these could help in planning, implementing, and evaluating, more imaginative thought could be employed. Textbook teachers become assistants to the text. Teachers who know how to use instructional support systems become more able to deal with spontaneity, variety, and children's individual pursuits. As they become more secure in their ability to draw upon available resources to meet instructional needs, they will be more willing to meet the challenges of life-centered career development programs. Instruction in the use of support systems could be based on the following outline of services and facilities:

1. Ways to utilize community resources
   a. Community resource file
   b. Parental involvement system
   c. School-community liaison workers
2. Administrative supports
   a. Staff development activities
   b. Technical supports, e.g., learning centers
3. Pupil guidance system
   a. Biographical information system
   b. Coordinated guidance programs

The teachers in the previous examples had their students explore and visit local businesses. Others who follow in their footsteps may find it easier to plan and implement career education activities because the names, addresses, time schedules, special features, costs, meal arrangements, and types of presentations were recorded and placed on file in the school office. Such a community resource file can be supplemented by the names and addresses of receptive parents with notations of their occupations, hobbies, and talents. Relevant information can be gathered by means of questionnaires and then organized on a card for the file system.

A coordinated parental involvement system could be based on class visits by such parents and on other meaningful forms of communication between school and home. The career resource system can also be profitably extended by utilizing, for career education purposes, the work of the school-community liaison workers. If a school has none, social workers or even community volunteer workers could help with home contact and coordination of visits.

Other teachers in the Chicago school became involved in career education through listening to experienced teachers describe their activities. An administrative support system would foster such sharing of ideas by sending teachers to workshops and conferences on career education and by setting up formal and informal meetings in schools to explore career education ideas.

In a large district, a "cadre-system" might be established by appointing two or three teachers from each school to attend monthly workshops and to be responsible for informing faculty about what was done at these workshops. Other important administrative supports are technical facilities, such as learning centers, where students and teachers can get information and equipment to set up such life-centered enterprises as banks and popcorn companies. In addition, an effective school administration can provide those essential motivational supports which fledgling programs require.

Finally, recall how the teachers in the example noted a marked improvement in attendance and a decline in discipline problems as career education unfolded in their classrooms. Documentation of such results in individual students could lead to maintenance of a "biographical information system" which would facilitate a teacher's planning for the personal development of each student. It would also provide a secure base for coordinated guidance programs between classroom teachers and counselors.

Such instructional support systems need not require great additional expense and effort, and they promote not only career education programs but the general welfare of the school. Working together, teachers in any school can take advantage of a pool of managerial talents and organize the support systems available to them.

College students should learn to develop a school-wide community resource file, work with school-community liaison workers and interested parents, participate in and learn from staff development activities, and utilize guidance and information systems to promote the personal development of their students.

College students should learn to expect instructional support systems to serve their needs as teachers. If school districts do not have effective systems in operation, our young professionals should know how to initiate their creation and development. This may mean that our novices will have to be aggressive in building the structures within which they will work. This approach would be a change in attitude perhaps from "fitting into the norm" and "getting along" with others in an employer-employee relationship.

Recommendations

In this section we were to have outlined new kinds of college organizations, including the utilization of advisory committees; indicated how a biographical information system on the collegiate level would not only facilitate pre-service planning and evaluation, but also serve as a model for learning how to work with one designed for the elementary schools; and illustrated how unit planning techniques could be enhanced by incorporating systems approaches to the management of ideas, time, and resources.

However, in keeping with our developmental approach we have decided to suggest only ideas that could be initiated almost immediately, at little cost, and with a minimum of reorganization of courses and resources.

I. In-service programs for college faculties should include:
    A. Communication with resource people from "the world of

work" through advisory committees, seminars, and task force teams.

    B. Consultant help in utilizing systems-planning in instructional activities and in making these systems visible to students.

    C. Suggestions for involving students in a wide range of professional activities: committees, research, conferences, conventions, etc.

    D. Opportunities to work with children in a variety of settings, in class and out of class.

II. Teacher education programs should encourage activities leading to a diversification of talents related to the work of teaching.

    A. Students can be selected for pre-service programs on the basis of life experiences as well as on the basis of grade point average.

    B. Students can be evaluated through descriptive measures (many self-evaluative in nature) and out-of-class activities planned for individuals on the basis of the information obtained through subjective sources.

    C. All students should not be expected to learn exactly the same content or to attain the same level of competency. Evaluations of competencies should be comprehensive, but should encourage individuals who have mastered the basic areas to work on development of more advanced skills in selected areas of their choice. Skills which may not have to be learned within regular academic courses include:

        1. Community development
        2. Group dynamics
        3. Systems analysis
        4. Human relations

III. Programs leading to teaching for specific purposes should be clearly delineated and priorities for activities within the diverse programs should be agreed upon by the college faculty and students.

    A. Students should have opportunities to examine instructional offerings in a variety of community settings and then share their perceptions of how the activities met the career development needs of children. A case study approach, treating alternative plans and consequences, is preferable to one based upon the accumulation of information from so-called key disciplines of knowledge. Decision-making in terms of subject-schedule dimensions must be replaced with ways of planning relevant to the lives of people.

    B. Students should have the opportunity to learn how people in the world of work see their relationship to the programs of the schools by activities such as:

1. Interviews with active adults to discover who people think they are and what they believe the school should be doing.
2. Volunteer, apprentice, and full pay experiences to provide effective content regarding the world of work as well as information about specific skills and processes.
3. Experience within teams of faculty, college students, and teachers practicing in the schools as task forces to perform relevant educational work.
   a. New instructional activities could be planned, implemented, and evaluated.
   b. Support systems within a school could be strengthened.
   c. Planners might identify available resources and specify possible approaches to alternative solutions to meet emerging problems.
4. Access to individuals actively involved in contemporary issues. Issues might be:
   a. School finance
   b. Affirmative action programs
   c. Political approaches to peace
   d. Quality of the environment
   e. Labor relations
5. Sharing sessions with a wide variety of representatives of adult interests and occupations to provide for the expression of contemporary concerns from the working world, the academic world, the professional educator's world, and the world of the student preparing to teach in the public schools. These can be developed within courses or through special teacher-preparation seminars.

In brief, our suggestions are meant to create more doing activities for college students and college faculties, more active participation in a variety of community settings. We see the introduction of new courses such as "The History of Career Education," "The Philosophy of Career Development," "Preparing for the World of Work," and "The Administration of Career Education Programs" as unnecessary, and possibly dangerous, overhead.

Most teacher education programs can be changed through imaginative refocusing of existing course requirements and support systems within colleges of education. Career education could be alive and well if individual teachers and their students actively involve themselves in life-centered activities.

Reference

Wernick, Walter, *Teaching Career Development in the Elementary School: A Life-centered Approach*, Charles Jones Publishing Co., Worthington, Ohio, 1973.

The ABLE Model Program was originally funded as The World of Work as an Organizing Center for the Curriculum of the Elementary School by the Division of Vocational and Technical Education, Illinois. Dr. Wernick is project director.

52

Involvement
in Learning*

Gene Meyer

C areer education means getting involved in life's activities. It means bridging the "generation gap," and getting interaction between people in the community and the schools. In career education, the curriculum is focused on people. . . . Discovering these definitions proved an exciting experience for twenty-four Northern Illinois University student teachers who saw career education in action at the Peoria, Illinois, conference sponsored jointly by Peoria Schools and ABLE Model Program.

Our group quickly recognized that career education can fit about anywhere in the classroom. It can serve to motivate, stimulate, and help to build positive self-concepts in children's attitudes, feelings, and abilities. The group also saw that utilizing the resources in a community can upgrade the academic program; the community and the world become the classroom. They felt enthusiastically that lessons learned through contact with the community were more relevant. But best of all, they realized that the children they observed were interested in their lessons—they were having fun in their learning because they were seeing, hearing, AND doing. The group recalled an already familiar precept:

*Reprinted by permission from the author.

I hear – – – I forget
I see – – – I remember
I do – – – I understand.

I was able to observe during the course of the conference that the same precept also holds true for student teachers. Hearing speeches—even though interesting and thought provoking—did not stimulate much mental involvement and did not leave a lasting impression. The students became more alert when they saw slide programs of classroom activities with the same teacher's enthusiastic commentary of what actually was being done when the slides were made. They began to interact and began to comment that they could do similar activities with their students. But by far the best part of the conference for the group of seniors was visiting elementary schools and going on "career visits" to participating industries to "see" and "do" activities that opened many new possibilities for presenting language arts, math, reading, art, science, and social studies.

By accompanying a third-grade class on a trip to a donut shop, the students saw possibilities for integration of various subject areas into total learning. They saw that language arts could be introduced by writing letters to set up the visit, by making telephone calls to finalize arrangements, by interviewing the workers at the shop, by discussing and spelling words the workers had used, and through the thought processes involved in actually helping to plan the project and in solving the problems that arose in carrying it out. The seniors saw that math became real when students started figuring weights and measures for donut making, as well as the cost of items used at the shop, salaries, overhead for operation, and necessary markup for selling the products. The seniors saw drawings and paintings the children had made as a result of other career visits. They saw how reading could be motivated by a desire to investigate the development of machinery such as a donut maker, by wanting to learn more about food, or even by reading a card of instructions posted for employees. Lessons in social studies could be related to social interactions within the community, such as those between the people in the donut shop and the people they serve or between the shop owner and workers and other businessmen in the community. Science could include studying health standards and health laws, pollution, ecology, and the effects of population. The seniors realized that there were a great many directions they could go to stimulate and motivate children while utilizing individual resources and talents.

In comparing their visits in Peoria with other field trips, they remarked on the stimulation provided by the interaction with people in the community. It was even stimulating to them to see interested and enthusiastic children and teachers getting involved in life's activities outside the classroom. They felt that when parents and other community members became involved in the school, there would be a better understanding of the social, economic, and minority problems within the community. Also, the children would be better able to understand about their parents' careers, thus helping the family to become a closer social unit.

I felt the trip to Peoria was worth the extra planning it involved, because of the active content that the conference provided for my students. They actually saw how children can become interested in learning as they see the need to read, write, know math, interact socially, etc. They saw involved, self-confident children carrying out cooperative activities. They saw teachers utilizing the various interests and abilities of the children, as well as using the parents and the community to make learning fun. And they experienced career visits to several businesses and industries, with each small group later sharing their particular experience with the other groups. In the busy day and a half at this conference my students learned more about being humanistic, being person-centered, and exposing children to first-hand experiences than I could have taught them in two weeks in the classroom. What is more, they had a good time—and they came away eager to explore and try other possibilities for career education. In the words of one student, they felt it was "such a privilege to be able to attend." During follow-up discussion, these twenty-four students agreed that

Career education involves people
People are the world
The world is the classroom.

53

Preparing Elementary School Teachers for Career Education

Terry Whealon
and Janet Whealon

A major emphasis in the field of education today is the area of career education. In the near future, teachers at all grade levels will be involved in career education activities. It is for this reason that teacher education institutions must develop programs which will adequately prepare teachers in this area.

Career education has two major goals—the development of attitudes and values about people and jobs and the use of people who work as a means of making education more relevant. The question is this—what kind of career education activities will meet these needs? I feel that by putting children in direct contact with adults we can accomplish the first goal. When a person has the opportunity to interview a real person who does a job, he tends to become better aware of the value of that work because he has an opportunity to know the value of that person. Therefore, a career education program must provide opportunities for the students to inquire from primary sources (people).

We at the university level tend to tell teachers how to teach rather than set up opportunities for them to experience how to teach. Before a teacher can accomplish the goals of career education, he must have gone through the process as a learner. A teacher must be aware of his own biases concerning various jobs before he can plan a set of experiences that are designed to help students clarify their attitudes and values toward careers. Thus, in a graduate workshop on career education that I recently taught, I tried to provide the kinds of experiences for the teachers that I felt would help them do this. I first asked the individual students to rank a list of careers from those they considered most desirable to those they considered least desirable. The range was very wide. The class was structured so that each session we met with resource people from the community who were involved in different kinds of occupations. I brought in welders, electricians, draftsmen, sales people, nurses, secretaries, operators of small businesses, sheet metal workers, machinists, waitresses, managers, farmers, etc. The class would interview the resource persons and then divide into small groups and actually perform the activities which these people would do on their jobs. In this way, the teachers were able to develop a keen insight into the individual person and his view of his job. One could walk into the classroom and find elementary teachers actually welding, doing mechanical drawing, hammering, or taking each other's blood pressure and pulse. The authority to whom they turned was a real person who was engaged in that particular career. As a result of these type of "hand-on" experiences, I again asked them to rank the same list of careers from most desirable to least desirable. The range diminished.

It is my contention that these teachers have acquired an effective method of educating students about attitudes and values in career education. By seeing the changes that took place in their own attitudes and values, through their direct contact with the people engaged in various occupations, they are now better prepared to use this same process in varying degrees in their own classrooms.

This leads me to the second goal of career education—the use of people who work as a means of making education more relevant. It seems to me that education would become more meaningful if we, as teachers, demonstrated that the skills we ask students to learn are applicable to things that real people do in life. Making classroom activities life-centered and focusing our attention upon the people who actually do these activities will motivate students to learn.

The teachers in my workshop saw the potential for this type of activity almost immediately. One evening, while they were involved in mechanical drawing, I overheard many comments which demonstrated that they were identifying the basic skills involved in this activity and that they were thinking about the implication this had for their own students. An upper intermediate teacher was analyzing what skills she was using that were the same as those she was trying to teach her students. She said, "My students could develop their math skills by drawing a floor plan of our school." Each teacher began analyzing the activity they were doing and making some part of it applicable to their students. They realized that some aspect of this activity could be employed at their particular level to teach some skill that they were trying to get across. They began to see that in this manner, the children would find the information more meaningful because they would see a relationship between school and the real world.

Activities of this type also point out the interrelationships of subject or content areas. The academic subjects can be taught through life-centered activities. The teachers in this workshop engaged in the planning of activities whereby their students could develop language arts, math, science, social studies and art skills through a study of nursing. Each teacher had a unique insight into how students could be involved in an activity that would integrate various subject areas.

I have attempted to give one example of how a teacher training institution can develop activities that will help prepare teachers to work with career education in the classroom. One of the accomplishments was that each teacher left the workshop with a number of ideas and plans on how to implement career education in his own classroom. This allows for growth. Now I would like to challenge educators involved in the training of teachers to take my example and see where it leads you.

54

Career Education—
It's the Real Thing

*Janet Whealon
and Terry Whealon*

Career education—It's the Real Thing—at least that's what the sign said. To me, career education at the elementary level was one of many new ideas being discussed among educators. But what did it actually involve?

My principal mentioned in a recent faculty meeting that one of the things we as teachers might acquaint ourselves with is career education. My first reaction was—at the elementary level? Isn't that a bit early to begin worrying about an occupation? He related that career education had been named as one of the top priorities by the Office of the Superintendent of Public Instruction in our state and that he would like to see our building head in this direction. A few weeks later I received a notice about an upcoming conference on career education being held at Northern Illinois University in DeKalb. Since I had very little knowledge of the current thoughts concerning career education, I requested permission to attend. My principal was delighted to see my interest.

The conference, which was sponsored by Northern Illinois Cooperative in Education and Able Model Program, proved to be a worthwhile experience. During the morning session, we were allowed to browse through materials related to career education and to look at displays. This experience allowed me to acquaint myself with some general concepts about career education. I began thinking that this might be used as a motivating factor in my own classroom. After all, kids were interested in jobs.

After listening to the speakers on the program, my interest became even greater. Their talks stimulated me to find out more about this area of study and how I might incorporate career education into my classroom. One idea particularly struck me—that of humanizing the curriculum. Sure—that made sense. We would actually be studying people—the people who did the work. I liked that.

There were still many questions which concerned me, but the possibility of motivating my children with a curriculum which emphasized people led me to pursue other resources.

During the afternoon, small group sessions were held with teachers who had already incorporated career education. I happened to attend a group conducted by Mrs. Virginia Weston and Mrs. Doris Miller of Willow Grove School. These teachers were working at the first and second grade levels respectively. Mrs. Weston began the session by relating the types of activities which she had undertaken this year. Her class of first-graders began by studying the school personnel. The class had already interviewed the superintendent, the principal, a school board member, and school secretary, and the custodian. She told how the children had prepared for these interviews by role-playing before the visitors came. Mrs. Weston showed us samples of the work which the children had done as a result of these activities. They had dictated stories to her. A vocabulary list including such words as *instruction, principal,* and *facilitator of learning* was constructed. She said that most of the children were able to read these words—mainly because these words had real meaning to the children. The class drew pictures of the people and were able to verbally express their feelings about them. Mrs. Weston said that the children felt very close to their principal and all of the drawings of him showed him with a smile on his face. With a little help, these first-grade children discovered the word *pal* at the end of *principal.*

Mrs. Miller then talked about her activities with the second-graders. They had already studied the scientific method by inviting a scientist to their classroom who actually demonstrated the five steps which make up the scientific method. This led them into a study of animals and a trip to the zoo for the purpose of classifying animals.

Due to these presentations, I began to see career education in a totally different light. It was not another subject, another area of study for which time must be allotted. It was a means by which the entire curriculum could be interrelated. Subject areas could be taught by organizing study around people—people who did work—people who used skills. I could see that the types of activities in which Mrs. Weston and Mrs. Miller had engaged their children were actually being used to teach reading, writing, oral communication, science, mathematics.

When I returned to my classroom, I mentioned the idea of studying people and their jobs to my children, and the response was encouraging. The children seemed interested in finding out about the people who worked on a newspaper, so we began pursuing this area.

I remembered that one of the basic components in this type of program was interviewing. Thus, we began working on interviewing skills. For practice, we decided that they could interview me. I divided my class into five groups and each group wrote two questions which they wanted to ask. They then elected a spokesman for the group and a person who would serve as recorder during the interview. This type of organization proved to be successful and the interview went quite well.

I then scheduled a visit to our local newspaper for the following week. I was astonished by the amount of cooperation which I received. I explained that we were interested in finding out about all aspects of the newspaper business so that we could put out a school newspaper. Mr. Dunn, the editor, suggested that it would probably be beneficial if he came to our classroom before we visited the paper. I thought his was a great idea.

Before Mr. Dunn came to school, we discussed the types of questions we would be interested in asking him. Again, each group wrote two questions and elected a spokesman and a recorder. The children roleplayed the situation before his visit. Also, I was able to send Mr. Dunn a list of questions that he might be prepared to answer as a result of these activities. He seemed to appreciate this.

In order to find out more about a newspaper and how it operates, we decided to interview other people involved in the business. We invited an advertising manager, a cartoonist, a photographer, a reporter, the circulation manager and a newsboy to our classroom. Before each visit, we prepared in the manner I described before. From each visit we discovered the various aspects of journalism and we also discovered a great deal about the person whom we interviewed.

We then visited the newspaper office and saw these people at their various work stations. This experience brought even more meaning to our previous experiences and we became even better prepared to operate our own newspaper.

The number of skills which the children were acquiring as a result of this study was fantastic. The improvement in oral communications skills and writing skills was obvious. We wrote thank-you letters to each visitor. We wrote letters to the parents explaining our program and the purposes behind it. We had both oral and written reports about each visitor. Kids who were virtually non-verbal began to communicate. The vocabulary list grew and grew. The children wrote experience stories and made their own reading books based on these activities.

We then organized our own school newspaper. Each child selected the job he was interested in doing. They were required to change jobs for every new edition. They worked up a work schedule for each student every month.

Our first edition was a smashing success. We charged 2 cents per copy and began saving this money for use on future projects.

The parents' reaction to this entire undertaking was very rewarding. Their cooperation and enthusiasm were outstanding. People began calling me and asking how they could help. We decided that we would survey the parents and find out what types of jobs they had so that we could use them as resource people for our next project.

The most rewarding result of this project was the enthusiasm of my class. The children were interested; they were involved. The motivation was there and school became a place to enjoy learning.

We've been planning our next project now. We're going to study the bank. After all, we need a safe place to keep the profits from the newspaper.

Bibliography

1. Adkins, Winthrop. "Life Skills Education." *Adult Leadership*, June 1973, pp. 55-84.
2. *American Assembly, Report of 43rd.* New York: Ardon House, Columbia University, November 1-4, 1973.
3. Appelgate, William K. "Meeting the Demand: Personnel Development in Career Education." *Illinois Journal of Education*, September/October 1972, pp. 52-53.
4. Arnold, Jean M., and Otte, Max R. "Continuing Professional Education—A Joint Partnership." *Adult Leadership*, February 1973, pp. 251-268.
5. Bane, Mary Jo, and Christopher Jencks. "The School and Equal Opportunity." *Saturday Review of Education*, September 16, 1972, pp. 39-42.
6. Byrnes, Agnes. "We're Not All Famous But Everyone Is Important." *K-Eight*, November/December 1972, pp. 28-31.
7. "Career Education." Special Report by *Nation's Schools* and *College & University Business*, December 1972, pp. 35-40.
8. Carroll, Riley O. "Vestibule Training Takes Hold in Wake County." *American Vocational Journal*, March 1972, pp. 44-45.
9. Connolly, John J. "New Careers: A Challenge to Adult Education." *Adult Leadership*, December 1972, pp. 187-188.
10. Cravens, Raymond L. "The Four-Day Work Week and Its Educational Problems." *Adult Leadership*, March 1973, pp. 278-281.

11. Crew, Stephen. "Private Vocational Schools Thrive." *Chicago Tribune*, 29 April 1973.
12. DeBernardis, Amo. "What Career Education Means for the Community College." *Community Junior College Journal*, May 1973, pp. 9, 11, 42.
13. Diminico, Gerald. "You and Work: An Instructional System for Children in Elementary School." *American Vocational Journal*, December 1969, pp. 22-23.
14. Dull, Lloyd W. "The Cluster Concept in Career Education." *Educational Leadership*, December 1972, pp. 218-221.
15. Ellis, Charles. "Career Education and Culture." *Illinois Career Education Journal*, Spring 1970, pp. 17-20.
16. Farmer, James A., and Williams, Robert G. "An Educational Strategy for Professional Career Change." *Adult Leadership*, April 1971, pp. 318-320.
17. Fuller, Coreen. "Of Careers and Little People." Original manuscript, March 1974.
18. Fuller, Jack W. "Serving the Community Through Marketing and Management Seminars." *Journal of Business Education*, December 1972, pp. 117-119.
19. Gambino, Thomas W. "Junior High: The Exploratory Years." *American Vocational Journal*, March 1972, pp. 56-57.
20. Gabino, Thomas W. "Putting Plans to Work—Some Who Have." *Instructor*, February 1972, pp. 54-55.
21. Gysbers, Norman C., and Moore, Earl. "Guiding Career Exploration: Any Teacher Can." *Instructor*, February 1972, pp. 52-53.
22. Gysbers, Norman C., and Moore, Earl. "Career Development: A New Focus." *Educational Leadership*, December 1972, pp. 257-260.
23. Hedrich, Vivian. "Seattle's Concentration on Careers." *American Education*, July 1971, pp. 12-15.
24. Hendrickson, A. "Problems and Issues in Career Education for Adults," *Adult Leadership*, February 1973, pp. 266-272.
25. "How Much Career Education in Science," *Science Teacher*, April 1973, pp. 28-30.
26. King, Arthur R., Jr., and Brownell, John A. "The Claim for Occupational Man on the Curriculum." *The Curriculum and the Disciplines of Knowledge*, New York: John Wiley & Sons, 1966, pp. 3-8.
27. Kopelke, Phyllis B., and Koch, Moses S. "A Community College Perspective on New Careers." *Community Junior College Journal*, June 1971, pp. 14-16.

28. Laramore, Darryl. "Career Education Concept Filters Down." *American Vocational Journal*, September 1972, pp. 45-47, 78.
29. Madless, D. "Careers from A-Zoo." *American Education*, May 1973, pp. 15-21.
30. Marland, Sydney P. Jr. "Career Education: Every Student Headed for a Goal." *American Vocational Journal*, March 1972, pp. 34-38.
31. Matheny, Kenneth B. "The Role of the Middle School in Career Development."*American Vocational Journal*, December 1969, pp. 18-21.
32. Meyer, Gene. "Involvement in Learning." Original manuscript, 1974.
33. Mitchell, Edna. "What About Career Education for Girls?" *Educational Leadership*, December 1973, pp. 233-236.
34. Moss, Ruth. "Careers: Age Doesn't Limit the Interest." *Chicago Tribune*, 13 May 1973.
35. Nash, Robert J. and Agne, Russell M. "Career Education: Earning a Living or Living a Life." *Phi Delta Kappan*, February 1973, pp. 373-378.
36. Palmer, Ronald. "Schooled Vocational Experiences: Some Modest Proposals," *Clearinghouse*. In press.
37. Peterson, Marla. "Occupacs for Hands on Learning." *American Vocational Journal*, January 1972, pp. 40-41.
38. Ristau, Robert A. "Career Exploration: Why, When, and How." *The Balance Sheet*, February 1973, pp. 196-198.
39. Rosenthal, Nina. "Career Guidance in the Elementary School: The Classroom Corporation." *Elementary School Guidance and Counseling*, December 1973, pp. 129-130.
40. Smith, Joel. "The Need for Math Seemed Endless." *American Vocational Journal*, March 1972, pp. 50-51.
41. Stell, Mary. "Career Guidance in the Elementary School: Take an Idea and See Where It Leads You." *Elementary School Guidance and Counseling*, December 1973, pp. 126-127.
42. Svicarovich, John, and Hagans, Rex. "An Employer Based Career Education Model." *Educational Leadership*, December 1972, pp. 222-224.
43. Sylvester, Robert, and Mathews, Esther. "Four Big Questions Children Need to Ask and Ask and Ask." *Instructor*, February 1972, pp. 46-52.
44. Tuckman, B. W. "Getting at the Attitudes Problem: Career Development and the Affective Domain." *American Vocational Journal*, January 1973, pp. 47-48.

45. Vacca, Richard. "Reading Development Through Career Education." Original manuscript.

46. Venn, Grant. "Thirteen Ways to Improve Your Occupational Program." *Nation's Schools*, December 1971, pp. 41-48.

47. Wernick, Walter; Ellis, Charles; Luce, Linda; Meyer, Norma; Nielsen, Karen; Peterson, James; and Whealon, Janet. "Career Education for Elementary School Teachers." *Journal of Teacher Education*, Summer 1973, pp. 97-102.

48. Weston, V., Whealon, Janet, and Wealon, Terry. "Boutiques, Banks, and Bakeries." *Illinois Career Education Journal*, Winter 1973, pp. 22-24.

49. Whealon, Janet, and Meyer, Norma. "Basic Content People." Original manuscript, June 1974.

50. Whealon, Janet, and Whealon, Terry. "Career Education—It's the Real Thing." Original manuscript, May 1974.

51. Whealon, Janet, and Whealon, Terry. "Integrating the Curriculum Via Careers." Original manuscript, February 1974.

52. Whealon, Terry, and Whealon, Janet. "Preparing Elementary School Teachers for Career Education." Original manuscript, July 1974.

53. "Where the Action Is." *College and University Business*, December 1971, pp. 46-49.

54. Wykle, James H. "To Business Teachers—On Career Education." *The Balance Sheet*, April 1973, p. 291.

Jack W. Fuller, Ph.D., is dean, extended day and summer programs, Pima Community College, Tucson, Arizona. His work has appeared in several professional publications, including *Journal of Business Education* and *Community Education.*

Terry O. Whealon, Ph.D., is chairman of urban education, department of elementary education, Northern Illinois University, DeKalb. He has published widely on career development in journals such as *Secondary School Principal's Bulletin* and the *Journal of College Placement.*